Island World

THE CALIFORNIA WORLD HISTORY LIBRARY

Edited by Edmund Burke III, Kenneth Pomeranz, and Patricia Seed

Island World

A HISTORY OF HAWAI'I
AND THE UNITED STATES

GARY Y. OKIHIRO

UNIVERSITY OF CALIFORNIA PRESS

Berkeley   Los Angeles   London

University of California Press, one of the most distinguished
university presses in the United States, enriches lives around the world
by advancing scholarship in the humanities, social sciences, and natural
sciences. Its activities are supported by the UC Press Foundation and
by philanthropic contributions from individuals and institutions.
For more information, visit www.ucpress.edu.

University of California Press
Berkeley and Los Angeles, California

University of California Press, Ltd.
London, England

Library of Congress Cataloging-in-Publication Data

Okihiro, Gary Y., 1945–.
Island world : a history of Hawai'i and the United States / Gary Y. Okihiro.
    p.   cm. — (California world history library ; 8)
Includes bibliographical references and index.
ISBN: 978-0-520-25299-8 (cloth : alk. paper)
1. Hawaii—History.   2. Folklore—Hawaii.   3. Popular culture—Hawaii.
4. Hawaiians—History.   I. Title.
DU625.O37   2008
996.9—dc22   2007044588

Manufactured in the United States of America

17 16 15 14 13 12 11 10 09 08
10 9 8 7 6 5 4 3 2 1

The paper used in this publication meets the minimum requirements of
ANSI/NISO Z39.48–1992 (R 1997) *(Permanence of Paper)*.

For Amparo

CONTENTS

ILLUSTRATIONS

FIGURES

MAPS

ACKNOWLEDGMENTS

I have learned much over the course of this book's formation and have benefited greatly from the generous advice and kind research assistance of many, from the islands of Hawai'i to America's Pacific and Atlantic coasts, including Carl Kalani Beyer, Dale Cockrell, Vicente M. Diaz, Lissy Marina Henriquez, Marina A. Henriquez, Frances Karttunen, Derek Kauanoe, J. Kehaulani Kauanui, James Little, Michelle S. Liu, Davianna Pomaka'i McGregor, Kekela Kuhia Miller, Colin I. R. Okihiro, Jonathan Kay Kamakawiwo'ole Osorio, Walter Pitman, Joseph P. Reidy, Greg Robinson, Brenda M. Romero, Leslie Rowland, Ted Solis, Amy Ku'uleialoha Stillman, Elda Tsou, and Michael Nevin Willard; Lucinda P. Cockrell at the Center for Popular Music, Middle Tennessee State University; Vivian Gutierrez of the Mission Houses Museum; Linda L. Hall of the Williams College Archives and Special Collections; Lynn K. Manuel of the Lyman House Memorial Museum; Dawn Oberg at the Country Music Hall of Fame and Museum; Laura Pereira of the Kendall Institute, New Bedford Whaling Museum; Ann Schillinger and Eddie Bigelow of the Cornwall Historical Society; and the archivists at Bishop Museum, the Hawai'i Volcanoes National Park Archives, the Hawaiian Historical Society and Hawaiian Mission Children's Society, and Hamilton Library Special Collections, University of Hawai'i. Of course, although they helped steer me and point the way, I bear responsibility for this voyage and landing.

I also acknowledge my debt to Columbia University for granting me a two-year senior research associate position, which enabled me to complete *Island World* and the second installment, "Pineapple Culture," of my trilogy; to Ken Hakuta, whose subvention helped fund this book's illustrations; and to the anonymous reviewers and Niels Hooper and his colleagues at the University of California Press, who believed in the merits of *Island World* and made valuable suggestions that produced a better book. Colleagues and students at the following places have encouraged and aided me, having heard and commented upon excerpts from this work: Aristotle University (Thessaloniki), Barnard College, Boston University, Sarah Lawrence College, Tokyo University, University of Arizona, University of British Columbia, University of the Ryukyus, University of Southern California, University of Virginia, University of Washington, University of Wisconsin, Vanderbilt University, and Wellesley College. Above all, I am grateful to Marina A. Henriquez, to whom this book is dedicated, for her partnership on a remarkable journey from Kona and La'ie to New Bedford, Dover, and Hampton.

Introduction

Movement, the heartbeat of history, is a matter of perspective. I am referring not to history as past reality but to the writing of history or accounts of the past. Despite claims of universality and timelessness, historians record the past from their present standpoint. Their texts thus carry tracings of their own time and place. To claim otherwise is a conceit and falsehood designed to discipline those who exceed the boundaries of the guild. Consider, then, history as evidence of the historian's presence as much as it is a shadow of the past. And from that vantage, contemplate the act of creation, the historian's craft, the formation of worlds on paper, moving across space and time, from their very beginnings.

It is a matter of perspective, according to some Polynesian navigators. Mau Piailug, a master navigator, referenced a star compass in his head. With Polaris pointing north and the Southern Cross south, selected stars rising indicated east, and others, setting, showed west. Locating the canoe's position on the open ocean depends upon estimates of speed and direction. Piailug plotted his progress in relation to a "reference island," which sat well out of sight over the horizon, and familiar stars whose rising and setting indicated directions. His object was to keep his canoe stationary as the imaginary reference island moved from the bearing of one horizon star to another until the island had moved past all the horizon stars, marking the completion of the voyage. Piailug's mental plotting system allowed him to break the voyage into manageable segments marked by the movement of the island from one horizon star to the next and enabled him to calculate his position.[1] In his world, thus, islands move and canoes reach their destinations by holding steady.[2]

In this book, I reflect upon islands and continents as revealed by relations between Hawai'i and the United States and, in effect, the world. Instead of the customary narrative of the United States acting upon Hawai'i, I present the Islands' press against the continent, causing it to move and endowing it, accordingly, with historical meaning. In this version of the past, Hawai'i is the center that, in its circuits, stirs and animates the United States. I take that perspective, I realize, as a strategic position to counter the prevailing bias; in the end, I hold that distinctions between islands and continents dissolve in the recognition of our "island world."

The book's title conjures literal worlds, seas and lands, into which Hawaiians and their deeds are entered and rendered historical, mainly in the United States but also virtually everywhere else on this earth. But it also alludes to a metaphysical world of ideas based upon my understanding of Hawaiian cosmology and is directed against some ill-conceived notions of time and space—history. The past, it seems to me, is impoverished if limited to humans and their initiatives, and discrete stations and linear progressions are but one variety of historical explanation. Like a Polynesian voyaging canoe and history itself, *Island World* is as much a vessel as an orientation.

The volcano and some of its representations helped mold and reaffirm aspects of American religion, art, and science, the subject of chapter 1. Oceania's fires might have conjured dread in the American mind, whereas its waters induced visions of tropical paradise, romance, and manly vigor, according to chapter 2. A reorientation of the United States from its westward march into the continent's interior to its watery crossings for the sake of overseas missions, as described in chapter 3, opened this new nation to the world, and the return of New England's religious diaspora in the person of Samuel Chapman Armstrong was pivotal in a brand of education for formerly enslaved African Americans and native peoples in the newly "acquired" territories on the continent and distant islands, the topic of chapter 4. In chapter 5 I outline Hawaiians' influences, mainly as sailors but also as soldiers, on the U.S. west and east coasts. Island music and its hold on the continent during the early twentieth century is my focus in chapter 6.

The ancient Greeks had it correct, I believe, in their concept of the "world island," which, as I explain in chapter 7, represented a landmass, the intersection of Europe, Asia, and Africa, surrounded by bodies of water. Although America and other lands and seas were left out of this geography, I find it fascinating to think of the earth as comprising islands that move, in Polynesian perspective, in fecund oceans that convey, rather than impede, biotic communities, producing perpetual transgressions of bordered spaces and peerless nativities. I'd like to think of all life as mere visitors to this planet earth, aliens all who, as migrants and kinfolk, bear responsibility as caretakers of its waters, airs, and lands devoid of privileges of possession claimed by priority or contract. Hugo of St. Victor, a twelfth-century monk from Saxony, put it this way: "The person who finds his homeland sweet is still a tender beginner; he to whom every soil is as his native one is already strong; but he is perfect to whom the entire world is as a foreign place." To this Edward W. Said sagely added, "Survival in fact is about the connections between things."[3] Worthy is that faith and conviction, a Hawaiian and Oceanic acumen, in an island world.

Island World is, despite appearances, a history, a rendition of the past. It is the first volume of a trilogy I intend to write on space and time, or history. Historians might easily miss my version of history as a species of their craft. In fact, as individuals and departments over the course of my career, historians have routinely barred my admission into their company and circle. Members only, the more vigilant, like Minutemen, insist. Borders must be patrolled, fences erected, erosions of the discipline shored up against. A history colleague once told me that she, as a historian of Africa, had "been to the edge" but that I had "gone over it." I delight in that revelation because history, like other disciplines and regimes, languishes if left to its own devices. It can, assuredly, burrow deeper into its staked territory and build elaborate edifices to itself, while failing to reach beyond its claims to equally wondrous worlds in other realms.

Three of my discipline's pieties include a linear progression of time, frequently standing in for causality or explanation; a discrete, managed space, sometimes presumed to be unique or exceptional; and humans as subjects with volition without regard for the agencies of other lifeforms both within and without humanity's orbit. I have those "truths" in mind in this history of Hawai'i and the United States, which I believe offers an alternative, what I conceive of as "historical formations," to those foundational assumptions, which to my mind carry much merit but should not exercise sole dominion over our field. Although implicit to this account, a fuller explanation of what I mean by historical formation must await "Disciplining Subjects," the third and final installment of this trilogy. The present volume and the second, "Pineapple Culture," offer examples of historical formations and violations of history as some conceive and practice it rather than their theorization.

There are other objectives at work in this book. If chronology fails to convey this telling, subject matters, especially individual lives, provide coherence, tracing routes that specify and ramify. Connections, like old friends, appear and reappear in different times and on occasion in delightfully divergent climes. Biotic communities, after all, move in an interrelated world, despite our best efforts to divide, classify, order, and therewith control, island-like.[4] Yet surely limits must be reached even within this version of history. *Island World* stops short of treading upon the more familiar ground of Pearl Harbor, World War II, and the "Pacific century," and it fails to travel over territories other than Hawai'i and corners of the United States, hardly exhausting islands and continents in their worldly plenitude. Hawai'i is also at the apex of northern and southern engagements as a vanguard of Polynesia and Oceania's sea of islands, whereas this study follows the conventional and frequently hegemonic flows of East with West. My choices in this historical formation are, even in its transient moments of resistance, I must confess, constrained by prior structures and discourses. Endowing islands with initiative, weight, and intellect, thus, contradicts their representations as feminine spaces while affirming the original attributions of "man" and "woman." The very idea of intervention, alas, presupposes a former condition.

The present, too, is alive in *Island World*. I write about Hawai'i, my birthplace and home, enabled and sobered by the persistence and resurgence of Hawaiian language and culture and by movements and demands for Hawaiian sovereignty and self-determination, including the right to script pasts.[5] The theft of the Hawaiian Islands by the United States was and continues to belie the republic's declarations of democracy and freedom, even as Hawaiian resistance gifts us with exemplars of identity and nation building. I also write, as an Asian American, amid a debate around the ahistorical notion of "settler colonialism," and from that point of view my relationship to the Islands is a vexed if not privileged one. Impossible to ignore, additionally, is my post–September 11, 2001, station in the United States and its government's determination to wage war against itself and the world for the installation of its new nationalism, empire, and world order.[6] Given those ambitions, my centering of Hawai'i as the "mainland" and marginalizing of the United States to the periphery appears misguided and puny indeed.

Other matters reflective of my intellectual moment compressed into *Island World* are my efforts to situate islands, like the Hawaiian Islands and Okinawa Islands, in comparative perspective,[7] to conceptualize a "black Pacific,"[8] and to advance a "Pacific civilization."[9] Those works address ideas prevalent in world historiography that favor lands over waters; continents over islands; the Atlantic and Atlantic civilization, including the "black Atlantic," over the "other" ocean and Oceania; and in the United States the black and white and nonwhite and white racial formations. *Island World* articulates instead the intersections of land and sea and their biotic communities, of the Atlantic and Pacific, of Hawaiians and Europeans, Africans, American Indians, and Latina/os, and it transgresses sites of nation, discipline, subject, and, at times, even narrative form. Fortunately, I stand upon broad shoulders and in good company in these projects of trespass, and it should not surprise readers in the least, accordingly, that my version of history resembles and speaks to some of the salient imperatives of my time and space.

Regions of Fire

Consider a mountain range 1,500 miles long, 500–600 miles wide, the summits rising 15,000 feet at its northwestern extremity and 30,000 feet at its southeastern end. More than 30 million years ago, through a vent in the earth's surface, magma and molten rock poured quietly to the surface, hardened, and piled up layer upon layer to form those immense mountains, the highest, unsurpassed on earth.[1]

When space turned around, the earth heated
When space turned over, the sky reversed
When the sun appeared standing in shadows
To cause light to make bright the moon,
When the Pleiades are small eyes in the night,

From the source in the slime was the earth formed
From the source in the dark was darkness formed
From the source in the night was night formed
From the depths of the darkness, darkness so deep
Darkness of day, darkness of night
Of night alone.[2]

So begins the epic song of genesis, the Hawaiian hymn of creation that celebrated the birth of the mountain range whose peaks, jutting up in the midst of Pacific waters, became a haven for life. In the night of the ocean's cold and silent depths, paired rocks, male and female, reproduced themselves during that chaotic and fecund period to form the Hawaiian Ridge, followed in succession by the births of Kumulipo (source-darkness), male, and Poʻele (night-blackness), female, tenuous polyps that gave rise to branching coral, grubs and worms, starfish, sea cucumbers, sea urchins, oysters and mussels, and seaweed and land plants swaying in liquid currents of water and air. The long night was pregnant with motion, with creativity.

> Filling, filling full
> Filling, filling out
> Filling, filling up
> Until the earth is a brace holding firm the sky
> When space lifts through time in the night of Kumulipo
> It is yet night.[3]

Even as the Hawaiian Ridge imposed itself upon the sea, the ocean wore upon the peaks as rainfall, waves, and currents that gnawed at the land's solidity. The mountain's mass engaged the ocean's kinetic energy. Thus locked in perpetual embrace are solid and liquid, stability and change. And their borders, their distinctions, dissolve in the mix, like molten streams of lava that become, upon cooling, fixed and solid. Land and sea together with their paired populations conspire in those acts of creation and correspondences: the "*coralline seaweed* living in the sea" and the "*bird's nest fern* living on land"; the "*fragrant red seaweed* living in the sea" and the "succulent *mint* living on land"; the "*manauea* seaweed living in the sea" and the "*manauea* taro living on land."[4]

> It is a night gliding through the passage
> Of an opening; a stream of water is the food of plants
> It is the god who enters; not as a human does he enter
> Male for the narrow waters
> Female for the broad waters[5]

About 15–20 million years ago, ringing the summits and in places shielded from lava flows, grew corals, colonies of plankton-eating animals and their single-celled algal symbionts.[6] The polyps of stony coral species secreted the calcareous cups, or hard exoskeleton, that formed the Islands' fringing reefs. For the colonies to survive and thrive, sufficient sunlight had to reach the algae within them for photosynthesis to occur. The Indo–West Pacific area, stretching from Indonesia to Okinawa, was the birthplace of those corals, along with most of the Hawaiian marine biota. From that region, millions of microscopic plankton (from the Greek *planktos,* "wandering"), mainly as larvae, began drift voyages that lasted for months. Because of the speed of the ocean currents, the distances traveled, and the limited lifespans of larvae, many of the species that made it to the islands of Hawai'i were remigrants from other Pacific islands, such as Wake, Kalama (Johnston), the Line Islands, and the Hawaiian Ridge, both at and below sea level. Some coral larvae, for instance, can survive 45–212 days, and molluscan larvae 200–300 days. Estimates of drift time to Hawai'i from Kalama range from 30 to 50 days, and from Wake 187 days,[7] suggesting the need for island hopping for many of Hawai'i's marine taxa.

From coral anchors grew more complex algae—seaweeds—carried as plankton near the water's surface for the sunlight necessary for photosynthesis. Hawaiian waters are too warm for certain species of seaweeds, notably kelps, and other cold-water marine biota, and too cool for others, which are stunted in Hawai'i as compared with their size in warmer parts of the Pacific. The basal trophic seaweeds supported herbivores, including mollusks like snails, clams, and octopuses, and vertebrates like the small inshore fishes upon which the larger pelagic fishes fed. Seaweeds, thereby, filled the ecological niche occupied by their terrestrial green plant counterparts as food for herbivores, which are, in turn, consumed by carnivorous predators in the water and on the land.

The likely sequence of migration from the Indo–West Pacific area and settlement in Hawai'i involved corals, then marine algae, then mollusks and fishes, although these movements were also simultaneous and recurrent once the foundations had been laid. Larvae of small tropical fishes, sustained by feeding upon tinier plankton en route, survived for several months. Other larvae, hitching rides on ocean debris, whales, turtles, and large fishes, arrived and made homes in Hawaiian waters over the course of millions of years. That ability of larvae to travel, along with the constant flows and exchanges facilitated by the movements of the ocean and its populations, produced greater continuities and less speciation among marine life in the Pacific than the endemism more characteristic of the Hawaiian Islands' terrestrial biota. Life on the land, accordingly, proved more disruptive than life in the sea. That fact of relative oceanic homogeneity is particularly remarkable because of Hawai'i's near isolation from other havens of sea life, a feature that would ordinarily favor endemism, and because terrestrial forms had much less time for speciation than marine forms.[8]

The conceit of the Kumulipo, the Hawaiian creation song, is that although recounting life's formation in its entirety the poem's core is about humans and the stages of human growth—the gestation, birth, and maturation of a child. Thus, in Chant One, the fecund wash of sea creatures conjures images of an infant world, and the sliding and twisting of sea and land plants suggest the halting gestures of a newborn baby. The fishes that appear in Chant Two, including an elegant child born in the shape of a brilliantly colored fish, the wrasse *(hilu)*, allude to babyhood and the first solid food fed to children, which influenced their futures.

> Born a child of the gentle wrasse that swims
> Is the *hilu* whose tail fin marks
> The renown of Pō-uliuli[9]

The *hilu* fish, among the most beautiful in Hawaiian waters, ensured the good looks of the child, and the red-eyed *kole* fish gave the child a rosy skin color. The oceans that circled the Islands were the playground for active children, like the brightly colored *opule* fish (the sea is thick with them) that surfaced for gulps of air and quickly turned to dive and disappear under the sea. The landed counterparts of the ocean's depths were the verdant, secluded valleys, home of the gods and the children of chiefs, where they could be reared away from commoners to preserve their high rank and the taboo *(kapu)* that precluded contact with them.[10] Born swimming were the sea creatures, including the porpoise, shark, goatfish, crab, octopus, stingray, bonito and albacore, mackerel, mullet, *ono, moi, weke,* and *ulua.*

> Black as night the opaque sea,
> Coral sea in the dark cliffs of Paliuli,

Land that slid away from them,
Dark shore passing into night—
It is yet night.[11]

In the Kumulipo—this pairing of sea and land, parent and offspring—light dawns at the birth of gods and humans, whose genealogies constitute the final eight sections of this creation song. That closing affirmed the connections of present with past and of self with society, and it pointed to a future of recurrence and design. As was pointed out by ethnographer Martha W. Beckwith, who was born in New England but grew up in Hawai'i, the poem was composed for and dedicated to the birth of a child, firstborn son and heir to a powerful chief on the island of Hawai'i. The cosmos and its origin simply offer analogies to the phases of human development from conception to birth. And as a birth chant and genealogy, the focus is on the celebrated child and the processes of reproduction and the cycles of life.[12] The hymn, in particular, was the name song *(mele inoa)* for Lono-i-ka-makahiki or Ka-'Ī-i-mamao, ancestral figure of the agricultural year and as such progenitor and sustainer of life.[13]

By contrast, the Islands' history long predated the arrival of humans, and its tale of continuities and changes was told in the ocean's washes, the earth's engagements with the sea and then the air, and the life that traveled on those liquid currents to colonize the Hawaiian Ridge. Seaborne traffic was long-standing and continuous, as is emphasized by the fact that of Kalama's 300 total fish species, it shares 285 inshore species with Hawai'i, even though the two islands are separated by some 500 miles of open sea. At the same time, oceanic discontinuity formed a part of the story in that migrants were not uniformly successful in traversing distances or adapting to new environments. Thus, although there are about 2,500 species of bony fishes in the Philippines, in the Indo–West Pacific triangle of origin and dispersal there are some 940 in adjacent Micronesia but only about 530 in the distant Hawaiian Islands.[14] Apparently, only the hardy and lucky survived the diaspora.

Attenuation among the seaborne traffic paralleled the filtering experienced by the Islands' flora and fauna. Although there are some one hundred palm genera on the islands of the southwest Pacific, there is only one native palm genus in Hawai'i.

Among animals the break is even more marked. There are no native amphibians or nonmarine reptiles and only two native species of bats. Buoyant seeds, branches, and objects of human manufacture, with occasional passengers, floated on ocean currents, other lifeforms took flight on the wings of migratory birds and bats, and some butterflies and dragonflies flew from other Pacific islands and the continental rim of Asia and America. Invertebrates and other organisms were borne from the Asian continent to the Hawaiian archipelago on winds whipped by storms and the jet stream with gusts of more than 100 miles per hour. Like its marine biota, Hawai'i's terrestrial plants and animals originated mainly in Southeast Asia and the southwest Pacific region.[15]

ISLANDS AND CONTINENTS

"Oceanic islands," a well-known professor of geology began, "are small, young, isolated, simple, and subjected to a limited range of environmental factors." Accordingly scientists, famously Charles Darwin in the Galápagos Islands, have found them to be ideal research laboratories because of their finite variables and controlled conditions. By contrast, this geologist continued, "consider the continents. They are aggregates of every type of rock produced for billions of years, and most of their history is obscure. . . . The whole is obscured by every type of soil and by plants. Across the continents migrate animals and plants in constant flux. One can have little reason to hope that nature has conducted many controlled experiments on the continents."[16] Those scientific sentiments—those attributions of simplicity and complexity, stasis and movement, to islands and continents—are neither unique nor confined to that branch of human knowledge. Unlike some Pacific islands, which appear solitary, moored in the apparent monotony of a vast and vacant sea, geology flourishes in a teeming and fecund pond of Western intellectual life from which emerges a common sense about continents and islands.

Yet even geology points to the abundance of islands, which are, geologically speaking, mostly the tips of volcanoes that rise above the water's surface, along with the more than two thousand identified seamounts, which are mainly subma-

FIGURE 1. Isolated peak in a seemingly vast sea. Yann Arthus-Bertrand. Courtesy of Corbis Corporation.

rine volcanoes hidden from sea-level view. In the Pacific where they predominate, approximately ten thousand volcanoes rise more than a kilometer from the ocean floor, and one hundred thousand more reach less than a kilometer. In fact, volcanoes are a prominent feature of the Pacific Basin sea floor, and their extrusions have been far more intense in volume and scale than their continental counterparts, perhaps as much as one hundred times greater.[17] Further, rather than being isolated, Pacific volcanoes, both above (islands) and below (seamounts) the water's surface, tend to group into collections throughout and in certain parts of the basin.[18] Fault lines along which volcanism occurs have determined that pattern and distribution.

Volcanism is associated with some of the oldest known rocks on earth, and its structural conditions have modified and continue to modify the planet's surfaces both above and beneath the seas, pushing up mountain ranges and tearing apart

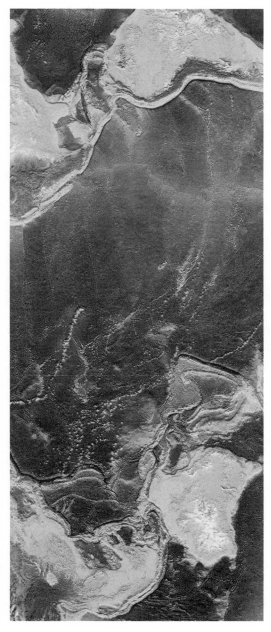

MAP 1. Numerous peaks and vast mountain ranges shape the landscape beneath the ocean's surface. Courtesy of Office of Naval Research.

great rifts that might extend for thousands of miles along the earth's crust. A spectacular example is the "ring of fire" that encircles the Pacific Basin, stretching from New Zealand northward to Melanesia, the Philippines, Japan, Kamchatka, the Aleutian Islands, and Alaska and southward along the Americas' west coast down to Chile. About three-fourths of the earth's active volcanoes lie within the Pacific ring and its outliers, and the study of volcanoes, earthquakes, and the ocean floor during the 1960s led to the new science of plate tectonics.[19]

The unstable ground where volcanoes and earthquakes predominate, the theory of plate tectonics hypothesizes, marks the edges of plates that constitute the earth's oceanic and continental mantle. Magma ascends to the surface from the collisions and cracks of plate edges as volcanic eruptions, earthquakes result from the sliding caused by plate movements along fault lines, and the plates, though rigid, are in constant motion across the globe's surface, like islands floating on a molten sea. Viewed from that perspective, continents are not marked by the water's edge but form continuous landmasses, albeit of different densities, with vast portions of the ocean's floor, and plates that might begin mid-ocean demarcate the planet's mantle.[20] The Eurasian plate extends from Japan westward across Asia and Europe to the mid-Atlantic ridge, Africa sits on a plate with sides in the Atlantic and Indian oceans, and the Australian-Indian plate unites the Indian subcontinent with the Australian continent. A map of the globe from the projections of plate tectonics, accordingly, presents a picture at odds with the familiar contours of land and sea, continents and islands.

Volcanoes that erupt along the plate margins deposit magma that enables plate expansion, and where two plates meet, due in part to that spreading, one's edge slides beneath the other's in a process called subduction. Volcanism and subduction are related in that the former requires the latter to be at roughly the same rate, because the earth cannot accommodate only growth. In that way, volcanoes are a key to the main processes affecting the earth's mantle, the generation and destruction of its plates. The study of volcanoes in Hawai'i prompted a break from continental geology, which dominated the science and postulated a thin, flexible shell that contracted through heat loss, accounting for folding, as demonstrated in mountains such as the Appalachians and Andes.[21] Instead, the vast volcanic sea bottoms

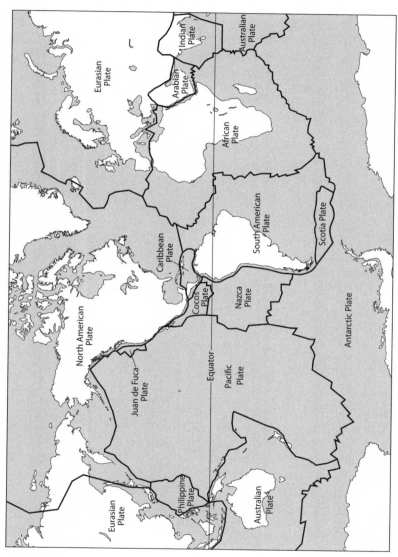

MAP 2. One view of the earth's landmasses and their distinctions. Redrawn from a U.S. Geological Survey map.

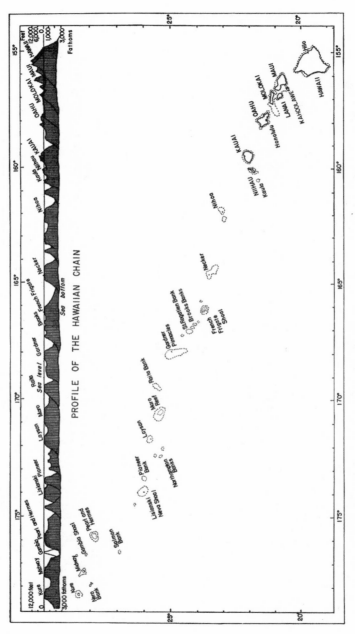

MAP 3. Profile and aerial views of the Hawaiian Ridge. E. H. Bryan Jr. Courtesy of Bishop Museum.

suggested a thick mantle, bordered by fracture lines and edges that settled, scraped, and collided against each other, producing earthquakes, volcanic eruptions, and massive buckling and uplifts. The Hawaiian hot spot in the middle of the Pacific plate, which accounted for the mountains called the Hawaiian Ridge, indicated the speed and direction of that plate's movement.[22]

Although only eight islands—Niʻihau, Kauaʻi, Oʻahu, Molokaʻi, Lanaʻi, Maui, Kahoʻolawe, and Hawaiʻi—make up more than 99 percent of the Hawaiian chain's emergent land area, they represent a mere fraction of the archipelago's entirety when seen from the ocean's bottom.

Scientists believe that the Hawaiian hot spot began at least 75–80 million years ago near the Aleutian Trench off Alaska, moved southward creating the Emperor Seamount Chain, and turned toward the east to form the Hawaiian Ridge. The oldest of the Hawaiian chain and its northwest extremity, Kure, is about 30 million years old, and its youngest, the Big Island of Hawaiʻi, is still in formation. Indicative of that work in progress, to the Big Island's southeast is Lōʻihi, a submarine volcano that will eventually form another peak on the island. Hawaiians accordingly call the northwest islands, banks, and reefs the "*kupuna* [ancestor] islands," indicating origins, genealogy, and kinship.

The fates of islands and continents, the sea and the land, are more related than seen in the customary view at sea or shore level. Beneath the waters that cover most of the earth's surface await connections to be made by discerning eyes. As the founding director of the Hawaiian Volcano Observatory declared, "Continental life came out of the sea, and original life comes continually from the earth core."[23]

CREATION SONG

To Hawaiians, poetry *(mele)*, a complex, integrated system of rhythm, melody, and movement, is inseparable from life and its intricacies.[24] Like life, poetry consists of a time pattern and structure and relies upon the engagement and imagination of its community of listeners. It forms relationships, shares secrets, and is passed from one generation to the next, intact and altered. It is old and new, constant and modulated. Words are poetry's brushstrokes, painting exquisite imageries that, with their multiple meanings, conceal as well as reveal their beauties. *Haku mele* (to weave a song) refers to the sorting out, selection, and stitching of bird feathers of varying quality and color, which oscillates depending upon the light and perspective, for the cloaks *('ahu 'ula)* and standards *(kāhili)* of chiefs. The work requires great skill, artistry, and discipline.[25]

Some poetry traces descent and, with it, memberships and privileges, placing individuals within lineages and with ancestors, the environment, and all things in the universe. These *mele* are *ko'ihonua*—genealogical poems that are, at core, creation songs. As such, they are origin stories, explaining the beginnings of the sky and land, gods and humans, and plants and animals along with their relationships both lateral and vertical, as peers and as superiors-inferiors.[26] The Kumulipo is perhaps the best known of those historical epics. Composed long before the arrival of Europeans to the Islands, the Kumulipo is perhaps the oldest genealogy and provides an opening to a truly Hawaiian concept of origins. "In the conception and birth of the chief is the analogy of the conception and birth of the universe," explains Hawaiian scholar Rubellite Kawena Johnson. "As man is born into the universe, so is the universe reborn in him; he is the intelligent survivor of cosmic creation in the highest form of organic life on earth."[27]

Queen Lili'uokalani, Hawai'i's last reigning monarch, claimed the Kumulipo as her family's genealogy, connecting her back to the first light, the first spark of life in the cosmos. After having been imprisoned in her own land by foreigners who had deposed her, the queen translated into English and published the epic poem in 1897. Eight years earlier, her brother and predecessor, King Kalākaua, had published it in the Hawaiian language.[28] Like the family it traces, the Kumulipo is an aggregation of name chants composed and revised by "masters of song" over time to incorporate those joining the lineage and to enhance the prestige and secure the power of the persons being celebrated.[29]

Recitation of a completed chant requires careful and skillful utterance because a wrong breath taken, a hesitation, a mistake, might bode ill for the individual or family being praised. Samuel Manaiakalani Kamakau, a nineteenth-century Hawaiian scholar, described the exacting performance in which "the voice took a tone almost on one note *(kamakua)*, and each word was enunciated distinctly. There was a vibration *(kuolo)* in the chanting together with a guttural sound *(kaohi)* in the throat and a gurgling *(alala)* in the voice box. The voice was to be brought out with strength *(haanou)* and so held in control *(kohi)* that every word was clear."[30] The hush occasioned by the recitation of the Kumulipo must have matched the silence that marked the birth of the universe.

Lili'uokalani's translation of creation's song into the tongue of her usurpers was fitting because her removal by English-speaking foreigners marked genealogy's end, at least of the ruling chiefs. There would no longer be high chiefs for whom *mele inoa* (praise songs) could be composed and sung. Instead, in 1820, with the coming of Christian missionaries from New England, *'oli* (religious songs) were suppressed and *himeni* (hymns) were encouraged. Other kinds of music, called "Hawaiian," played mainly on imported instruments, would take hold in the Islands and make their way back to their originating sources, the continents marked as America, Europe, Africa, and Asia and islands in other seas. The deposed queen would herself become an accomplished composer of music that blended native with alien elements. And despite the monarchy's end, Hawaiians continued to praise past chiefs in *mele inoa* and voice origin poems such as the Kumulipo, to provide themselves with a clear sense of history, identity, and community. Like the poetic process, the death of the old gave way to the birth of the new.

In fact, Lili'uokalani's family, the Kalākauas, as master composers of *mele* and *'oli*, established themselves as sovereigns of the existing order, and by assimilating European forms of music and blending the old with the new they affirmed their standing as peers among Europeans. Lili'uokalani's translation of the Kumulipo substantiated her claim to sovereignty insofar as its genealogy proved her descent from and kinship with Hawai'i's very creation. Her usurpers, fraudulent "natives," could not legitimately claim a similar estate, having no creation song that tied them to the gods and ancestors, the land and the sea.[31] Devoid of rhythm, beauty, and imagination, in this instance of dominion, they were silent and without song.

As songs, religious prayers, praise poems to gods and chiefs, and genealogies and

Danse des hommes dans les îles Sandwich

FIGURE 2. Louis Choris, *Male Dancers of the Sandwich Islands* (1822). Courtesy of Bishop Museum.

historical narratives animated the past for the present; poetry as movement was the hula, which as a poetic form *(mele hula)* highlighted words and their nuances and shades of meanings. Before the arrival of whites, experts taught students in hula schools *(halau hula),* which were often subsidized by chiefs for whom *mele inoa* with hidden designs *(kaona)* were composed and performed. Once conceived, the *mele hula* was an offspring of the school's patron and lineage, and each song/dance and its melodic contour, choreography, and instrumentation bore the traits of that family. The aesthetic and intellectual challenges of those distinctions heightened creativity among artists and interest among their audiences. After European contact, dance translated Hawaiian literature for undiscerning linguistic and cultural tourists, and it thus came to resemble simple pantomime rather than the complex poetic expression it was. The kingdom's end and decline in use of the Hawaiian language hastened the transformation of the *mele hula* and, with it, the power of words in the poetics of dance.[32]

PELE AND HIʻIAKA

A patron of the hula is Hiʻiaka, the younger and much beloved sister of Pele, goddess of volcanoes.[33] Prayer chants *(mele pule)* named for Hiʻiaka were designed to honor her. As a young girl, Hiʻiaka first learned to dance watching her close friend Hōpoe perform the hula by the sea at Nanahuki in the Puna district of Hawaiʻi. For Hōpoe, Hiʻiaka planted the groves of lehua trees with their red and white blossoms, which lent *hōpoe* its meaning as "fully developed" or "well rounded," as a lehua flower. Hiʻiaka performed the hula when Pele asked her sisters to entertain her with dance. All of them declined except Hiʻiaka, who had gathered lehua flowers for wreaths for her sisters. "Yes, I have a song," Hiʻiaka responded to Pele's request, and sang a simple chant, that of a young girl:

> Puna is dancing in the breeze
> The hala groves at Keaʻau dance
> Haʻena and Hopoe dance
> The woman dances
> (She) dances at the sea of Nanahuki
> Dancing is delightfully pleasing
> At the sea of Nanahuki

The imagery of wind blowing over the grasslands of Puna suggests movement, and waves beating against the sea cliffs rhythmically conjure the sound of an *ipu* (gourd drum). Swaying, swirling, and swinging like a pendulum, all referenced in the chant, the line of dancers forms a string of islands.[34] Delighted with the performance, Pele urged Hiʻiaka for more, which prompted:

> The voice of Puna resounds
> The voice of the sea is carried.

While the lehua blossoms are being scattered.
Look towards the sea of Hopoe
The dancing woman is below, towards Nanahuki
Dancing is delightfully pleasing
At the sea of Nanahuki.[35]

"The hula associated with these deified sisters [Pele and Hiʻiaka]," a Pele family member and *kumu hula* (hula teacher) wrote, is "pure original movement and pure sound."[36]

The Pele story is probably indigenous to Hawaiʻi and is one of the most elaborate narratives throughout Polynesia.[37] The account includes a biography of the goddess—her genealogy and birth, migration with family members to Hawaiʻi, search for a suitable home for them in the Islands, and torrid love affairs and epic contests with rivals. Associated with Pele are the worship of volcano deities, the development of the hula, and various geological formations throughout the Islands. In fact, Pele's most common chant name is Pele-honua-mea, or "Pele of the sacred earth."[38] Whether as a body form in the fire of lava or a spirit in its red glow, Pele is associated with both creation and destruction in the formation of land and the fire that consumed and buried forests and all that stood in her way.

"According to Hawaiian myth," the principal recorder of the Pele story notes, "Pele, the volcanic fire-queen and the chief architect of the Hawaiian group, was a foreigner, born in the mystical land of Kuai-he-lani, a land not rooted and anchored to one spot, but that floated free." That ocean, like land, was covered with lushness, "a vision to warm the imagination," and connoted Java, the Asiatic cradle of the Polynesian peoples.[39] With the aid of her brother, a skilled navigator, Pele and her companions sailed from "my kindred beloved" to "an unknown land below the horizon" and made landfall at the northwest extremity of the Hawaiian chain and then at Niʻihau. Like the moving hot spots explained by plate tectonics, Pele's workings began on the oldest and continued on the newest of the Hawaiian chain, where she dwells today. Her search for a suitable home took the expedition from island to island, where she left her mark. These were craters—like Lēʻahi (Diamond Head) on Oʻahu and Haleakalā on Maui—which Pele excavated with a divining rod and digging stick to find land that would shelter the group and be impervious to water.[40] Transformed into a goddess on Maui after a fierce battle with her older sister and implacable enemy, the ocean, Pele moved on to Hawaiʻi, where in the caldron at Kīlauea she settled to become "the Woman who dwells in the pit."[41]

Pele and her family members were a mixed group of spirit and human, powerful and vulnerable. Once a human, Pele became a deity but retained a measure of humanity. Her sister Hiʻiaka, likewise, was human and yet exercised the powers of the heavens (sun, moon, stars, wind, rain, thunder, lightning) from the spiritual power *(mana)* given to her by Pele. The sisters possessed human-like desires and hunger, loves and hatreds, but wielded nonhuman-like powers that violated the limits imposed by time and space. "Pele, on her human side at least," the compiler of her story explained, "was dependent for support and physical comfort upon the fruits of the earth and the climatic conditions that made up her environment." Yet in the account, Pele straddles "that border line which separates the human from the superhuman, but for the most part occup[ies] the region to the other side of that line, the region into which if men and women of this work-a-day world pass they find themselves uncertain whether the beings with whom they converse are bodied like themselves or made up of some insubstantial essence and liable to dissolve and vanish at the touch."[42]

Such a blurring of demarcations was unexceptional to Hawaiians. *Kupuna,* thus, meant both "ancestor" and "grandparent," indicating the smooth transition from the living to the dead. Upon death, *kūpuna* become *ʻaumākua,* spiritual bodies and natural forms of the sky, ocean, and earth such as birds and fishes, wind and rain.[43] Pele and Hiʻiaka were female *ʻaumākua* of families, and their male counterparts like Ku and Lono were similarly associated with volcanism—clouds and rain (Lono) and lightning and thunder (Ku). Family members called out to their *ʻaumākua* for guidance and help, and these calls were in the form of *mele.* Most Pele chants come from the Pele-Hiʻiaka cycle, "the fountain-head of Hawaiian myth" and "the matrix from which the unwritten literature of Hawaii drew its life-blood."[44]

The delicious taste left by the Pele-Hiʻiaka account involves a great romance and love story but also a contest of wills and a sweet and unexpected surprise ending. The story begins when Pele, in the form of a beautiful woman, attends a hula performance and wins the devotion of Lohi'au, a young chief on the island of Kaua'i. From her home on Hawai'i, Pele entrusts her devoted and innocent sister Hi'iaka with the task of going to Kaua'i and bringing Lohi'au to her. With her women companions, Hi'iaka braves evil spirits, monsters, and nature's obstacles to learn, upon her arrival on Kaua'i, that Lohi'au has committed suicide over Pele's sudden disappearance after their night of lovemaking. Using her powers, Hi'iaka restores Lohi'au to life, and together they journey back to Hawai'i, where an impatient Pele has assumed the worse, that Hi'iaka has betrayed her trust. Acting on impulse, Pele reduces Hi'iaka's beloved lehua forests to ashes and turns her dear friend Hōpoe to stone. Having been faithful to her sister, Hi'iaka defies her by embracing Lohi'au in full view of Pele, who promptly engulfs the young lovers in flames. Lohi'au is consumed but Hi'iaka, with a divine body, escapes to restore Lohi'au to life once again and wrap him in her embrace.

In that reunion, the storyteller concludes, "two human streams of characters so different, in defiance of powerful influences that had long held them apart, were, at length, turned into one channel—that of the man, not wholly earthly, but leavened with the possibility of vast spiritual attainment . . . ; that of the woman, self-reliant, resourceful, yet acutely in need of affection; human and practical, yet feeling after the divine." And as metaphor, the story revealed that "the old order," the state in which the will of Pele had ruled almost supreme, had passed away, and in its place was the order of the younger, that of humans who were fast peopling the land that was once Pele's alone "in the making." In this love story, thus, "a new spirit has leavened the whole mass, a spirit of dissent from the supreme selfishness of the Vulcan goddess, and the foremost dissident of them all is the obedient little sister who was first in her devotion to Pele, the warm-hearted girl whom we still love to call Hi'iaka-i-ka-poli-o-Pele [Hi'iaka in the bosom of Pele]."[45]

Impressive, indeed, were Pele and her family of volcanic deities who lived high above the sea to keep the sacred fires burning, who shook the earth and caused the land to quake, who darkened the skies with smoke and clouds from which rumbled thunder and flashed lightning, and who exploded in eruptions and poured forth in fountains and rivers of fire, stone, and molten rock that cascaded into the ocean, causing it to boil and steam. But they were also knowable to the Hawaiians, some of whom held them to be their ancestors, who, like them, migrated from lands to the south and became indigenous to the islands they made and called Hawai'i. A version of Pele's migration remembers Hi'iaka making the long voyage as a fertilized egg carried by her older sister wrapped in her skirt as it incubated and, upon arrival, hatching in Hawai'i.[46] Unlike the immigrant Pele and like the colorful, tropical reef fishes who drifted around the Pacific as larvae, thus, the gentle spirit of the hula was, by birth, Hawaiian.

FIRE AND BRIMSTONE

To some foreigners, Pele and her family were superstitions to be exposed and purged. One of the first non-Hawaiians to write about Pele's manifestations was William Ellis, an English missionary who visited the Islands in 1822 and 1823. The hula, Ellis lamented, attracted large audiences. "The beach was crowded with spectators," he wrote, "and the exhibition kept up with great spirit." To the rhythms of drums, two nine-year-old children, a boy and a girl, danced "in honor of some ancient of Hawaii," dressed "in the dancing costume of the country, with garlands of flowers on their heads, wreaths around their necks, bracelets on their wrists, and buskins on their ankles." Ignorant of the fact that Pele and her clan were the principal patrons of the hula and that the dance linked the people with their ancestors, Ellis and his company proposed substitution of "religious truths" for the "mirth" occasioned by the hula and without apology preached to the multitude at the next hula performance. In his sermon, Ellis, quoting from scripture, urged the people to "turn from these vanities unto the living God, which made heaven and earth, and the sea, and all things that are therein."[47]

Ellis's account of his visit to Pele's domain appears crafted to illustrate the chaos and turbulence that accompanied "idolatry." Barren lava beds, he recorded, greeted the expedition as it headed for the caldron.

> We . . . traveled about a mile across a rugged bed of lava, which had evidently been ejected from a volcano more recently than the vast tracts of the same sub-

stance by which it was surrounded. It also appeared to have been torn to pieces, and tossed up in the most confused manner, by some violent convulsion of the earth, at the time it was in a semifluid state. . . . in many places, it seemed as if the surface of the lava had become hard, while a few inches underneath it had remained semifluid, and in that state had been broken up, and left in its present confused and irregular form.[48]

To Hawaiians, the missionary speculated, a volcanic eruption must have presented a "spectacle awfully sublime and terrific," and "with what consternation and horror must it have filled the affrighted inhabitants of the surrounding villages, as they beheld its irresistible and devastating course, impressed as they were with the belief, that Pele, the goddess whom they had offended, had left her lightning, earthquake, and liquid fire, the instruments of her power abode in the volcano, and was in person visiting them with thunder, and vengeance."[49] In fact, Hawaiians spoke with and prayed to Pele and gave her their respect and devotion, as was practiced by the people at Ka'ū as late as the 1890s, who prayed "The Coming of Pele" on the beach in the early morning before dawn to celebrate the start of the new day:

> From Kahiki came the woman Pele,
>   from the land of Polapola,
>   from the rising reddish mist of Kāne,
>   from clouds blazing in the sky, horizon clouds.
>
> Restless desire for Hawai'i seized the woman Pele.
> Ready-carved was the canoe, Honua-i-Ākea,
> your own canoe, O Ka-moho-ali'i,
>   for sailing to distant lands.
> Well-lashed and equipped, the canoe of high gods,
> your canoe, Sacred-hewer-of-the-land,
> Stood ready to sail with the ocean current.

The prayer continues the account of Pele's voyage in the company of "royal companions" and "gods" and concludes:

THE SACRIFICE TO THE GODDESS PELE.

FIGURE 3. "The Sacrifice to the Goddess Pele," *Harper's Weekly*, April 16, 1859, 249. "Vast numbers of hogs, some alive, others cooked, were thrown into the craters during the time they were in action, or when they threatened an eruption; and also, during an inundation, many were thrown into the rolling torrent of lava, to appease the gods, and stay its progress." William Ellis, *Journal of William Ellis: Narrative of a Tour of Hawaii, or Owhyhee; with Remarks on the History, Traditions, Manners, Customs and Language of the Inhabitants of the Sandwich Islands* (1827; reprint, Honolulu: Advertiser Publishing, 1963), 173.

Jets of lava gushed from Kahiki.
Pele hurled her lightning,
vomit of flame, outpouring of lava was the woman's farewell.[50]

Between descriptions of volcanic devastation, Ellis inserted scenes of battles waged among "supporters of idolatry," women warriors, the abolition of the priesthood and "idolatry," Captain Cook's death, human sacrifices, war and warfare, and funerals and mourning. When a chief died, Ellis charged, "the whole neighbourhood exhibited a scene of confusion, wickedness, and cruelty, seldom witnessed even in the most barbarous society. The people ran to and fro without their clothes, appearing and acting more like demons than human beings; every vice was practised, and almost every species of crime perpetrated. Houses were burnt, property plundered, even murder sometimes committed, and the gratification of every base and savage feeling sought without restraint."[51] In missionary hands, in fact, the volcano becomes a site of contest, both literal and metaphorical, between Christianity and truth, idolatry and superstition.[52]

In response to his guide's fear that the missionaries might offend Pele and cause her to erupt, Ellis assured him that "we did not apprehend any danger from the gods; that we knew there were none; and should certainly visit the volcano." With that confidence, the band proceeded toward Kīlauea, which, in the distance, issued columns of "smoke and vapour." Nearing the crater, Ellis and his companions endured dense smoke and heat from "subterranean fires" that "nearly scorched" their legs, hands, and faces. Kīlauea, Ellis described, was "a vast plain . . . fifteen or sixteen miles in circumference, and sunk from 200 to 400 feet below its original level. The surface of this plain was uneven, and strewed over with large stones and volcanic rocks, and in the centre of it was the great crater." Descending the steep rim of the crater, Ellis stood transfixed peering into the volcano's depths. The view, he wrote, was "sublime and even appalling. . . . 'We stopped and trembled.' Astonishment and awe for some moments rendered us mute, and, like statues, we stood fixed to the spot, with our eyes riveted on the abyss below."[53]

Before the group "yawned an immense gulf, in the form of a crescent, about two miles in length, from north-east to south-west, nearly a mile in width, and

FIGURE 4. Engraving of Kīlauea as sketched by William Ellis in 1823, *Polynesian Researches,* volume 4 (1829). Courtesy of Bishop Museum.

apparently 800 feet deep." Within, lava filled the bottom, creating "one vast flood of burning matter, in a state of terrific ebullition, rolling to and fro its 'fiery surge' and flaming billows." Islands dotted "the burning lake," and Ellis counted twenty-two spouts, which "vomited from their ignited mouths streams of lava, which rolled in blazing torrents down their black indented sides into the boiling mass below." Besides the churning lava on the crater's surface, "dense columns of vapour and smoke" rose to impressive heights, and the whole presented "an immense volcanic panorama, the effect of which was greatly augmented by the constant roaring of the vast furnaces below."[54]

To Christian eyes, the "immense volcanic panorama" presented a "spectacle" that was hard not to recognize. "After the first feelings of astonishment had subsided," Ellis testified, "we remained a considerable time contemplating a scene, which it is impossible to describe, and which filled us with wonder and admiration at the almost overwhelming manifestation it affords of the power of that dread Being who created the world, and who has declared that by fire he will one day destroy it."[55] Yet unexpectedly, near those "regions of fire" and scenes of hell and death everlasting, Ellis and his companions found pools of sweet, fresh water that had formed from the steam from Pele's vents, steam that never touches a cliff, the face of Kā-moho-aliʻi, Pele's eldest brother, and that was condensed by the cool breezes that descended the slopes from the snow of Poliʻahu, Pele's rival, whose white mantle capped the summits of Mauna Kea and Mauna Loa. And ringing those pools grew "flags, rushes, and tall grass" that "flourished luxuriantly."[56] Amid death and barrenness, from a Christian worldview, leapt life abundant.

VOLCANO SCHOOL

The U.S. South Seas Exploring Expedition led by Charles Wilkes visited Pele in 1840–41.[57] The expedition's purposes, as outlined by the secretary of the navy, were to advance "the great interests of commerce and navigation" and to "extend the bounds of science and promote the acquisition of knowledge."[58] Its distinguished scientists, among them Charles Pickering and James B. Dana, and less notable artists accordingly recorded and classified natural phenomena and exotic specimens and presented those renderings as objective and realistic. On this expedition was Titian Ramsay Peale, naturalist and scientific illustrator, member of Stephen H. Long's 1819–20 trans-Mississippi expedition, and son of one of the most influential portraitists of the early republic, Charles Willson Peale. Like his son, the elder Peale held an Enlightenment faith "that the encyclopedic cataloging of descriptive phenomena would yield knowledge and mastery," according to a biographer.[59] His self-portrait, *The Artist in His Museum* (1822), was his masterwork and the painting for which he is best known, and it sums up his central tenet and life's work.

Like Ellis, the expedition's members, both scientists and artists, nevertheless saw through lenses colored by their beliefs, as when Charles Wilkes conjured up the originating evil in the Garden of Eden and mankind's fall by likening the lava on Kīlauea's floor to "hideous fiery serpents with black, vitreous scales."[60] Titian

FIGURE 5. Charles Willson Peale, *The Artist in His Museum* (1822). Lifting the veil, the artist reveals life as studies captured on canvas and in museum cases. Courtesy of Pennsylvania Academy of the Fine Arts, Philadelphia. Gift of Mrs. Sarah Harrison (The Joseph Harrison Jr. Collection).

Ramsay Peale rendered a Romantic portrait of the caldera, which bore the hall-marks of a "volcano school" of painting and its culture-bound associations with creation and primal energy, procreative powers, female genitals and the womb, consuming and transforming fire, original sin and hell, the subterranean world.[61] Embedded thus within a scientific expedition were Romanticist sentiments that rebelled against the ideas of objectivity, order, and explanation—and volcanoes were a fertile and irresistible symbol of elemental chaos that, for Romantic pens and brushes, defied description or control, even as these instruments inscribed representations that masqueraded as science.

Victorian traveler Isabella Bird, daughter of a Presbyterian vicar, was one of the first foreign women to visit and describe for her homebound, curious readers Hawai'i's natural wonders—the "Palm Groves, Coral Reefs, and Volcanoes." Like others who would follow her, Bird traveled to the Islands to regain her health and benefit from the climate, open air, and exercise, "exploring the interior, ascending the highest mountains, visiting the active volcanoes and remote regions which are known to few even of the residents, living among the natives, and otherwise seeing Hawaiian life in all its phases."[62] Those acts of recovery, of self and self's others, constituted the core of Victorian travel writing and scientific observation. An author, plumbing Bird's unpublished letters, reported that the rebel who sickened with "terror and disgust" at the "tyrannies of our aggravated [Victorian] conventionalities" saw in the volcano the face of her "fire and brimstone" clergyman father.[63]

Despite her revulsion of confining precepts, Bird drew generously from stock treatments of Pele's fires. Genesis-like, she described her arrival near the caldron's edge:

> The scene started out from the darkness with the suddenness of a revelation. We felt the pungency of sulphurous fumes in the still night air. A sound as of the sea broke on our ears, rising and falling as if breaking on the shore, but the ocean was thirty miles away. The heavens became redder and brighter, and when we reached the crater-house at eight, clouds of red vapour mixed with flame were curling ceaselessly out of a vast, invisible pit of blackness, and Kilauea was in all its fiery glory. We had reached the largest active volcano in the world, the "place of everlasting burnings."[64]

FIGURE 6. Titian Ramsay Peale, *Kilauea by Night* (1842). Positioned in the foreground, in this rendition of the "consuming fire," are voluptuous Hawaiian women draped in classical Greek-style garments. Courtesy of Bishop Museum.

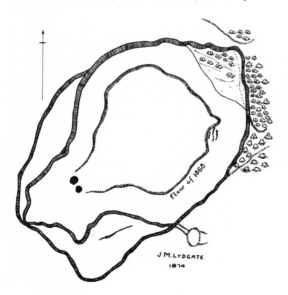

FIGURE 7. Anxiety producing, perhaps, from a man's perspective, a gaping orifice and wound—life and death, ejecting and consuming, Paradise gained and lost. J. M. Lydgate, "Survey of Kilauea," 1874. Courtesy of Bishop Museum.

As she peered into the "invisible pit of blackness," words failed her:

> I think we all screamed, I know we all wept, but we were speechless. . . . The
> words of common speech are quite useless. It is unimaginable, indescribable,
> a sight to remember for ever. . . . Here was the real "bottomless pit"—the "fire
> which is not quenched"—"the place of hell"—"the lake which burneth with fire
> and brimstone"—the "everlasting burnings"—the fiery sea whose waves are never
> weary. . . . there were groanings, rumblings, and detonations, rushings, hissings,
> and splashings, and the crashing sound of breakers on the coast, but it was the
> surging of fiery waves upon a fiery shore.

"But what can I write!" she despaired. But write she did, and recapitulated the totality of the experience with this: "It was all confusion, commotion, force, terror,
glory, majesty, mystery, and even beauty."[65]

An earlier and less reverent visitor to the volcano was Mark Twain, at the time
a correspondent for the *Sacramento Union*. Perhaps Bird was referring to his entry
dated June 7, 1866, in the Volcano House Register, which from 1865 on provided a
record of tourists' impressions, when she noted dismissively that its pages contained
"an immense quantity of flippant rubbish, and would-be wit."[66] Read against missionary accounts, like those by Ellis, Twain's satire is revealed.[67] Traveling with his
fictitious companion, "Mr. Brown," Twain offered, upon arrival at Volcano House:
"But I know there was a protecting Providence over us all, and I felt no fear." Their
visit to the crater was "a thrilling adventure" punctuated by drink, which gave out
"in the careless hands of Brown," who dropped and broke the gin bottle, and ended
with a caricatured confession: "I mused and said 'How the stupendous grandeur
of this magnificently terrible and sublime manifestation of celestial power doth fill
the poetic soul with grand thoughts and grander images, and how the overpowering solemnity . . .'"[68]

The few Hawaiian reflections contained in the Volcano House Register resist
the phantasmic and hackneyed language of the foreigners for whom words had
failed. They often wrote in Hawaiian. "Aloha to you, Pele, the Chiefly Woman of
the Pit," bid Jesse Peliholani (Peleiholani) Makainai of Honolulu on November 22,
1895. "I looked at the bottom of the Pit this morning at nine; there was no fire at

this time—only the aa [a kind of lava flow] below was to be seen, and the steam. I give my full thanks for the beauty and comfort of this place, the Volcano House. Aloha." And Wm. Puaoi on November 23, 1910, reported simply: "The eruption of The Woman was beautiful in the dark of night, and I saw the magical works of The Woman of the Pit and I saw Halemaumau and the top of Uwekahuna, so there was much seen. And so I give my deep aloha to the people who live here at this Hotel. The child of Kauai where the sun sinks into Lehua now goes home."[69]

By the end of the nineteenth century, Kīlauea was apparently the most commonly recognized image of Hawai'i outside the Islands, a status achieved by the productions of writers and visual artists from Europe and the United States and their patrons who financed those representations.[70] Volcanoes as a force of nature occupied the European mind perhaps as early as the Vesuvius eruption in A.D. 79 and its destruction of the Roman cities of Pompeii, Stabia, and Herculaneum. Hawai'i's volcanoes entered the romance novel genre with British missionary Ellis's depictions and the 1825 visit of the H.M.S. *Blonde,* which carried the bodies of King Liholiho (Kamehameha II) and his queen, Kamāmalu, both of whom had died in London of measles during a state visit. Accompanying his majesty's body was his retainer, Naukane, and an English artist, Robert Dampier, whose rendition of Kīlauea, which graced the official 1826 narrative of the H.M.S. *Blonde* as frontispiece, was the first published picture of the volcano.[71]

Scores of artists followed, including Enoch Wood Perry, an American praised for his ability to take a lowly subject and invest it "with a poetry of feeling and delicacy of expression," and Constance Fredericka Gordon Cumming, a Scottish travel writer and amateur artist whose *Fire Fountains* was published in 1883.[72] Charles Furneaux of Massachusetts was one of the most influential of Hawai'i's volcano painters. William T. Brigham, Harvard geologist and later founding director of Hawai'i's Bernice Pauahi Bishop Museum, discovered Furneaux's paintings at a Boston Art Club exhibition.[73] Expecting a major eruption, Brigham invited the artist to accompany him to the Islands to paint and record the phenomenon, "to preserve for scientific study . . . those appearances that the camera does not retain and which are so difficult to describe." Together, Brigham and Furneaux climbed Mauna Loa in July 1880, and later that year when the mountain obliged with a

FIGURE 8. "The precipice from which we had a fine view of the crater itself," wrote an apprehensive Robert Dampier, "was difficult & dangerous to descend: on all sides were yawning chasms & vast apertures seemingly of very great depth. . . . The sight was most extraordinary & appalling." *To the Sandwich Islands on H.M.S. Blonde* (1826). Courtesy of University of Hawai'i Press.

lava flow that threatened the town of Hilo, Furneaux documented the historic, two-year event with more than forty field sketches, many of which found a permanent home in Bishop Museum.[74]

Brigham, the scientist, saw the volcano as more than a specimen for dissection, because science, he admitted, stood mute in its presence, "in this mighty laboratory where God seems to be showing us His most wonderful ways," and where "man must confess without shame to his own ignorance and failure to comprehend." Similarly, Realism could not capture the art of the volcano in its totality. "Many photographs were taken . . . but they fail to give an impression of the outflow at all satisfactory," Brigham reported. "They might represent a dead lava bed as well." Instead, he offered, "I feel that the three views made by Furneaux show more completely than any pictures I have seen, the beginning, course and end of

FIGURE 9. Charles Furneaux, *John Hall's House after July 21, 1881* (1881). "This John Hall," the *Hawaiian Gazette* of August 3, 1881, reported, "is the only one as yet that has lost his home by the lava; but he is a man of much heathenism, believing in old traditions." Furneaux, born in Boston, went to Hawai'i to document the volcano's flow more accurately than the camera, according to geologist William T. Brigham. Courtesy of Bishop Museum.

an Hawaiian lava flow: even without the color, as we have them here, they show better the sublimity of the scene."[75]

In Honolulu, away from his "laboratory," Furneaux painted oil renderings of the volcano in color from notes scribbled on his black-and-white sketches. Critical acclaim greeted his exhibits, and the king, who would foster a revival of Hawaiian arts, Kalākaua, commissioned the painter to record for posterity his newly built 'Iolani Palace and 1883 coronation.[76] Gratitude was short-lived, and a mere four years after having served his royal patron, Furneaux joined white foreigners and the children of American missionaries born in the Islands in a "Hawaiian" League that sought, "by all necessary means," to seize power by curbing the king's prerogatives.[77] Furneaux exhibited a will to exert mastery over his subjects and, accordingly, captured in reality as well as in the imaginary, science, art, and politics. After suffering several strokes and left virtually helpless, Furneaux spent the last years of his life dependent upon Ah Hu, his Chinese American manservant, and his wife, Mary.[78]

Befriended by Furneaux was French-born painter Jules Tavernier, who arrived in Honolulu in 1884. An illustrator in London and New York City, Tavernier headed for California to sketch American Indians and the American West. Debt ridden, he escaped arrest in San Francisco by fleeing to the Islands, where he soon supplanted Furneaux as the principal interpreter of the kingdom's chief tourist attraction.[79] Entranced by Tavernier's 1885 exhibit, a reviewer pronounced one of his paintings "not merely a picture" but "the lake itself, glowing, flashing and sluggishly rolling within massive walls of lava."[80] The copy, for this critic, had supplanted the original, and the volcano's essence was revealed not in "the lake itself" but in the "picture." Tavernier's output was directed, in part, to feed his appetite for alcohol, and he taught students in his Honolulu studio and inspired and tutored another of Hawai'i's volcano school painters, D. Howard Hitchcock, Island-born grandson of missionaries, who, "like a parasite," in his own words, followed Tavernier to Kīlauea to watch him work.[81]

One of the most influential American painters of Pele's fire was muralist, stained-glass innovator, writer, theoretician, and teacher John La Farge (1835–1910). Called by a critic "perhaps the most cultivated of all American artists," La Farge visited Hawai'i in the company of Henry Adams in 1890.[82] Perhaps more memorable than his watercolors of Kīlauea were his written accounts, which conveyed a mood that hung over the crater and its environs like dark, heavy clouds. "Besides the undefined terror and spookiness of the thing," he wrote of the volcano, "there is great boredom. There is nothing to take hold of, as it were—no center of fire and terror—only inconvenience and a faint fear of one thing—but what?" That inchoate yet palpable sense of fear in the volcano's presence was inspired by the otherworldliness of the place. He said of his work, "As I looked and tried to match tints, I realized more and more the unearthly look that the black masses take under the light. A slight radiance from these surfaces of molten black glass gives a curious sheen, that far off in tones or mirage does anything that light reflected can do, and fills the eye with imaginary suggestions." The glitter, La Farge wrote, was "like that of

FIGURE 10. John La Farge, *Crater of Kilauea and the Lava Bed* (1890). The (ghostly) light off the lava beds, the artist felt, "fills the eye with imaginary suggestions." Courtesy of Toledo Museum of Art. Gift of Edward Drummond Libbey, 1912.530.

the moon on a hard cold night, and the volcano crater I shall always think of as a piece of dead world."[83]

Scenes of Pele's fires reflected Romanticism's tinge, whether in the writings of British visitors like William Ellis or Isabella Bird or in the visual renderings by European and American painters. Romanticism's primary concern was the individual's response to nature, and the concept of the romantic sublime expressed an intensely felt relationship to the natural world. Since the mid-eighteenth century, favorite images for British artists and writers of the sublime had been thundering waterfalls, tempestuous seas and violent storms, and destructive volcanoes that evoked an astonishing, powerful, and overwhelming sense of nature. Although the nineteenth-century American sublime grew from British roots, it flourished on a much grander scale because of America's amazing wilderness, from the Hudson River Valley and

Niagara Falls in the Northeast to the thickly wooded forests and rugged coastline of the Pacific Northwest. It is thus unsurprising that the British Ellis would describe his view of Kīlauea as "sublime and even appalling," or that William T. Brigham, the American scientist, would refer to Charles Furneaux's lava flow painting as showing better "the sublimity of the scene." To Americans, the ideas of pain and danger were Romantic, religious, including Transcendentalist, and expansionist sentiments. The American West, thus, and the extracontinental U.S. empire constituted key sites for the sublime. And as with the disciplining of unruly nature with brush and pen, the volcano school sought, as Romanticists, to capture Pele's essence and, as scientists, to harness her energies.

BOMBING PELE

The scientific study of Kīlauea commenced when, in 1911, Thomas A. Jaggar of the Massachusetts Institute of Technology and R. A. Daly of Harvard founded the Hawaiian Volcano Observatory. Enabled by a gift of the Whitney Fund for the study of earthquakes and related phenomena to protect human life and property, the Volcano Observatory depended for its daily operations upon the contributions of local business and professional men interested in the volcano. Because the observatory was in constant need of financial support, its ownership was passed from MIT to the federal government, to the U.S. Weather Bureau, the National Park Service, and the U.S. Geological Survey.[84]

Science in the service of mankind suggested making war on Pele; as put by a 1939 summation of thirty years of volcanology in Hawai'i, the study moved "from geological chemistry to defensive engineering." Jaggar likened that turn to war: "Hawaii was the place where the war of the skyways broke out on December 7, 1941," he recounted, "and where the war against volcanoes had been going on systematically since 1911. Both wars have much in common, demanding services of intelligence, scouting expeditions, mapping, photography and supply, while the main base is essentially a listening post with all the resources of science, invention and industry brought to bear on detection of the strategy of the enemy."[85]

With the precision of a military operation, the first plane took off from Hilo on December 27, 1935, at 8:45 A.M. and was followed by four others at twenty-minute intervals. "Each plane was loaded with two 600-pound demolition bombs, armed with 0.1 second delayed-action fuse, and two 300-pound practice bombs for sighting shots. The bombs were dropped from an altitude of 12,000 feet, approximately 3,500 feet above the target. Two photographic airplanes accompanied the bombers and carried cameras for still and moving pictures." The mission, conceived by Jaggar and his observatory, was designed to divert Mauna Loa's lava flow, which threatened the town of Hilo. At a press conference, Jaggar and Col. Delos C. Emmons of the U.S. Army's air corps noted that "public opinion demanded that something be done to divert or stop this lava flow." Further, as if to warrant his offensive action, Jaggar claimed, "Mauna Loa has definitely mobilized and declared war." Pronounced by him a "victory over Nature," the bombing offered "very valuable tactical training" and was "well worth the cost," according to Emmons, who would later gain promotion to general and, after the Pearl Harbor disaster, responsibility for the defense of Hawai'i.[86]

Viewed from another perspective, surely not represented by the "public opinion" that was alleged to demand it, Pele's bombing was an assault against and desecration of the sacred earth, the gods and ancestors, and the Hawaiians. It has been an ongoing act of war, from the invasive landing of British captain James Cook's expedition on the morning of January 18, 1778, to the occupied present. For Hawaiians, Pele was not "the enemy," in Jaggar's martial idiom, but a revered ancestral figure, as was believed by David Alapa'i, who during the flow of 1919 stood in a cave under the surging lava while chanting his prayer to Pele to spare her beloved people:

Beautiful art thou O Pele of the Pit,
You make such swishing sounds,
You put your beauty on display,
Glowing red before the face of the clouds.
So you are gone to 'Ālika,
The land bedecked with *lehua* blossoms.

Be kindly in your behavior,
Be merciful to your beloved people.[87]

A Hawaiian man, while loading up his truck with his possessions in December 1986 as lava destroyed part of the village of Kalapana, acknowledged: "I love my home; live here all my life, and my family for generations. But if Tūtū [grandparent, as in Tūtū Pele] like take it, it's her land."[88]

Palikapu Dedman, a leader of the Pele Defense Fund during the 1980s, explained: "For us Hawaiians that is what this land is—our religion, and our history. You cannot separate the land from Hawaiian culture. The land shaped us to speak for it; we are what the land made us, we are its soul."[89] Another Fund leader, Noa Emmett Aluli, added: "At its root, Aloha ʻAina is the belief that the land is the religion and the culture. Native Hawaiians descend from a tradition and genealogy of nature deities . . . the sky, the earth, the stars, the moon, water, the sea, the natural phenomena such as rain and steam; and from native plants and animals. The native Hawaiian today, inheritors of these genes and mana [spiritual power], are the kino lau or alternate body forms of all our deities."[90]

"Hawaiians believe that all the land is alive," wrote Hawaiian scholar Davianna Pomakaʻi McGregor, "especially the land which is hot, steams, and has magma under it. As long as there is steam coming out of the earth, Pele lives. The earth where the steam vents belongs to Pele and is sacred." The volcano supplies spiritual power for Pele's descendants, hula masters and dancers, and worshippers, and its various manifestations are sacred. "Come to see my display," the crater beckons, "to see the movements that I do," recited *kumu hula* master Pualani Kanakaʻole Kanahele. "To view my inner parts and how I dance and how I move. But you are not welcome to take what is mine. Whatever hot here is mine. Whatever is hot here is sacred."[91] The land is alive and moves, and breathes, inhaling and exhaling in rhythm as fire and steam.

2

Oceania's Expanse

How shall we account for this nation's
having spread itself in so many detached islands,
so widely disjoined from each other, in every quarter
of the Pacific Ocean? We find it from New Zealand in
the south, as far as the Sandwich Islands to the north, and
in another direction, from Easter Island to the Hebrides; that
is, over an extent of sixty degrees of latitude, or twelve hundred
leagues north and south, and eighty-three degrees of longitude,
or sixteen hundred and sixty leagues east and west! How much
farther in either direction its colonies reach is not known;
but what we know already, in consequence of this and
our former voyage, warrants our pronouncing it to
be, though perhaps not the most numerous,
certainly by far the most extensive,
nation upon earth.

The Voyages of Captain James Cook
Round the World, vol. 2, 256

FIRE AND WATER

Pele, keeper of the sacred fires, engaged in eternal contest with the sea, which strived
to extinguish her fires and erode her creation—the land. A version of Pele's origins
tells of her older sister, Na-maka-o-kahaʻi, a sea deity who anticipates that Pele's fas-
cination with fire will result in trouble for their floating homeland, Kuai-he-lani.

True to form, Pele erupts one day and engulfs the land in a flood of lava. Pele flees Namaka's wrath in the famed canoe Honua-i-a-kea with her brothers and sister Hi'iaka, but Namaka pursues and confronts her in an epic battle on the island of Maui. "To destroy my enemy, to destroy Pele," is Namaka's pledge. She subdues Pele, dismembers her body, and casts its parts about. And yet, in her moment of apparent triumph, Namaka spots Pele's smoke rising from and the skies glowing red above the summits of Mauna Loa and Mauna Kea on the neighboring island of Hawai'i. "She is invincible; she has become a spirit," her brother declares.[1]

Despite their apparent opposition, fire and water are related, as illustrated by the facts that Pele and Namaka are sisters, that Pele's fires emit steam, and that the land and sea and their populations form correspondences. Even islands and continents, falsely distanced by water, float as if adrift on single plates, which ground them. Life, too, can hardly be distinguished from its environments and from one body to another, whether plant or animal, fish or human. "Without piscine ancestry," ichthyologists point out, "man might never have evolved."[2]

Those arteries of animation are a Hawaiian insight, a systematics of the cosmos and all that dwell therein, unifying as well as ramifying as genealogies, which branch but also send roots that connect with deep pasts, distant places, and other bodies. One of those kinship lines tells of the renowned fisherman Kapuhe'euanu'u (the large-headed octopus), who snags and hauls up a mass of coral, which, upon instruction, he throws back into the sea in several pieces with a prayer and a sacrifice. From each piece arises an island in a chain of islands that become Hawai'i:

A land found in the ocean,
Thrown up out of the sea,
From the very depths of Kanaloa,
The white coral in the watery caves
That caught on the hook of the fisherman,
The great fisherman of Kapaahu,
The great fisherman, Kapuhe'euanu'u.[3]

Oceania is both water and fire, "the very depths of Kanaloa" and "a land found in the ocean," extending from Southeast Asia, the birthplace of much of the region's sea and terrestrial life, eastward to clusters of islands called by Europeans Micronesia, Melanesia, and Polynesia. The Hawaiian Islands form the apex of an immense triangle whose area is twice that of the continental United States, with New Zealand and Easter Island at its other corners. The approximately 290 islands within that triangle, along with a few outside of it, constitute Polynesia, an area called by James Cook "by far the most extensive, nation upon earth." Despite their geographic spread, the languages and material cultures of Polynesia's peoples are remarkably similar, like the marine communities of Oceania, which, with its currents, islands, and seamounts, favors rather than deters migrations that distribute, connect, and fortify populations across vast distances.

Skilled seafarers and horticulturalists in Southeast Asia, proto-Polynesians in their well-crafted canoes, like coral and fish larvae but against prevailing winds and currents, island-hopped toward the rising sun. Off New Guinea's northeastern end, they formed "Lapita culture," named for its distinctive pottery, around 1500 B.C., and from that base they ventured eastward, establishing settlements along the way and reaching the eastern end of Melanesia about 250 years later. These were not the original inhabitants on many islands but migrants who were probably useful to their hosts, serving as intermediaries for trade goods and skilled artisans, sailors, and cultivators. From Melanesia they spread to parts of Micronesia, and around 1000 B.C. they reached western Polynesia. In the process of moving, settling, and interacting, Lapita peoples adapted and changed, like their Lapita ware, which, without its characteristic surface decoration, became Polynesian plain ware. In Tonga and Samoa, the Polynesian homeland and dispersion center, pottery making ceased altogether sometime between A.D. 200 and 500.[4]

As their canoe technology improved, involving larger and more seaworthy vessels, Polynesians became capable of traveling greater distances.[5] Two hulls lashed together with a passenger platform between them carried humans and their household goods, domestic animals, water and food, and plant seeds and shoots for propagation. Propelled almost entirely by the wind in their sails, these canoes transported migrants to the Marquesas around 100 B.C., Easter Island and Hawai'i as early as

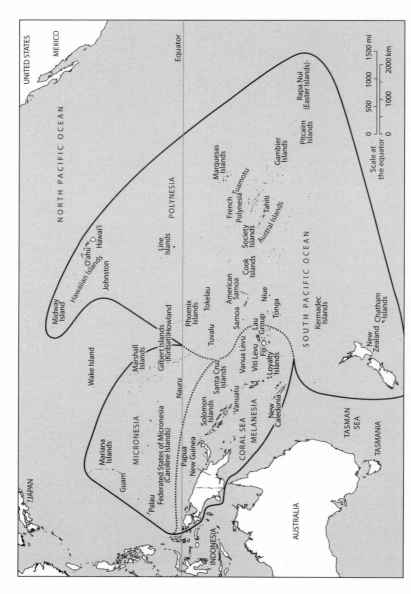

MAP 4. Oceania and the Polynesian triangle. Used with permission of the Center for Pacific Island Studies, University of Hawai'i. Cartography by Manoa Mapworks.

A.D. 300, and New Zealand about 500 years later. The expeditions to the Hawaiian Islands were exceptional in that the spread of Lapita peoples who became Polynesians was generally in an eastward direction. Hawai'i lay to the north in a vast, uncharted territory for those seafaring peoples. It must have required imagination, skill, and daring to reorient the tried and true convention and long-standing practice of movement toward the east. It went against the grain, the inertia of tradition.

"What struck me about voyaging was that before you set out to find a new island you had to have a vision of that island over the horizon," was the lesson learned by Hawaiian Myron "Pinky" Thompson, a leader of the Polynesian Voyaging Society during the 1980s and '90s. "Then you had to figure out how you are going to get there; you had to make a plan for achieving the vision. You had to experiment to try new things. Finally, you had to get out there and take a risk. And on the voyage you had to bind the crew to each other with aloha so they could work together to overcome the risk and achieve the vision."[6] Those objectives were gained in the process of voyaging, in the act of recovering Hawaiian ways of thinking, learning, and doing, and they likely were the same principles employed by Polynesians hundreds of years earlier. They supply an answer to James Cook's puzzlement over "this nation's having spread itself in so many detached islands, so widely disjoined from each other, in every quarter of the Pacific Ocean."

Intention must have inspired those voyages. And because expeditions left islands that were not likely overpopulated, resource poor, or convulsed by wars, the attractions of life at sea and the prospects of renewal rather than expulsions probably underwrote those momentous movements.[7] Oceania to Polynesians of that first diaspora almost certainly suggested an immense and expanding habitat of endless seas and lands, and of opportunities for continuities and changes that awaited them just beyond the next horizon. As put by Thompson, "like our ancestors," voyagers "envisioned new lands and new hopes for ourselves and the generations that will follow us," and they sailed in pursuit of those dreams.[8] Virtually all of them assuredly felt an intimacy with water and land equally and a genuine kinship with their universe, a physical and spiritual world made real through ideas conveyed in poetry, song, and dance, and specialists developed keen senses and accu-

FIGURE 11. Herb Kawainui Kane, *The Discovery of Hawaii*. © 2007 Herb Kawainui Kane.

mulated considerable bodies of learning to detect, systematize, and make use of the resources all around them.

Navigators, like the shark, Pele's brother Kā-moho-aliʻi, who led her expedition to Hawaiʻi, maintained prodigious knowledge of the sea and sky to convey voyagers to their destinations. Wind direction, the color of the water, surface drift objects, birds in flight, cloud formations, and the location and movements of the sun, moon, and stars all figured in a calculus of location, direction, and distance.[9] "With their many types of ocean-going canoes, their use of the stars and other natural phenomena for navigation, and their sensual and emotional familiarity with the sea," wrote the anthropologist and sailor Ben R. Finney, "these Pacific Islanders were able to treat the ocean as an avenue, not a barrier, to communication."[10] And though Polynesians left islands in search of other islands, their lives at sea, the days, weeks, and even months spent there, were influential in shaping their belief systems, their economic activities, and their social relations insofar as voyaging constituted a way of life. So, although intention steered travelers toward land, it also directed them to the open sea.

Oceania has been renamed and reconstituted since the 1970s by some who have claimed its existence and birthright. Instead of a vast and empty ocean dotted by paltry bits of islands and reefs as depicted on European maps, or an Oceania of the colonial regimes of the nineteenth century, Oceania the "sea of islands" as conceived by writers Albert Wendt of Samoa and Epeli Hauʻofa of Tonga conjures "a large world in which peoples and cultures moved and mingled, unhindered by boundaries of the kind erected much later by imperial powers."[11]

> Oceania is vast, Oceania is expanding, Oceania is hospitable and generous, Oceania is humanity rising from the depths of brine and regions of fire deeper still, Oceania is us. We are the sea, we are the ocean, we must wake up to this ancient truth and together use it to overturn all hegemonic views that aim ultimately to confine us again, physically and psychologically, in the tiny spaces that we have resisted accepting as our sole appointed places, and from which we have recently liberated ourselves. We must not allow anyone to belittle us again, and take away our freedom.[12]

Hawaiians and Pacific Islanders are thus indigenous to "a large world" consisting of fire and water, and an estate and home all the same.

WAVE SLIDING

Hawaiians are a mixed group of Polynesians who arrived in the Islands as early as A.D. 300 from the Marquesas and around A.D. 1100 from the Society Islands, coming in waves that continued for at least 200 years. Each group brought with them new ideas and material cultures, crops and relations of production, religions, and ruling genealogies and chiefs, and because they developed in relative isolation over hundreds of years, Hawaiian social relations diverged from those of their equally dynamic Polynesian branches to the south. That process of endemism, accordingly, was not the result of passivity or mere isolation but was stimulated by ingenuity and innovation as much as by the new environment's demands and constraints upon the immigrant. Surfing was one of those imports carried from Oceania to its northern frontier in Hawai'i, where it was modified and reached its highest expression.

Surfing, "sliding down the slope of a breaking wave on a surfboard,"[13] was at the center of Hawaiian social and religious life. It also revealed origins, movements, and histories, which melded disparate Polynesians into a distinctive people, the Hawaiians. A nineteenth-century poem composed during the reign of Kalākaua recalled that past in a "surfing song," in the act of riding "the big wave" at Kona, the surf rolling in from Tahiti, a Hawaiian homeland, "waves worthy of Wākea's people," one of the ruling lineages that came to Hawai'i, and "waves that build, break, and dash against our shore," suggestive of migrations and their effects upon "our shore."[14] Although found throughout Oceania for more than a thousand years, riding the waves was transformed by Hawaiians from a prone to a standing position on long boards. A migrant to Hawai'i like much of the Islands' flora and fauna, surfing rooted itself and drew from the pristine lands and waters and became indigenized and uniquely Hawaiian.

Before making a surfboard, the craftsman carefully selected a tree and buried a red fish among its roots or surely made an offering in gratitude and exchange. Other rites usually followed during the board's construction and, upon completion, dedication to ensure its seaworthiness and good fortune. Hawaiians valued the surfboard highly, and, according to a visitor in 1823, it was "an article of personal property among all the chiefs, male and female, and among many of the common people."[15] At least one *heiau* (temple) on the island of Hawai'i's Kona coast, near the shore where the breakers rolled, was reported to be dedicated to the sport, complete with a deep, stone-lined freshwater pool for washing the devotee's body and surfboard of salt from the sea. Surfing contests were a part of the annual Makahiki festival, marking the agricultural season and honoring its deity, Lono, whose bodies included thunder and rain. The Hawaiian year, the *makahiki,* as referenced in the Kumulipo, consisted of both twelve months and this four-month season of sports and tax collecting.[16] And as was true for all sports, particularly ones that threatened life and limb, prayers for divine intervention asked not only for protection but also for assistance in achieving unequaled feats of skill and strength.[17] The prestige garnered from such demonstrations constituted social capital, affirming chiefly rank and powers and earning commoners fame and, at times, sexual partners.

"There are perhaps no people more accustomed to the water than the islanders of the Pacific; they seem almost a race of amphibious beings," speculated missionary William Ellis, who visited Hawai'i during the 1820s. Although fraught with problematic suppositions and imagery, Ellis's observation appears accurate for many Hawaiians: "Familiar with the sea from their birth, they lose all dread of it, and seem nearly as much at home in the water as on dry land."[18] Men and women participated equally in the sport, which occupied much of their leisure time. In fact, news of high surf might threaten even the necessities of daily labor. "Sometimes the greater part of the inhabitants of a village go out to this sport," reported Ellis, "when the wind blows fresh towards the shore, and spend the greater part of the day in the water. All ranks and ages appear equally fond of it."[19]

The surfers' daring and feats astonished European guests like Ellis. "The higher the sea and the larger the waves," he remarked, "in their opinion the better the sport." They paddle their boards "a quarter of a mile or more out to sea," and there "they adjust themselves on one end of the board, lying flat on their faces, and watch the approach of the largest billow; they then poise themselves on its highest edge, and, paddling as it were with their hands and feet, ride on the crest of the wave, in the midst of the spray and foam." Watching surfers, he concluded, left an indelible impression: "To see fifty or a hundred persons riding on an immense billow, half immersed in spray and foam, for a distance of several hundred yards together, is one of the most novel and interesting sports a foreigner can witness in the islands."[20]

The importance of wave sliding is seen in the large number of surfing terms in the Hawaiian language and their richness. These describe in detail board types, the kinds of waves and the distances between them, how they break, positions on the board, riding styles and wave angles, and the techniques of catching and quitting a wave. Beaches especially noted for high surf appear favored as places for settlement. Thus, for example, the Kona coast on the island of Hawai'i was dotted with surfing beaches, as was the Waikīkī area on O'ahu, and these were areas of high population density. Place-names of surf spots specify the waves and their actions, such as Waipi'o

FIGURE 12. Earliest European rendition of surfing, published in 1829 in William Ellis, *Polynesian Researches,* volume 4.

(curved water) and ʻĀwili (swirl), and dozens of stories and songs commemorate surfing legends and recount tales of sex, love, and courtships played out in the surf and on the beach.[21] A son described his aged father's retirement to and great affection for the famous curving surf of Makaīwa (mother-of-pearl eyes) beach:

> He is dwelling in ease in Kauaʻi
> Where the sun rises and sets,
> Where the surf of Makaiwa curves and bends,
> Where the kukui blossoms of Puna change,

FIGURE 13. Surfing, called by David Malo "a national sport of the Hawaiians," attracted men and women, young and old, and thereby helped to create a sense of community. David Malo, *Hawaiian Antiquities,* trans. Nathaniel B. Emerson (Honolulu: Bishop Museum Press, 1951), 223. Engraving by Roberts. Courtesy of Bishop Museum.

Where the waters of Wailua stretch out,
He will live and die on Kaua'i.[22]

European and American travelers described the sport to their audiences. The first observations were those of scientist and astronomer James King of Captain Cook's expedition, which in 1778 was the earliest contact of Europeans with Hawaiians:[23]

But a diversion the most common is upon the Water, where there is a very great Sea, & surf breaking on the Shore. The Men sometimes 20 or 30 go without the Swell of the Surf, & lay themselves flat upon an oval piece of plank . . . they wait the time of the greatest Swell that sets on Shore, & altogether push forward with their Arms to keep on its top, it sends them in with a most astonishing Velocity,

& the great art is to guide the plank so as always to keep it in a proper direction on the top of the Swell.[24]

American author Mark Twain recalled during his 1866 stay in Hawai'i happening upon

> a large company of naked natives, of both sexes and all ages, amusing themselves with the national pastime of surf-bathing. Each heathen would paddle three or four hundred yards out to sea, (taking a short board with him), then face the shore and wait for a particularly prodigious billow to come along; at the right moment he would fling his board upon its foamy crest and himself upon the board, and here he would come whizzing by like a bombshell! It did not seem that a lightning express train could shoot along at a more hair-lifting speed.[25]

Such accounts may have intrigued their readers, but surfing remained largely an Island affair although carried to the continent as early as 1885, when three Hawaiian princes surfed California's waves at Santa Cruz. Jonah Kūhiō Kalaniana'ole and his brothers, David and Edward, attended St. Matthew's Military School in San Mateo, and during a visit to nearby Santa Cruz they astonished crowds on their long boards hewn from local redwood. "The young Hawaiian princes were in the water enjoying it immensely and giving interesting exhibitions of surfboard swimming as practiced in their native land," reported the *Santa Cruz Daily* on July 20, 1885.

George Freeth, an expert Hawaiian surfer, introduced the sport to Southern California in 1907, under the sponsorship of the Redondo–Los Angeles Railroad Company, to promote water recreation for passenger business between the city and the shore. And five years later, Duke Kahanamoku, on his way to the 1912 Stockholm Olympics, where he won a gold medal in the 100-meter freestyle and a silver medal in the 4-by-200-meter freestyle relay swimming events, surfed Southern California's beaches on his redwood board.[26]

Hawai'i's publicists, Alexander Hume Ford among them, seized upon surfing as a way to command national attention and bring tourist dollars to the Islands. In 1907, Ford and Freeth taught surfing at Waikīkī to writer Jack London, who

FIGURE 14. "Surf-bathing—Success," from Mark Twain, *Roughing It* (Hartford, Conn.: American Publishing Company, 1872), 525.

FIGURE 15. Jonah Kūhiō Kalanianaʻole, David Kawananakoa, and Edward Keliʻiahonui, nephews of Queen Kapiʻolani, in their military uniforms. Rieman and Pray (San Francisco). Courtesy of Bishop Museum.

promptly published "A Royal Sport" in *A Woman's Home Companion* in October of that year. In the article, London whetted women's appetite for "the salty edge of things"; the "majestic surf thundering in on the beach to one's very feet" with its sound, force, and fury; the "thrill of apprehension, almost of fear"; and a "sea-god," a man with "black shoulders, his chest, his loins, his limbs—all is abruptly projected on one's vision." A picture of masculinity, the surfer is "standing above them all, calm and superb, poised on the giddy summit, his feet buried in the churning foam, the salt smoke rising to his knees, and all the rest of him in the free air and flashing sunlight, and he is flying through the air, flying forward, flying fast as the surge on which he stands. He is a Mercury—a brown Mercury. His heels are winged, and in them is the swiftness of the sea."[27] An activity in which men and women participated equally among Hawaiians was translated by London into a spectator sport for the imagined home-staying, white American woman who thrilled vicariously over the strength and speed of a bronzed man, "a Kanaka, burnt golden and brown by the tropic sun,"[28] forbidden fruit and the master of wild waters.[29]

Ford himself published an article on surfing in one of the leading periodicals of the time, *Colliers National Weekly*, in 1909, and through his own *Mid-Pacific Magazine*, launched in January 1911, he promoted surfing as a means for recovering health and manliness. In its inaugural issue, Duke Kahanamoku wrote a lead article, "Riding the Surfboard," for the magazine's white American readers in words reminiscent of Jack London's famous account: "Perhaps the ideal surfing stretch in all the world is at Waikiki beach, near Honolulu, Hawaii. Here centuries ago was born the sport of running foot races upon the crests of the billows, and here bronze skinned men and women vie today with the white man for honors in aquatic sports once exclusively Hawaiians, but in which the white man now rivals the native."[30] That acknowledgment, by the Islands' most accomplished and recognized waterman, affirmed the ability of whites not only to "go native" but also to rival the native in a sport that was uniquely and centrally Hawaiian.[31]

During the early twentieth century, surfing grew in popularity along California's coast, surf clubs sprang up, and in 1928 the sport held its first Pacific Coast Surfriding Championships at Corona del Mar. Surfers competed for trophies for the eight years the championships were held, until World War II ended the event.

FIGURE 16. One of the earliest published photographs of a surfer. *Mid-Pacific Magazine* 1, no. 1 (1911), cover.

Although influenced at first by styles crafted in Hawai'i, surfing in California soon took its own path, including board designs like the lighter and easier-to-ride balsa boards manufactured after 1945. California, with its many beach towns and swelling ranks of surfers, nurtured businesses linked to surfing, such as board building and beachwear. The state produced thousands of balsa and plastic foam boards and became the world's leading producer and market for that industry.[32]

Starting in the 1920s, California surfers made pilgrimages to Hawaiian waters, the sport's fountainhead, and brought with them new board designs and riding techniques, which surfers in the Islands indigenized. Those flows between continent and Islands increased, especially after World War II. The surfboard's development exemplifies the nature of those exchanges, in which "Californians provided many of the ideas; Hawaii provided ideas as well as the waves that challenged the board builders' ingenuity."[33] As boards gained in efficiency and availability, more people surfed, and likewise techniques improved with the involvement of greater numbers of riders. Hawaiian hardwoods were gradually replaced by redwood and pine from California, and boards became sleeker and lighter. Californians perfected the tail fin, or skeg, which provided stability, and covered balsa boards with fiberglass to strengthen and waterproof them. On California's beaches, a *Popular Science* article claimed, "there are schoolboys who easily rival the best Hawaiian experts in the thrilling sport of surf-board riding. That is partly because of the superior surf boards they use—light, buoyant, and beautifully finished."[34] Those innovations swept the beaches of California and Hawai'i by the end of the 1940s and led to new techniques and board materials like the solidified plastic foam of the 1950s.[35]

Adaptations were induced by local conditions of waves—their height, break, speed, and motion—and by temperatures, currents, winds, and shorelines. Those complications and openings increased with the sport's spread along the U.S. west and east coasts and the rest of the world. In 1915, Duke Kahanamoku, while in Australia for swimming events, fashioned a board from local woods and thereby prompted renewed interest in surfing on that island continent's shores. Carlos Dogny, a Peruvian visitor to Hawai'i during the 1930s, took up the sport, and with a board from the Islands he introduced surfing to the beaches near Lima in his homeland. Dogny and others organized Club Waikiki on the beach at Miraflores in 1942, and Hawaiian surf champion George Downing competed in a 1955 tournament in Peru. The following year, Dogny entered the international championships at Mākaha on Oʻahu.[36] Those Pacific crossings of wave sliding extended eventually to other oceans and seas, continents and islands.

A distinctively Hawaiian creation at the center of identity and community, surfing and its mastery by foreigners paralleled foreign powers' influence over the kingdom's political and economic fortunes. European and American sailors, missionaries, and merchants visited the Islands and introduced diseases, ideas, and manufactures that led to a precipitous and horrific human population decline and widespread and destabilizing demands upon the biotic communities of the Islands' waters and lands. At around the time of initial contact with Europeans in 1778, for instance, Hawaiians numbered more than 400,000. But largely because of measles, smallpox, and venereal and other diseases alien to the Islands, Hawaiians were without immunities and suffered massive losses through deaths and sterilization such that by the 1890s only about 40,000 survivors of the biological invasion remained.[37]

Surfing and other aspects of Hawaiian culture suffered similar declines encouraged by a deliberate campaign waged by some foreigners to eradicate all traces of "savagery" and replace them with the blessings of "civilization." Others sought to escape civilization's materialism and "feminization" by assuming the natural state of the savage.[38] Christian missionaries, an 1838 visitor claimed, were the principal censors of Hawaiian sports. "A change has taken place in certain customs," the traveler charged. "I allude to the variety of athletic exercises, such as swimming, with or without a surfboard, dancing, wrestling, throwing the javelin, etc., all of which games, being in opposition to the strict tenets of Calvinism, have been suppressed."[39] Missionaries such as Hiram Bingham, of the first company sent by the American Board of Commissioners for Foreign Missions, denied their role in the downturn of Hawaiian sports, which he attributed to "the increase in modesty, industry and religion" with civilization's advance.[40] Still, surfing's associations with idleness and sexual freedoms must surely have bruised and scandalized tender missionary moral sensibilities.[41]

In addition to undergoing those externally induced societal changes, Hawaiians participated in establishing new relations through gender and class contestations, such as when Liholiho, the son of Kamehameha I, ended the *kapu* system in 1819 and with it a set of religious beliefs and practices and certain chiefly and manly privileges. With the system's overthrow, the annual Makahiki festival, with its sports and games, along with the Hawaiian calendar ended soon thereafter, and according to some visitors surfing became a rare sight in the Islands during the second half of the nineteenth century.[42] The sport's apparent resuscitation during the next century, as claimed by foreigners such as Alexander Hume Ford and Jack London, bent upon their bodily rejuvenation as whites and as men in the Islands and on the continent, narrates the familiar colonial trope of "going native" and, for the sake of natives, enacting cultural and environmental rescue and preservation. For those new "natives," civilization might have encouraged the taking up of that redemptive role and racialized burden with their attendant attractions and restorative powers.

HEALTH IN PARADISE

During the early 1900s, the *Mid-Pacific Magazine* pitch for white tourists and settlers, or those "who have become enchanted with the lure of the Pacific," was shaped by sexual and racial anxieties held by many in the temperate zone of life in the tropical band.[43] An essayist, in "Hawaii for the White Man," declared unambiguously that "Hawaii is the one land within the tropics created by Nature for the white man," and he claimed that the Islands were ordained as "the white man's paradise" and that white men would thus benefit from visiting and settling in Hawai'i.[44]

A key concern was the ability of whites to live in the tropics, with its heat, diseases, and peoples of color. "Can the white man live in the tropics?" asked the magazine's Frederic J. Haskin in its 1920 issue. "Although a great deal has been said and written on the subject of the white man's health in tropical lands," he observed, "it has never been determined exactly what effects, good or bad, the tropical climate has on the man with a light skin." With whites increasingly seeking homes and "free or cheap agricultural lands" in the tropics, he continued, the question of health

FIGURE 17. Naked Polynesian youth beckon to white men from the pages of *Mid-Pacific Magazine* 1, no. 2 (1911), and 3, no. 5 (1912).

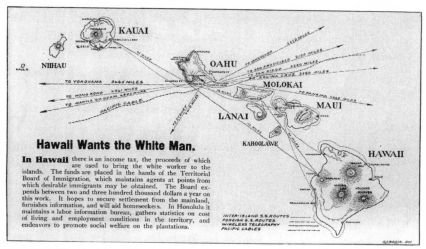

Hawaii Wants the White Man.

In Hawaii there is an income tax, the proceeds of which are used to bring the white worker to the islands. The funds are placed in the hands of the Territorial Board of Immigration, which maintains agents at points from which desirable immigrants may be obtained. The Board expends between two and three hundred thousand dollars a year on this work. It hopes to secure settlement from the mainland, furnishes information, and will aid homeseekers. In Honolulu it maintains a labor information bureau, gathers statistics on cost of living and employment conditions in the territory, and endeavors to promote social welfare on the plantations.

FIGURE 18. Board of Immigration's advertisement in *Mid-Pacific Magazine* 1 (1911): 146 (insert).

and morbidity was becoming more important. Hawai'i, with its cool sea breezes and mountains that "reach literally out of the tropics by reason of their elevations," posed an exception to the conditions that whites usually encountered in the torrid zone. In fact, whites born in Hawai'i were "among the star athletes of Yale and Harvard," the writer boasted, and "young Hawaiian athletes of Anglo-Saxon blood, who have spent so much of their time riding the surf" have "tanned to a very dark hue—darker indeed than the native Polynesians." By thus acquiring "the dark skin of the native," a form of endemism, Haskin concluded, whites had successfully adapted to life in the tropics.[45]

Water sports played an important role in this call to convince whites on the continent that their well-being and interests were well served in the Islands. "The Lure of Hawaii," the magazine proposed, was its bearing as "the natural playground of the Pacific." Here the visitor would discover that activity, rather than passivity, was the real entertainment. Even amateurs, with practice, could master the "sport of kings." "Anyone who swims with a little patience learn[s] not only to ride the surfboard, but to come in before the great rollers standing erect upon even a tiny bit of plank," the article promised. "Duke Kahanamoku and a dozen other swimmers who hold world records of some sort are there every day, companions of the new comer in the surf at Waikiki." In the Islands' waters, "brilliant colored fish as they dart across the coral reefs in the shallow waters" would delight visiting fishermen. "Old Hawaii is dying out," the essay lamented, but a revival of "the old sports for which the Hawaiians were famous a century ago" was under way.[46]

A model for Ford's *Mid-Pacific Magazine* was *Paradise of the Pacific*, founded in January 1888 to promote "the business interests of the Hawaiian Islands in diffusing abroad, for the benefit of tourists and others, reliable information on all points relating to climate, natural scenery and volcanic wonders, tropic life and travel, agricultural and commercial interests."[47] Faithful to that promise, the magazine featured descriptions of the Islands' climate, natural beauty, and indigenous peoples. Hawaiians, the periodical tried to reassure its white readers, were not "naked, black creatures, whose principal occupation was blowing conch shells, brandishing thigh bones, and dancing a horrible cancan around a fire where a human carcass was roasting." Rather, "physically they are rather large, and have a light brown color, straight hair, and are handsomely formed, of good bearing, and well featured. The women also are pleasing and comely. There is nothing about them savoring of the squaw, hag, or wench, which is almost universal among so many of the primitive dark-skinned races."[48]

Like the writings of Victorian traveler Isabella Bird, whose visit to Hawai'i was prompted, in part, "for health" and "the benefit which I derived from the climate,"[49] those descriptions of "the white man's paradise" were creations of alien whites who became, through their claims and conquests, native, like their pale skins tanned dark by the tropical sun. And white men, by mastering rough water sports like surfing, might reclaim their manliness, which had been attenuated by the gentility of civilization. As the presses printed the first issue of *Paradise of the Pacific,* the Hawaiian kingdom stood on its last legs. The year before, with Kalākaua on the throne, whites had formed the "Hawaiian" League, whose members claimed "Hawaiian" status by "birth, parentage and affiliation," and whose purpose was unbridled control of Hawai'i's government. "Revolutions do not go backwards," wrote one of the plotters, "and there was sufficient determination and force behind the revolution of 1887 (bloodless as it was), to persuade the dusky monarch into subjection."[50] Under that threat of arms, the king signed the Bayonet Constitution of 1887, which curtailed his executive powers and prerogatives and contributed to the end of the Hawaiian kingdom, finally realized with the 1893 overthrow of Queen Lili'uokalani, who had tried to revoke the 1887 constitution.

Seemingly above that political fray, the October 1890 *Paradise of the Pacific* featured legends of the volcano, a brief mention of "ancient Hawaiian voyages," and a report, "Hawaii for Health," written by "a medical visitor to these islands." "It is not surprising that a trip to the Hawaiian Islands should be recommended in cases of sickness in which a change of climate is considered necessary for cure," the author confirmed. "In Honolulu the invalid throws off his heavy wraps and basks in the lovely atmosphere." For those afflicted with pneumonia or "acute diseases generally, as contracted in San Francisco . . . the rest and quiet life, the agreeable temperature and lovely scenery are invaluable."[51]

Charles Warren Stoddard, American writer and friend of Mark Twain and Robert Louis Stevenson, once described Kalākaua: "Oh, what a king was he! Such a king as one reads of in nursery tales. He was all things to all men, a most companionable person. Possessed of rare refinement, he was as much at ease with a crew of 'rollicking rams' as in the throne room."[52] Writing in *Paradise of the Pacific,* Stoddard described his "Halcyon Hawaii" about two years after Kalākaua, the "dusky monarch," had signed the Bayonet Constitution: "To sail over placid seas in sight of my summer islands; to lie off and on before the mouths of valleys that I have loved, those in my youth, I have been in ecstacy *[sic]*; but never again to set foot on shore, or to know whether it be reality or a dream—this is the dance my imagination leads me; this is the prelude to many an unrecorded souvenir." His Hawai'i, Stoddard claimed, and its

> soft cadence of the evening breeze, the caress of drooping boughs, and the silent showers of rose petals in the unvisited arbor . . . will lead one ever to think of the place and to speak of it very much in the spirit of Peter Martyr, who thus wrote long ago of the queen's garden in the Antilles: "Never was any noisome animal found there, nor yet any ravaging four-footed beast, nor lion, nor bear, nor fierce tigers, nor crafty foxes, nor devouring wolves, but all things blessed and fortunate."[53]

SCREENING OCEANIA

The early magazines' vision of a tropical paradise, with its gentle trade winds and nursery rhyme monarchs, laid the foundation for Hollywood's films of the "South Seas," in which the sea and land and their biotic communities were the sets and backdrops for featured white actors who moved across that dreamy stage. One survey counted sixty-six movies made in or about Hawai'i between 1898 and 1939. The first two, both produced in 1898, were the filmic counterparts of the then-popular travel writings of far-off and exotic places. An Edison Company film crew, on their return voyage from Asia, disembarked to record a Honolulu street scene and "natives" diving for coins tossed by boat passengers, and a travel lecturer and his cinematographer filmed canoes riding the surf, U.S. troops on their way to the warfront in the Philippines, and a *lu'au* (feast). Others in this genre, like *Kilauea—*

The Hawaiian Volcano (1918), *Hawaii* (1919), and *Oahu and Its Pineapple Fields* (1921), introduced the Islands to audiences on the continent.[54] Travelogues, whether filmic or textual, offered their readers vicarious and real pleasures in the acquisition of empire through overseas investments in and purchases of land, labor, commerce, and goods and exertions of control over virgin territory and servile subjects.[55]

In defining "South Seas cinema" as a separate genre, a film historian noted as its most distinguishing feature the theme of "Paradise," of the islands of Oceania as "earthly Edens." Hollywood, he postulated, depicts paradise as tropical abundance, simplicity, and tranquility as opposed to competition and survival of the fittest.[56] Those attributes of Oceania's islands—pregnant, plain, passive—are feminine qualities bestowed similarly upon its dark women, who await the embrace of heterosexual men, especially white men from the continental United States.[57] Accordingly, a favored story line since 1913, with the release of *The Shark God* and *Hawaiian Love,* the first Hollywood productions shot on location in Hawai'i, has been the romance of brown women, often played by white women or Latinas, by white men set amid scenes of white-sand beaches and gently swaying palm trees.[58] Those interracial couplings of men and women offer parallels for spatial ravishments of islands by continents.

The fictive quality of South Seas romances was enhanced by the indecipherable racializations of Polynesians, especially women, who were played by actresses with a range of colors and looks, including whites such as Virginia Brissac as a "pretty Hawaiian girl" in *Hawaiian Love* (1913) and Clara Bow as a hula flapper in *Hula* (1927) and Mexican-born Dolores del Rio in *Bird of Paradise* (1932).

Billed as the "Epic Romance of All Time," *Bird of Paradise* the movie followed on the success of the 1912 Broadway production of that same title and cut the pattern that became the South Seas romance. Famed King Vidor directed a stellar cast, including Joel McCrea playing Johnny, an American tourist who falls in love with Luana (del Rio), the native princess whom he abducts and takes to a lush and isolated isle where they live in tropical splendor. The natives, however, despoil their paradise by recapturing Luana and preparing her as a sacrifice to appease the volcano god, Pele. Johnny and his friends rescue her, but Luana chooses to stay with her people. After sharing a final, tender moment with Johnny, Luana walks toward

FIGURE 19. Hollywood cast such white actresses as Dorothy Lamour (top left), the "sarong girl," along with Japanese Reiko Sato (top right) and Mexican Movita Castenada (bottom right) as "Polynesians." Courtesy of Luis Reyes Archives.

FIGURE 20. Clara Bow, idealized as the thoroughly modern "Roaring Twenties" flapper, went native, dancing as Hula Calhoun on her father's spread in the Islands. *Hula* (1927). Courtesy of Luis Reyes Archives.

her redemption and destiny in the volcano's fires. According to Vidor, David O. Selznick, the movie's producer, instructed him: "I don't care what story you use so long as we call it *Bird of Paradise* and Del Rio jumps into a flaming volcano at the finish."[59]

Born Lolita Dolores Martinez Asunsolo López Negrete, Dolores del Rio starred in many silent films but was frequently typecast in exotic, ethnic roles, especially with the advent of sound. Unhappy with Hollywood and its limits imposed upon her career as an actress, del Rio returned in 1943 to Mexico, where she made many important films.[60] Other Latinas who played Polynesians include Mexican-born Raquel Torres, who starred in MGM's first feature-length movie that synchronized dialog, music, and special effects, *White Shadows in the South Seas* (1928), and María Montez of the Dominican Republic, one of the most notable of the "dark ladies," whose big break came with *South of Tahiti* (1941), in which she played a jungle beauty.[61] Torres, as a South Seas native in *Aloha* (1931), marries an American businessman, causing his family in San Francisco to disown him. Returning to her island home, the doomed lover leaps into the volcano, as did Luana in the model

FIGURE 21. Dolores del Rio dances topless under her leis and reveals her navel. *Bird of Paradise* (1932). Courtesy of Luis Reyes Archives.

Bird of Paradise, sacrificing herself to Pele and thereby atoning for her miscegenation and restoring her man and, in effect, white society to normalcy. Montez danced the hula in *Moonlight in Hawaii* (1941), and Lupe Vélez, the popular comedienne of the "Mexican Spitfire" series, played a Mexican nightclub performer who is crowned Miss Honolulu in the 1941 movie *Honolulu Lu.*[62]

In Hollywood's feminization of Oceania, the primal, fertile earth frees white men from the confines of modernity and allows them to shed social inhibitions such as nudity and interracial sex. In landscapes of endless summers and perpetual

FIGURE 22. "Christian finds release from his responsibilities . . . in the arms of Maimiti, beautiful native girl," assures a lobby card for *Mutiny on the Bounty* (1935). Pictured here are Clark Gable and Mamo Clark. Courtesy of Luis Reyes Archives.

contentment, near-naked women and men cavort and sing, like Betty Grable in *Song of the Islands* (1942):

> Everybody feels terrific
> And romantically prolific
> And you never see a face without a smile
> It's against the law to wear a frown
> Down on Ami Ami Oni Oni Isle.[63]

In the MGM Oscar-winning *Mutiny on the Bounty* (1935), Hawaiian actress Mamo Clark and Mexican Movita Castenada go topless as Tahitian beauties who

FIGURE 23. Behind the camera, Bing Crosby during a shoot for *Waikiki Wedding* (1937). Courtesy of Luis Reyes Archives.

fall in love with the mutinous crew of the H.M.S. *Bounty,* led by Clark Gable as Fletcher Christian.[64] Having broken the bonds of a humorless taskmaster, the ship's captain, played by Charles Laughton, the rebellious sailors find freedom in the islands and arms of seductive and sexually available brown women who leave their homes to accompany the white men to an isolated island paradise, which is, instructively, only temporary because of the defiant crew's recapture by the persistent captain and their court martial in England under the laws and strictures of civilization.

South Seas cinema, thus, contained lessons for white American audiences. Tropical paradise, like the biblical one, was planted with the temptation of evil embodied by a seductress, an uninhibited brown woman. In *Never the Twain Shall Meet* (1931), Latina actress Conchita Montenegro plays opposite Leslie Howard in a morality play of the evils of miscegenation between a Polynesian woman and a white American man.[65] The movie's title comes from the famous line that begins *The Ballad of East and West* (1889) by British writer Rudyard Kipling: "Oh, East is East, and West is West, and never the twain shall meet." In 1898, Kipling published *The White Man's Burden,* a racialized and gendered load, to prod the United States into assuming its manly duty of empire in the Pacific: "Come now, to search your manhood," the poem chides, "Have done with childish days."[66] But empire was fraught with perils, South Pacific romances showed, even as Bing Crosby crooned "Sweet Leilani," written by Hawaiian composer Harry Owens and winner of that year's Oscar for best song, from *Waikiki Wedding* (1937). The movie critic for the *Honolulu Advertiser* blasted the film for its "pseudo-Hawaiian narrative," "headdresses reminiscent of Indians," and "tapas like Roman togas." *Waikiki Wedding,* he concluded with a sense of finality, was "purest hokum."[67]

3

Pagan Priest

On October 15, 1819, at the Park Street Church in Boston, a company of seven missionaries and their wives and children, along with three Hawaiians, were formed into "a Church of Christ" to convert Hawai'i's "heathens" to Christianity. Although the focus of that crowded assembly may have been upon the white American missionaries and their imminent departure for distant and dark lands, the three Hawaiians must have been eager to leave New England's approaching winter for Hawai'i's sunshine and warmth, having spent several years marooned on those alien shores. One of the Hawaiians, Thomas Hopu, addressed the crowd, and to the *Boston Recorder* reporter at the scene his performance was both wonderfully moving, "a most affecting spectacle." It was ironic to see a native of Hawai'i preaching the gospel to "the citizens of Boston" and "calling on them to . . . believe in Jesus Christ." Hopu would soon thereafter disappoint his missionary patrons with his backsliding, but on this day he, as "spectacle," bore witness to the transformative power of Christianity and civilization's benevolence. More than five hundred souls received Holy Communion at the farewell service, so great was the interest among Boston's citizens, and on Saturday morning, October 23, at Boston's Long Wharf, the crowd lifted their voices in hymn, singing "Blest Be the Tie That Binds" and "When Shall We All Meet Again?"[1]

HAWAIIANS IN NEW ENGLAND

"I was born about the year 1795," began Thomas Hopu in his memoirs, written shortly before his departure from Boston.[2] Reared by his aunt and uncle until the age of four, Hopu lived the next eight years with his birth parents, although his mother died when he was about nine years old. In 1807, Hawai'i's king, Kamehameha, charged Hopu and another Hawaiian, 'Ōpūkaha'ia, with attending to his twelve-year-old son, bound for America on board a ship from New Haven, Connecticut. The commercial vessel left Hawai'i for the Pacific Northwest, where it had left some of its men to collect the fur pelts exchanged in the China trade,[3] but upon its return to the Islands before setting out for China, Kamehameha changed his mind about the young prince's education in America and removed him from Capt. Caleb Brintnall's ship and care. Having tasted the excitement of travel, however, Hopu and 'Ōpūkaha'ia asked to remain on board and headed westward for Asia, and then America.[4]

In choppy seas en route to China, Hopu fell overboard while drawing up water to wash his dishes. Despite the high winds, he managed to call out to a mate at the helm, who in turn cried out, "Thomas is overboard." Still, it took some time to slow the vessel and turn it around, and in the high surf and wind Hopu soon lost sight of the ship and despaired of drowning. "I considered myself in the greatest danger of being swallowed up in the mighty ocean," he recalled. "I expected to die before the ship would reach me." A good swimmer, he somehow managed to stay afloat until rescued, although "I could not speak a word to any one of my shipmates, because I was almost dead when I got on board the ship."[5] After a six-month stay in Macao and Canton, the trade vessel, heavy with goods, sailed across the Indian Ocean for South Africa's Cape of Good Hope and northward for North America's east coast.[6] In the fall of 1809, Hopu and 'Ōpūkaha'ia stepped ashore at New York harbor.

Dazzled by the city's exoticism, Hopu wrote, "I perceived many new things, that I never had seen before in all my life. It seemed sometimes that it would make one almost sick, to see so many kinds of curiosities."[7] Part of those "curiosities" may have been the Christian doctrine taught to him later in nearby New Haven by his host, O. Hotchkiss, who told him of heaven and hell and of life and death without end. In turn, Hotchkiss and others persisted in asking him about Hawai'i, especially about its (primitive) peoples and their (false) religious beliefs.

After two or three years with Hotchkiss in New Haven, Hopu returned to the sea on about a dozen voyages. Captured by the British during the War of 1812, he was imprisoned for several months on the Caribbean island of St. Kitts, where he witnessed the barbaric enslavement of Africans and native peoples by Europeans. "I did not . . . like to see them abuse the slaves so cruelly: and sometimes they starved them, and would not give them any bread to eat, though they worked ever so hard; and but little other provision," Hopu reported. "I had often seen the white people, on these Islands, put chains on their slaves' necks, and on their legs, as long as they lived."[8]

Sickened by the inhumanity of island slavery, Hopu managed to return to the United States, where he spent the winter in New Haven. On his next voyage to the Caribbean, the ship on which he was sailing was overturned by high winds, and he and several crew members drifted in a lifeboat for six days before reaching an un-inhabited island. There they found three black fishermen, who gave them water and took them to a nearby inhabited island. "These Negroes were very kind to us," testified Hopu, "and did all that they had in their power to do us good."[9] That kindness, Hopu must have noticed, contrasted markedly with the treatment shown blacks by whites under slavery. After about two months on the island, Hopu tried to return to the United States on board an American ship, which was captured once again by the British, who took all of the crew's possessions, including the ship, before giving the crew members up to the Americans.

Hopu was deposited at Nantucket, and from there he returned to New Haven and worked as a family servant and coachman. He accompanied his employer to Whitestown in New York State, and after about nine months there he moved to Albany in September 1815 and from there to New York City. Hearing that Captain Brintnall planned a voyage to the South Pacific and intent on returning home to Hawai'i, Hopu set out for New Haven, where "Christian friends" prevailed upon him to obtain an education before returning to the Islands. Possibly unknown to Hopu, those friends intended to use him for missionary work in Hawai'i. Passed from one home to another and all the while receiving religious instruction, Hopu and fellow Hawaiians 'Ōpūkaha'ia (now known as Henry Obookiah) and William Kanui eventually met in Goshen, Connecticut. They remained in that vicinity for more than a year, attending James Morris's South Farms Academy in Litchfield, and in the spring of 1817 the group joined other students, mainly American Indians, at the newly built Foreign Mission School in nearby Cornwall.

William Kanui came to New England, like Hopu and ʻŌpūkahaʻia, on board an American ship. Born on the island of Oʻahu but reared on neighboring Kauaʻi, Kanui was probably well acquainted with the foreign vessels that landed near his Waimea home to replenish their supplies of fresh water and food and take on Hawaiians to replace crews that were frequently diminished by death, illness, and desertion. Kanui was eleven or twelve years old when he, along with his brother and four other Hawaiians, joined the crew of a Captain Davis of Boston. The ship sailed to Alaska and the Pacific Northwest before heading back across the Pacific to Asia and Africa. At the Cape of Good Hope, Davis arranged for the transfer of Kanui and his companions to a Boston-bound ship while he headed for England. The Hawaiians landed in Boston in 1809.

Working for their keep for several years as servants and farm laborers, the young men yearned to return to the sea to escape the drudgery of landlocked existence. Like Hopu, Kanui and his brother joined the U.S. Navy and fought in the War of 1812. After the war, while the two were on their way to New York City to find work, Kanui's brother was taken ill and died in Providence, Rhode Island. Alone and in grief, Kanui trained as a barber in New Haven, though he felt "so bad he did not care if he lived or died."[10] It was in New Haven that ʻŌpūkahaʻia found Kanui in 1815 and persuaded him to join the company that eventually studied at Cornwall's mission school in preparation for their return to Hawaiʻi.

Henry ʻŌpūkahaʻia was the poster child for the missionary endeavor in Hawaiʻi. He was, as engraved on his tombstone, "eminent for piety and missionary Zeal." Born to commoners in about 1792, ʻŌpūkahaʻia was orphaned as a result of war and reared by his uncle, "a high priest, to educate him for priestly service."[11] When he left with Hopu on Captain Brintnall's ship, ʻŌpūkahaʻia was about fifteen years old and apparently eager to explore the world beyond Hawaiʻi. After arriving in New York City in 1809, he and Hopu spent some time in New Haven, where, as the missionary story recounts, students at Yale College found him weeping at the threshold of one of the buildings. Upon being asked about his distress, ʻŌpūkahaʻia expressed his keen thirst for learning and his frustration over his inability to enter education's door. Touched by his story, Yale students, including Edwin W. Dwight, who would later write ʻŌpūkahaʻia's memoirs, tutored the Hawaiian castaway.

Samuel J. Mills, a recent graduate of Williams College in Williamstown, Massachusetts, on a recruiting visit to Yale for a secret missionary society, the Brethren, proposed that ʻŌpūkahaʻia continue his studies in Torringford, Connecticut, while living there with his parents. In a letter dated December 20, 1809, Mills described his Hawaiian subject: "His manners are simple; he does not appear to be vicious in any respect, and he has a great thirst for knowledge."[12] So while Hopu set off to sea, ʻŌpūkahaʻia left for the interior. Unlike his companion and friend, a missionary tract noted, Hopu "seemed inclined rather to rove than to study," and he accordingly chose "the life of a sailor."[13] The Mills family cared for ʻŌpūkahaʻia until 1813, when James Morris of Litchfield invited him to stay and study with him, and the next year the Litchfield North Consocation of Congregational Churches assumed sponsorship of ʻŌpūkahaʻia's education. "He is now about 21 years of age," the pamphlet published to raise money for the Foreign Mission School reported. "He is of amiable and affectionate disposition, modest and obsequious in his deportment."[14]

ʻŌpūkahaʻia was crucial to the missionary project. He was, in the words of one of his tutors and sponsors, "of essential service to the cause of Foreign Missions. [He] has silenced the weak but common objection against attempting to enlighten the heathen, that they are too ignorant to be taught."[15] ʻŌpūkahaʻia's conversion from pagan priest to evangelist for Christ, thus, was a deliberate and careful scripting of a man and a life. "He was considerably above the ordinary size; but little less than six feet in height, and in his limbs and body proportionally large," a praise-poem to ʻŌpūkahaʻia began. "His form, which at sixteen was awkward and unshapen, had become erect, graceful, and dignified. His countenance had lost every mark of dullness; and was, in an unusual degree, sprightly and intelligent. His features were strongly marked. They were expressive of a sound and penetrating mind. He had a piercing eye, a prominent Roman nose, and a chin considerably projected." This "whitening," this "Americanizing," of Henry ʻŌpūkahaʻia was uncommon in that Hawaiians were routinely racialized as "black" or "mulatto" in the United States during this time.[16] "His complexion was olive, differing equally

OBOOKIAH,
a Native of Owhyhee

FIGURE 24. Engraving of
Henry ʻŌpūkahaʻia from
Memoirs of Henry Obookiah
(Elizabeth-Town, N.J.: Edson
Hart, 1819), frontispiece.
Collection of the Cornwall
Historical Society, Cornwall,
Connecticut.

from the blackness of the African and the redness of the Indian," the apotheosis
continued. "His hair was black, worn short, and dressed after the manner of the
Americans. In his *disposition* he was amiable and affectionate. His temper was mild.
Passion was not easily excited, nor long retained. Revenge, or resentment, it is presumed, was never known to be cherished in his heart. He loved his friends."[17]

ʻŌpūkahaʻia began to translate a few chapters of the Bible into Hawaiian in
1815, and in the fall of the following year he traveled throughout Massachusetts on
behalf of the American Board of Commissioners for Foreign Missions to solicit do-

nations for the Hawaiian mission. Determined to become a preacher, according to his teacher and biographer, ʻŌpūkahaʻia entered the Foreign Mission School in Cornwall in 1817, where he worked on a Hawaiian grammar, dictionary, and spelling book. In 1818 he became seriously ill and had to quit his studies. On February 17 of that year he died of typhoid fever in a house that still stands near the site of the Foreign Mission School. The day before he died, according to his biographer, ʻŌpūkahaʻia called his companions to his bedside and spoke to them in Hawaiian: "My dear countrymen, I wish to say something to you all—you have been very kind to me—I feel my obligation to you—I thank you. And now, my dear friends, I must beseech you to remember that you will follow me. Above all things, make your peace with God—you must make Christ your friend—you are in a strange land— you have no father—no mother to take care of you when you are sick—but God will be your friend if you put your trust in him." The next day, "a few minutes before he breathed his last, his physician said to him, 'How do you feel now, Henry?' He answered, '*Very well—I am not sick—I have no pain—I feel well.*' The expression of his countenance was that of perfect peace." Soon thereafter, when he expired, "All sprang to the bed. The spirit had departed—but a smile, such as none present had ever beheld—an expression of the final triumph of his soul, remained upon his countenance."[18] The account bore the tracings of a beatification.

"In Memory of HENRY OBOOKIAH a native of OWHYHEE," ʻŌpūkahaʻia's tombstone reads.

> His arrival in this country gave rise to the Foreign mission school, of which he was a worthy member. He was once an Idolater, and was designed for a Pagan Priest; but by the Grace of God and by the prayers and instructions of his pious friends, he became a christian. He was eminent for piety and missionary Zeal. When almost prepared to return to his native Isle to preach the Gospel, God took to himself. In his last sickness, he wept and prayed for Owhyhee but was submissive. He died without fear, with a heavenly smile on his countenance and glory in his soul. Feb. 17, 1818, aged 26.

The grave, notable for its size and horizontal orientation, sits on the side of a hill in Cornwall Cemetery along Cemetery Hill Road, overlooking the valley where

FIGURE 25. ʻŌpūkahaʻiaʻs gravesite in Cornwall, Connecticut, 2003. Gary Y. Okihiro photograph.

the Foreign Mission School once stood. The people of Cornwall, despite criticism that the money should instead go to the cause of missions, donated the $28 needed to pay for ʻŌpūkahaʻiaʻs burial and headstone.[19]

When I made my pilgrimage to the site in the summer of 2003, visitors from Hawaiʻi, I was sure, had placed a lei and strands of seashells along with a piece of the aromatic sandalwood tree on the tombstone. A plaque at the foot of the grave indicated that ʻŌpūkahaʻiaʻs family had removed his remains in July 1993 and taken them home to Nāpōʻopoʻo, Kona, on the island of Hawaiʻi. ʻŌpūkahaʻiaʻs last wish, that he see Hawaiʻi, had finally been fulfilled. Wildflowers bloomed along the hillside littered with erect, thin granite slabs marking Cornwall's fallen citizens.

At ʻŌpūkahaʻiaʻs funeral, held the day after his death, the Reverend Lyman Beecher spoke of the mysteries of God and his ways and of the cause for which he had lived and died. "We thought, surely this is he who shall comfort Owhyhee," said Beecher of ʻŌpūkahaʻia. "We saw so plainly the hand of God, in bringing him hither; in his instruction, his conversion, talents, and missionary zeal . . . we were prepared undoubtedly to say, 'This is the Lord's anointed.'" That confidence had been shaken with his death, and "we behold the end of his race, and bury with his dust in the grave, all our high raised hopes of his future activity in the cause of Christ." But 'Ōpūkaha'ia did not die in vain, Beecher promised. "His death will give notoriety to this institution [Foreign Mission School]—will awaken a tender sympathy for Owhyhee, and give it an interest in the prayers and charities of thousands who otherwise had not heard of this establishment, or been interested in its prosperity." Thus, he concluded, "instead of being appalled by the darkness, we are cheered by it; instead of fainting under the stroke, we are animated by it, to double confidence in God, and double diligence in this work, forasmuch as we know, that our labour is not vain in the Lord."[20]

The presence in the Northeast of peoples who were the objects of that work, that civilizing mission, was critical to the pursuit of America's destiny. Related to but also distant from the continent's native peoples, American Indians, those island natives were brought to these shores by American ships that plied the highways of commerce. As described by historian Samuel Eliot Morison, "When independence closed our colonial trade routes within the British empire, the merchantmen and whalers of New England swarmed around the Horn, in search of new markets and sources of supply. The opening of the China trade was the first and most spectacular result of this enterprise; the establishment of trading relations with Hawaii followed shortly. Years before the westward land movement gathered momentum, the energies of seafaring New England found their natural outlet, along their traditional pathway, in the Pacific Ocean."[21] And as noted by Herman Daggett, principal of the Foreign Mission School, Hawaiians such as 'Ōpūkaha'ia and youth from "other parts of the heathen world" who were found "wandering in our land" were "the instrument of laying the foundation of this Seminary [Foreign Mission School]." They excited "prayer and liberality," spirituality and generosity in New England's churches, and 'Ōpūkaha'ia's life inspired the thought that "a new era was about to commence in relation to the Sandwich Islands."[22]

If 'Ōpūkaha'ia's death occasioned financial support for the Foreign Mission School and mission to Hawai'i, the life of George Kaumuali'i inspired a similar objective. The young men's sponsors, the American Board of Commissioners for Foreign Missions, ensured that end in the rendering and publicizing of their life narratives. Kaumuali'i's story, as told by the missionaries, was of a prince of Hawai'i who was divinely ordained to spread the gospel and do the mission's work. "George Prince Tamoree [Kaumuali'i] is son of a king of two islands of Hawaii," an 1816 fund-raising pamphlet for the Foreign Mission School began. "Capt [James] R[owan] brought him to Boston when he was about six years old. His father, Tamoree, has shown a partiality to Americans, and he entrusted his son to the captain and gave him 'property' sufficient for his son's education." The captain, however, consumed the prince's upkeep and left him destitute. "About three years ago, the Prince worked for a farmer, labored hard, was treated harshly, and received a bare subsistence." He left his employer, went to Boston, enlisted on an American man-of-war, and was wounded in battle in the War of 1812. As for his physical appearance, the writer described him in words reminiscent of 'Ōpūkaha'ia's "whitening": "Young Tamoree is of middling stature, light complexion and brown hair. He has very engaging features, appears mild and tractable in his temper."[23] Moreover, this "tractable" youth was eager for education and religious instruction and was the heir apparent to the dominion of all Hawai'i.[24]

Religious papers carried the prince's tale, and this story in which both father and son seemed favorably disposed to American and Christian influences received wide circulation in New England. The *Boston Recorder* of November 12, 1816, reported that Kaumuali'i's father on the island of Kaua'i dispatched his men to help save the *Enterprise,* a ship from New York City, from crashing on the reef during a storm. "An American ship, and the lives of several American seamen have thus been preserved by the humane exertions of King Tamoree," the writer reminded his readers.

Let every American then remember that Tamoree has a son in this country, that for several years past he has been enduring all the hardships attendant upon the life of a common sailor on board our frigates; that he fought in several of our battles during the late war, and was badly wounded; that he has recently been taken under the protection of the American Board of Commissioners, and sent to Connecticut to be educated, with view to his return to his native country. We trust that when our countrymen are called upon to contribute for the education of Heathen Youth, these facts will not be forgotten.[25]

A contemporary of Kaumuali'i, Samuel Cotting, sought to set the record straight on his earlier life. "The assertion that [Captain] Rowan received several thousand dollars to defray the expenses of the education of the lad, is wholly without foundation," an indignant Cotting wrote to the editor of the *Massachusetts Spy* on December 9, 1816. Instead, Rowan left the child in Cotting's care in Worcester when he was six years old. "It is not true that George was very much neglected by Capt. Rowan; but he was treated with great kindness and attention, until a reverse in his situation rendered this impossible. I rejoice at the favourable turn in the fortunes of the lad, but regret that his new friends should have encouraged and aided him in addressing a letter to his father,[26] so unfounded in many of its statements and devoid of gratitude for a single favor received during ten years of residence among a Christian people."[27]

Though the missionaries may have been using him for their purposes, Kaumuali'i could have been a willing accomplice for the promotion of his own ends. His intention, according to the London *Missionary Register,* was to embrace "the first favourable opportunity of returning to his own country."[28] Thus, when he stood with Hopu and the first missionary company at Boston's Long Wharf on October 23, 1819, he might have symbolized to Boston's citizens a divinely ordained vessel by which to convey to Hawai'i Christianity and civilization, but Kaumuali'i was also fulfilling his youthful ambition of simply returning home.

FOREIGN MISSION SCHOOL

According to the minutes of the meeting that established it on October 29, 1816, the Foreign Mission School was to be "a school for the education of heathen youth" such that "they may be qualified to become missionaries, schoolmasters, interpreters, physicians, or surgeons, among heathen nations, and to communicate such information in agriculture and the arts, as shall tend to promote Christianity and civilization." That pairing of Christianity with civilization, the school's agents noted, was of paramount concern because "Christianity and civilization go hand in hand, and ever have been, and ever will be mutual helps to each other." Thus, they mandated, this education of "heathen youth" "of acknowledged piety" was to include both their personal salvation and instruction in agriculture, commerce, and mechanics.[29]

Among the school's students in 1818 were six Hawaiians, two Society Islanders, two Malays, and eleven American Indians—seven Cherokees, two Choctaws, one from Pennsylvania, and another from Canada.[30] A report published in June 1825 listed six Hawaiians, four Chinese, fourteen American Indians, a Portuguese from the Azores, and a "Jew of England."[31] A poem titled "The Cornwall Seminary" written by a student, a Choctaw Indian named Miles Mackey, described the school in the fall of 1824:

> Now in Connecticut there stands
> On Cornwall's low and pleasant lands.
> A school compos'd of foreign youth
> For propagating gospel truth.
> And on this consecrated ground,
> Are those from many nations round.
> But mostly of the Cherokees,
> The Angloes, and the Owhyhees.
> The languages are now thirteen,
> Twelve nations are likewise seen.[32]

It is difficult, from the record, to ascertain the feelings, much less daily activities and thoughts, of the school's Hawaiian students. Even their names, like David Brainerd, John E. Phelps, Samuel J. Mills, and George Tyler, conspire to hide their identities. Their preserved writings, including the widely distributed ʻŌpūkahaʻia memoirs, were by and large devotionals penned to show their authors' religiosity and Christian piety. Still, there are glimmerings of individual aspirations and failings, as on September 5, 1824, when Charles M. Arohekaah (phonetic spelling of

FIGURE 26. Student drawing of the Foreign Mission School. Collection of the Cornwall Historical Society, Cornwall, Connecticut.

a Hawaiian name) confessed, "My labors, in this vale, have pleasant been, / Though mix'd with much unfaithfulness and sin," or when David Brainerd expressed his desire for recognition: "I will write a few lines in your book to remember me by."[33]

A glimpse of the students' indoctrination is revealed in their 1822 textbook, *The Missionary Spelling Book, and Reader.*[34] The lessons begin with sets of vocabulary, including parts of the body, household objects, nature and time, and relationships and work. By lesson twelve, students recite phrases such as "I am very well," "She is sick," "He is a Christian," and "Our bodies must die." Building upon those blocks, the subject of lesson nineteen is the destiny of all flesh.

We shall all die.
When our bodies die, our souls will go away from this world.

Angels will come, and take the souls of good men up to heaven.
They will see God. . . .
There they will be happy, and will live forever.
The souls of wicked men will go to hell.
There they will dwell with devils, and will be miserable forever.[35]

The students at the Foreign Mission School—"young men of many races"—
must have been a source of racial, gender, and sexual anxiety in the Cornwall area.
As put by a local historian, "Although the people of New England were more than
ready to offer both their blessings and their cold cash for the project of religiously
converting the heathens of far-away islands, their very natures rebelled at the idea
of accepting the converted and saved souls as equals."[36] The courtship and marriage of Sarah Bird Northrop, a white Cornwall woman, to John Ridge, a Foreign
Mission School student and member of a prominent and wealthy Cherokee family in Georgia, prompted a series of acidic articles by Isaiah Bunce, editor of Litchfield's *American Eagle,* attacking the Foreign Mission School, relations between
white women and men of color, and the Ridge-Northrop marriage. Intermarriage
with "the Indians and blacks of the missionary school at Cornwall," he wrote in the
March 22, 1824, issue of the *Eagle,* was an "affliction, mortification and disgrace."
The Northrop-Ridge marriage was particularly hard for Northrop's family because
Sarah thereby agreed to be "taken into the wilderness among savages" and has thus
"made herself a *squaw,* and connected her ancestors to a race of Indians."[37] He
went on to impugn the masculinity of Cornwall's white men, the "poor white boys"
of Cornwall Valley, chiding them for "their" women's alleged preference for darker
flesh. In reaction, eight of the valley's young men met in June 1824 to denounce
Bunce and his allegations and resolved "that though we feel no spirit of boasting
in this case, and though we do not profess to be 'Ladies Men,' still we spurn the
intimation that we have been cast into the shade, by our rivals, white or tawny."[38]

Feelings ran especially high when another of Cornwall's daughters, Harriet
Gold, asked her father's permission to marry Ridge's cousin and fellow Foreign
Mission School student, Elias Boudinot.[39] Both Boudinot and Gold came from
prominent families, and Gold's father, Benjamin Gold, was a deacon of the First

Church and an active supporter of the Foreign Mission School. Gold had encouraged his fourteen children to correspond with Indians of the Cherokee Nation, and he opened his home to students from the mission school. Amid heavy sentiment in the valley and in his own family against the marriage, Gold first refused, then gave his daughter permission to marry Boudinot. A mob assembled on the village green and burned Harriet Gold, Elias Boudinot, and Mrs. Northrop in effigy. Mrs. Northrop, Sarah's mother, had allegedly encouraged these unions of white women with Indian men. A letter from Harriet, dated June 25, 1825, described the scene:

> It being thought unsafe for me to stay at home, I left the night before and was kept in a chamber at Capt. Clark's where I had a full prospect of the solemn transactions in our valley. In the evening our respectable young people, ladies and gentlemen, convened on the plain to witness and approve the scene and express their indignation. A painting had before been prepared representing a beautiful young lady and an Indian, also on the same, a woman as an instigator of Indian marriages. Evening came on. The church bell began to toll, one would certainly conclude speaking the departure of a soul. Mr. John C. Lewis and Mr. Rufus Payne carried the corpse and Brother Stephen [Harriet's brother] set fire to the barrel of tar, or rather the funeral pile, the flames rose high and the smoke ascended, some said it reminded them of the smoke of their torment which they feared would ascend forever. My heart truly sung with anguish at the dreadful scene.[40]

The Gold family refused her marriage, then reversed themselves after Harriet was taken ill and failed to respond to ministrations. Finally, on May 1, 1826, Harriet R. Gold married Elias Boudinot in her family home.[41]

With sentiment running against the Foreign Mission School and its students, the American Board of Commissioners for Foreign Missions found it difficult to raise funds for its support and maintenance. In anticipation of the Gold-Boudinot marriage, on June 17, 1825, the school's agents—Lyman Beecher, who had predicted that ʻŌpūkahaʻiaʻs death would "give notoriety to this institution," Timothy Stone, Joseph Harvey, and Philo Swift—declared their absolute opposition to the union: "In closing this communication we feel bound to say, that after the unequivocal disapprobation of *such connexions,* expressed by the Agents, and by the christian public universally; we regard the conduct of those who have engaged in or accessory to this transaction, as criminal; as offering insult to the sacred interests of this charitable institution. For those who have been guilty of this outrage upon public feeling, we can offer no apology; all we have to request is that the christian public will not condemn the innocent with the guilty."[42]

To no avail. With declining financial support, in early November 1826 the board decided to terminate the mission school "as soon as practical."[43] The board directed that the students be dispersed to area families or returned to their homes and the school property liquidated and sold. The four remaining Hawaiian students, destined for an eventual return to Hawai'i as missionaries, were placed with local families and worked for their room and board.

NEW ENGLAND, THE UNITED STATES, AND THE WORLD

The American Board of Commissioners for Foreign Missions, the sponsor of the Cornwall Foreign Mission School and the 1819 mission to Hawai'i, was a product of the Second Great Awakening. Samuel J. Mills, one of its founders and one of the students who befriended 'Ōpūkaha'ia, was a student at Williams College in 1806 when he and four other students pledged themselves to mission service at the "haystack meeting." Set within a circle of trees in a quiet corner on the campus of Williams College today, the "Haystack Monument" celebrates that origin story of American foreign missions. "On this site in the shelter of a haystack during a summer storm in 1806," the plaque recounts, "five Williams College students dedicated their lives to the service of the Church around the globe. Out of their decision grew the American Foreign Mission movement."

Two years later, the students formed themselves into a secret society called the Brethren, and they continued to recruit others to the cause, notably Rufus Anderson, who became the longtime and influential corresponding secretary of the American Board.[44] After leaving Williams, Mills went to Yale, where he met 'Ōpūkaha'ia, and then enrolled at Andover Theological Seminary, the center for missionary recruitment. In 1810 he and other students formed the American Board of

FIGURE 27. The Haystack
Monument at Williams
College, Williamstown,
Massachusetts, 2003.
Gary Y. Okihiro
photograph.

Commissioners for Foreign Missions, but they had to wait until 1812 to receive its charter because some of the church elders saw the youth as stubborn and overly ambitious when fields needed tending at home.[45] But, as put by Mills, perhaps reflecting upon his charge, ʻŌpūkahaʻia, "Shall we not consider these southern islands a proper place for the establishment of a mission? Not that I would give up the heathen tribes of the west. . . . We ought not to look merely to the heathen on our own continent, but to direct our attention where we may, to human appearance, do the most good, and where the difficulties are the least."[46] Prominent Congregationalists like Jeremiah Evarts and Jedediah Morse supported the cause of foreign missions in their journal, the *Panoplist and Missionary Magazine.* In the summer of 1816, the *Panoplist* carried a series of articles on the education of "heathen youth" in the United States "with a view to employ them in civilizing and Christianizing the different nations to which they belong." These "natives," the magazine argued, knew the language and people and were physically better suited for the tropics. They were thus prime candidates for the work of missions.[47]

Mills was ordained in 1815, and although he never labored in fields abroad he ministered in the West and South under the Connecticut and Massachusetts missionary societies, and in 1816 he worked among New York City's poor. In July 1816 he proposed the idea of an African School along the lines of Cornwall's Foreign Mission School, which he helped establish later that year.[48] The African School, he envisioned, would produce African American teachers to uplift the race. On his fund-raising efforts for the school in the South, Mills confessed: "I received considerable aid from slave holders. I informed the persons on whom I called, that the object of the school was to qualify young men of colour for teachers of schools and preachers of the Gospel, in hope of exerting an influence in correcting the morals and manners of their brethren in our cities and large towns; and also to raise up teachers for these people, should an effort be made to settle them by themselves, either in this country or abroad."[49]

Following through on his intentions for African Americans, Mills helped organize in several cities auxiliaries of the American Colonization Society, which was formed in 1817. A historian of the colonization movement called Mills "a professional traveling agent for numerous benevolent societies and perhaps the best-known money gatherer of his time."[50] Later that year, the society appointed him as its agent for its "noble expedition" to explore Africa's west coast for a site to colonize America's free blacks. In a letter dated July 30, 1817, to Ebenezer Burgess, who became his companion on this expedition to Africa, Mills expressed his enthusiasm for the project:

> My brother, can we engage in a nobler effort? We go to make freemen of slaves.
> We go to lay the foundation of a free and independent empire on the coast of

poor degraded Africa. It is confidently believed by many of our best and wisest men, that, if the plan proposed succeeds, it will ultimately be the means of exterminating slavery in our country. It will eventually redeem and emancipate a million and an half of wretched men. It will transfer to the coast of Africa the blessings of religion and civilization; and Ethiopia will soon stretch out her hands unto God.[51]

Mills died on that mission in 1818 off the coast of Sierra Leone and was buried at sea.

Mills's brief but full life and career typify much about this period of U.S. history. The new republic, with its some four million inhabitants in 1790, embraced the rise of cities, a surging and diversifying economy, and the ideas of reason and individual freedoms of the Enlightenment and American Revolution. The religious revivalism of which Mills was a part was a response by New England churches to revitalize their flagging organizations amid widespread secularism and the emergence of a religious rationalism that rejected Christian "superstitions" and institutionalism. Coming after the religious fervor of the Great Awakening of the 1730s, the Second Great Awakening of the first half of the nineteenth century sought a return to evangelism and enthusiastic religion. Methodists, Baptists, and Presbyterians dispatched itinerant preachers from cities along the East Coast to the rural West and South, holding revival or camp meetings that attracted tens of thousands of adherents. Christian faith and fervor, not doctrine, were the essential glue that held together disparate denominations, creating a unifying sense of community and identity as Christians and as Americans.

That newfound feeling of unity, along with the traditional stress on Christian duty and benevolence, enabled and sustained the cause of foreign missions. Although the roots of missions ran deeper and broader than New England Protestantism, the impetus for overseas missions began and remained in a region "where cultural homogeneity was matched by religious and intellectual maturity."[52] New England supplied most of the money and missionaries for the gospel's spread overseas during the early years. And though religious revivalism spread rapidly away from the eastern coast to the western and southern interiors and was in several ways uniquely American, its inspiration came from across the Atlantic Ocean and the young republic's former master, Great Britain. Evangelical enthusiasm arose about the same time in both countries, but Britain was the first to send missionaries abroad, when the focus in the United States was on domestic missions to American Indians. Americans cheered the founding of the London Missionary Society in 1795 and followed closely the news of its evangelizing efforts in Asia and the Pacific. The chief instruments of evangelism, the tract and Bible societies, were British inventions that were adopted by Americans. Publications by those groups, of sermons, reports, journals and memoirs, were influential with their rapidly growing readership and established bonds among scattered believers and between them and the distant objects of their salvation and benevolence.[53]

The postcolonial influence of Britain on the United States in this matter of missions was sometimes direct. As reported by a religious magazine, in the fall of 1796 "a number of Ministers, in the city of New-York, being informed of the exertions which were then, and had been for some time, making in Great-Britain, to spread the knowledge of the Gospel among the heathen, became impressed with the duty of making a similar attempt in America."[54] The various New England missionary societies, however, unlike their British models, ministered primarily to American Indians and white settlers along the western frontier. Some worked among free and enslaved African Americans, and that field suggested looking to Africa, as when Congregational clergyman Samuel Hopkins, writing from the slave trading port city of Newport, Rhode Island, in 1773, informed Ezra Stiles, the future president of Yale College, of his plan to train two African Americans for mission work in Africa.[55]

American ambitions for foreign missions floundered in the current of westward migration and the immediacy of domestic relations. Thus, the plan for missions abroad redirected the young nation's view from westward continental expansion to eastward watery routes to distant islands and peoples. Of this dual initiative over land and sea, historian Clifton Jackson Phillips observed:

> It [foreign missions] opposed the flow of American life, then and later, for the youth of the nation to march east and not west. From the farms and villages of New England young men had already begun to emigrate in large numbers to the

Western valleys. But others, equally discontented with limited horizons, took ship at Portsmouth and New Bedford and a dozen other ports to carry the American flag to the seven seas and the exotic coasts of Asia and Africa. For New England faced in two directions: inland toward the trans-Appalachian country and overseas from its busy coast towns.[56]

Traveling companions ʻŌpūkahaʻia and Hopu made similar decisions at one point in their lives; ʻŌpūkahaʻia turned to the interior, while Hopu headed for the open sea.

In addition to that reorientation of the nation's attention as an impetus for missions, the ideals of duty and benevolence attracted white men and women alike. White women were at the heart of this evangelical movement and culture. Religious piety enabled greater egalitarianism between men and women, and white Christian women's status rose in contrast to that of women of color and "heathen" women, the objects of their maternal uplift and salvation.[57] If heathenism held women under bondage, the rhetoric alleged, then Christianity freed them. At the same time, evangelism promoted, rather than rejected, the cult of "true womanhood," in which women stood by as men's helpmeet, especially within the domestic sphere. Foreign missions, thus, came to require men missionaries who were married to pious women, like Adoniram Judson and his wife, Ann Hasseltine Judson, who was held up as a virtuous model for her gender.[58] The seemingly ubiquitous ʻŌpūkahaʻia boarded for a time with Ann Hasseltine's family.[59]

As well as promoting white women's groups and their social elevation, evangelism also provided an impetus and platform for the humanitarian and social reform movements of the nineteenth century, including the causes of antislavery, temperance, and missions. Evangelical religion carried both a sense of calling and commitment to social activism and change, and its doctrines of personal salvation and equality before God held out hope for the outcast, the excluded, and the enslaved. But once freed, former slaves might seek full equality and integration in a society unwilling to grant those gifts, leading to the creation of, from a white point of view, a "Negro problem." Solutions to that "problem" included racial segregation and its extension, the expulsion of free blacks from the United States in the colonization movement. As put by Thomas Jefferson, "The slave, when made free, might mix with, without staining the blood of his master. But with us a second is necessary, unknown to history. When freed, he is to be removed beyond the reach of mixture."[60] For the slave-owning and miscegenating Jefferson, emancipation unleashed the specter of racial mixing, which menaced social purity and public order. For abolitionists like Samuel J. Mills, the colonization of free blacks, a source of the "problem," would clear away an obstacle to emancipation in the United States and bring the light of Christianity and civilization to Africa's darkness. In addition, Mills tapped into a sentiment apparently held by those slaveholders who supported his idea for an African School that Christianity and civilization helped ensure docility on the part of free blacks.

The "problem," of course, was not African Americans or their freedom but white racism and the system of human bondage. Colonization advocates like Mills and the Reverend Robert Finley, who first proposed the plan to remove free blacks at a public meeting in November 1816, believed in the superiority of whites and inferiority of blacks and saw their mission as an act of benevolence. As fathers tending to their children, they knew what was best for their dependents. Free blacks, they held, would fail to develop in the United States—but in Africa, unfettered by race prejudice and competition with whites, they would be free to allow their innate capacities to emerge and flourish. Besides enabling emancipation in the United States and the self-improvement of free blacks in Africa, Mills and Finley held, colonization would implant Christianity and civilization in Africa and was thus a part of the cause of foreign missions. And like the initial idea of foreign missions, the British model in the crown colony of Sierra Leone, established in 1808 as a place of deposition for recaptured Africans after the British abolition of the slave trade, helped inspire and sustain the American colonization effort that resulted in the 1821 founding of neighboring Liberia.[61]

Hawaiians, brought to New England's shores by the tides of commerce that lifted the newly constituted ship of state from its moorings, were central figures in the cause of foreign missions. Insofar as they represented inferior specimens of humanity, according to their self-appointed, white overseers, Hawaiians, American Indians, and African Americans required schooling in Christianity and civilization, as was realized in the Foreign Mission School and African schools. And segregation

or removal from the possibility of mixture was the necessary resolution to the ir-
reconcilable differences and hierarchies of race because miscegenation, in the words
of the Foreign Mission School's agents, was "criminal" and an "outrage upon public
feeling." American Indians were an inward turn for missions, Hawaiians and free
blacks an outward turn to "foreign" missions in distant lands and peoples. As if to
underscore that move, among the second company of missionaries who arrived in
Hawai'i in 1823 was African American Betsey Stockton. Born into slavery in 1798,
Stockton was presented as a gift to the wife of the president of Princeton College.
Stockton, a domestic servant, attended evening classes at Princeton Theological
Seminary and was granted her freedom to serve as a missionary for the American
Board of Commissioners for Foreign Missions. On the island of Maui, Stockton
opened a school for the common people and taught there for about two years.[62]

Implicated in this story of Hawaiians in New England were some of the major
historical markers of the time, including the rise of mercantile capitalism, the growth
of cities and factories, and the social ferments around enthusiastic religion, the relations between men and women, and the campaign against slavery.[63] Moreover,
noted a religious historian, evangelicals deliberately set out to create a spiritual kingdom and its empire or domain. Writing of the Second Great Awakening, Martin E.
Marty explained, "Suddenly, just as the American chosen people were asking what
were the uses of chosenness, Protestantism was inspired with a desire to convert
people, to spread its civilization, to expand and conquer."[64]

John Ledyard, like Samuel J. Mills, was a son of New England and an exemplar of the lure of missions, expansion, and empire, which drew both men to their
graves in places far from Connecticut's shores. Ledyard was born in 1751 in Gro-
ton, Connecticut, and entered Dartmouth College's first class in 1772 with the intention of preparing himself to minister to America's Indians. That intention was
perhaps inspired by his mother's wish for him. According to Ledyard's biographer,
his mother "felt a strong compassion for the deplorable state of the Indians, and it
was among her earliest and fondest hopes of this her favorite son, that he would
be educated as a missionary, and become an approved instrument in the hands of
Providence to bring these degraded and suffering heathen to the knowledge of a
pure religion, and the blessings of civilized life."[65]

FIGURE 28. Betsey Stockton, teacher on Maui, circa 1863(?). Used with permission of the Hawaiian Mission Children's Society Library.

Ledyard, however, was unsuccessful in his application to the clergy and instead, like Hopu, took to the sea as a sailor. When in England, Ledyard enlisted in the marines and somehow gained an audience with famous British explorer and scientist Captain James Cook, who was preparing for his third expedition to the Pacific (1776–79). Hired as a corporal of the expedition's marines, Ledyard accompanied Cook to Polynesia, the west coast of North America, and Hawai'i, where Cook died in 1779 at Kealakekua Bay. Ledyard's observations, published as his "journal" in 1783, were important to European commerce in pointing out the abundance of animal furs and skins along North America's west coast and their trade value in China.[66] "They have foxes, sables, hares, marmosets, ermines, weazles, bears, wolves, deer, moose, dogs, otters, beavers, and a species of weazle called the glutton; the skin of this animal was sold at Kamchalka, a Russian factory on the Asiatic coast for sixty rubles, which is near 12 guineas, and had it been sold in China it would have been worth 30 guineas," he reported. "We purchased while here about 1500 beaver . . . , but it afterwards happened that skins which did not cost the purchaser six-pence sterling sold in China for 100 dollars. Neither did we purchase a quarter part of the beaver and other furrskins we might have done," he noted with regret, "and most certainly should have done had we known of meeting the opportunity of disposing of them to such an astonishing profit."[67]

Ledyard's advocacy of a lucrative American trade with China involving the furs and skins of the Pacific Northwest would soon become a means by which fortunes were made and Hawai'i drawn within New England's circuit of Pacific transactions, which included both commerce and missions. Although Ledyard was unsuccessful in lobbying prominent entrepreneurs into financing a ship for the China trade, his idea was influential in the 1784 departure of the *Empress of China* from New York's harbor. That inaugural venture reaped a 25–30 percent profit, and it presaged a future for the new republic on the world stage.[68] In 1785, Ledyard traveled to Paris, where he met and made a favorable impression on Thomas Jefferson. Thus, years before the Louisiana Purchase in 1803 and the Lewis and Clark expedition of 1804–6, both brokered by Jefferson as president, Ledyard's idea of westward expansion and American trade in the Pacific received a receptive ear from the American minister to France. "He [Jefferson] listened with interest to what Ledyard had to say," according to Ledyard's editor, "and shared his desire to see someone under American auspices explore the great lands between Mississippi and California."[69] As told by Jefferson, his discussions with Ledyard were directly connected with his instructions to the Lewis and Clark expedition "to explore the Missouri river, and such principal streams of it, as, by its course and communication with the waters of the Pacific ocean, whether the Columbia, Oregon, Colorado, or any other river, may offer the most direct and practicable water communication across the continent for the purposes of commerce."[70]

John Ledyard, would-be missionary to American Indians and Dartmouth dropout, gained fame as a member of Captain Cook's expedition that "discovered" Hawai'i in 1778 on its way to find the fabled Northwest Passage that supposedly connected the Atlantic with the Pacific. As a member of that scientific expedition dispatched to map the South Pacific and its flora and fauna, Ledyard volunteered to search Hawai'i's interior and ascend the snow-capped summit of Mauna Loa. The group turned back before achieving its object, but along the way Ledyard noted lava fields and evidence of "past eruption and fire." The island, he concluded, "has every appearance in nature to suppose it once to have been a volcano."[71] And although he failed to see his mercantile scheme realized, his enterprise was fulfilled in the 1787–90 voyage of the *Columbia,* which left Boston for the furs of the Pacific Northwest and the goods of Asia. That expedition, wrote historian Samuel Eliot Morison, was the inauguration of a trade "which enabled the merchant adventurers of Boston to tap the vast reservoir of wealth in China."[72]

In a reciprocal act of New England's expansion, stepping from the deck of the *Columbia* to Boston's streets in 1790, Morison informs us, was a Hawaiian: "Clad in a feather cloak of golden suns setting in flaming scarlet, that came halfway down his brown legs; crested with a gorgeous feather helmet shaped like a Greek warrior's, this young Hawaiian moved up State Street like a living flame."[73] Ledyard would die in Cairo in 1788, but his dream of an America engaging both frontiers of land and sea would take flight and open New England and the United States to the Pacific and its islands, Asia, and the world.

4

Schooling for Subservience

After years in the ocean, salmon return to their native streams to reproduce and die, having completed their circle of life. Missionary children, like Samuel Chapman Armstrong, born in Hawaiʻi in 1839, spent their college years at Williams College in Massachusetts, returning to the site of the haystack pledge that had inspired the foreign mission movement. Hawaiʻi in New England involved, in the first instance, the presence of native Hawaiians on those alien shores, and later the "return" of the offspring of New England's diasporic sons and daughters. Although foreign to New England and the continent, those Island mission children could more readily meld with the good citizens of Boston, Cornwall, or Williamstown than with their native Hawaiian counterparts because of their contrasting racializations and cultures.

NEW ENGLAND IN HAWAIʻI

Among the fifth company of missionaries sent by the American Board were the Reverend Richard Armstrong and his wife, Clarissa Chapman, who sailed from New Bedford and arrived in Honolulu on May 17, 1832, after an ocean voyage of 173 days.[1] Decades later, on the occasion of her eightieth birthday, Clarissa Chapman Armstrong would recall her early mission days in Hawaiʻi and the Marquesas as "a life amongst the heathens with the privilege of uplifting dark, degraded humanity," and as work among the "children of nature, with no knowledge of civilization whatever and given over to animal lusts and selfish degradation."[2] A mature Samuel Chapman Armstrong praised his mother: "It is wonderful how much you have gone through; you have taught a noble lesson to your children. You have helped me and have been in my work in a marvelous way."[3]

Richard and Clarissa Armstrong labored in the vineyards of Hawai'i and the Marquesas Islands, and they had ten children, including Samuel Chapman, their sixth child. Growing up on the island of Maui "amid the soft airs and noble scenery of that beautiful tropical archipelago," in the words of his daughter and biographer,[4] young Samuel played and went to school with his fellow mission children, who were unlike the "darkies," the Hawaiians to whom his parents ministered, and his family's Chinese servant, Ah-Kam, "a typical Chinaman" with a habit for stealing, he wrote.[5] Less charitably, Samuel bemoaned the Chinese as "rat-eaters" and "these sly pigtails" who come to "our Paradise" to despoil it, seeing Hawai'i as merely a place "to grind out money for their gambling . . . and their aged parents. Is the Chinaman capable of piety?" he pondered.[6]

His mother wrote similarly of Hawaiians that "to lie and steal seemed as natural as to breathe," and she considered them "very repulsive in their personal habits and immoral in the extreme." She despaired: "Week after week passes and we see none but naked, filthy, wicked heathen with souls as dark as the tabernacles which they inhabit. The darkness of the people seems to destroy the beauty of the scenery around us."[7] His father, the Reverend Richard Armstrong, described the Hawaiian objects of his affection: "The females are in great need of improvement. Their habits, conversation and mode of living are filthy. They are ignorant and lazy, lack everything like modesty, and hardly know how to do anything. Of course, the mothers being such creatures, you may judge what the children are. In multitudes of cases the pigs are as well taken care of as the children and are nearly as decent and cleanly."[8]

The son admired his father for "going native," in Samuel's words, because the intention of that cross-dressing was the saving of souls. "To know a race intimately and accurately does not imply a desire to help it," Samuel reasoned. "The young Southerner is reared in close association with the Negro; the plainsman knows the Indian; but [Richard] Armstrong absorbed from the atmosphere about him an attitude of protection and helpfulness toward the weaker race." And despite the apparent similarity of racial attitudes of slave masters and missionaries, the latter acknowledged the equality of all persons before God and sought the slaves' redemption. "The missionary fathers, like the slaveholders, practically regarded the Hawaiians as a type inferior to themselves as far as mental and moral fiber was concerned, but no missionary ever lost the point of view that the soul of each of these people was equal in the sight of the Almighty to his own." The "proper attitude" of Christians should be "to pity and to serve."[9]

His parents and their labors were pivotal in the life and work of Samuel Chapman Armstrong. As he acknowledged in his 1890 New Year's Eve letter, which was his last will and testament, "I am most thankful for my parents, my Hawaiian home, for war experiences & college days at Williams, and for life & work at Hampton."[10] His mother, Armstrong maintained, inspired him. "I more and more believe," he wrote, "that sons are of their mothers, and that daughters are of their fathers; for I see it constantly. In the most trying times of my life, I have felt a peculiar gift of girt and strength that seemed not of myself, but my mother in me."[11] His father directed much of Armstrong's career—his training at Williams College and his life's work at the Hampton Normal and Agricultural Institute—and he, despite his early death, was "a presence and power in our lives," Armstrong testified.[12] It was his father's wish that he study under Mark Hopkins at Williams,[13] and his idea for manual education at Hampton drew from his father's labors for the Hawaiian kingdom. "These schools, over which my father as Minister of Education had for fifteen years a general oversight," Armstrong credited, "suggested the plan of the Hampton School."[14]

Clarissa Chapman was born in Russell, Massachusetts, in 1805, graduated from Westfield Normal School in Massachusetts, and taught at a school in Brooklyn, New York, before her marriage to Richard Armstrong in 1831.[15] On the eve of her wedding, Chapman explained to a woman friend her decision to marry a missionary:

My faith seems immoveable—It has been growing *stronger & stronger,* & now is so firm, that I have given my life, to God. I expect soon, to leave my native land forever, to labor, toil & die in heathen lands. . . . The trial of leaving friends is of no ordinary kind—it tears the heart asunder. Without grace, I could not endure it—But I must forsake all for Christ—therefore must I leave my dear parents & only brother, even if it be as painful as plucking out an eye, or severing a limb from my body.[16]

About a month later, she set sail for Hawai'i.

On board the New Bedford whaler *Averick,* Armstrong was desperately ill. The wind and waves rocked the ship, she wrote in her journal, and the shaking increased "till the whole vessel was in commotion." "Four days my stomach would receive nothing but a little wine & water & could retain *that* but a short time— At length with great exertion, I could take a little water gruel, but *that too* seemed determined not to stay with me," she recounted. "The other missionaries suffered severely at the same time—some however much less than myself—others probably as much—I do not say more, for all admitted that my sickness was very severe."[17] And about two and a half months later and still at sea, "The old habit of vomiting has returned again, but not quite so violently as before. I have found french brandy the best remedy. One swallow of it has often prevented vomiting but it burned my throat prodigiously."[18]

Within a week of her arrival in Hawai'i, Armstrong reported to her friends, "my desires are granted in part—I am on heathen ground surrounded by thousands of natives & now I want to labor among them." Of her first encounter with Hawaiians she admitted, "I was somewhat shocked at seeing some of them although their external appearance is far better than when the first missionaries arrived. But few of them were entirely naked." Armstrong was likewise disabused of a prejudice: "I [had] supposed they [Hawaiian children] were all black little creatures, but they are as fair as American children." At the same time, she described the high chiefess Kīna'u as "a great, fat, black woman."[19] Apparently that maternal distaste for dusky flesh was passed on to her children. Teaching African American children in Norfolk, Virginia, her daughter, like her mother, reported that "the little nigs are dirty, ignorant lousy &c. They think Massa Linkum [Lincoln] is God."[20]

Clarissa Armstrong's journal entries, during the early years, reveal a displaced, alienated, and lonely woman whose husband was frequently on the road and engrossed in his work. "When he is gone," she wrote of Richard, "*all* is gone—at least

I think so."[21] Her children, accordingly, occupied her thoughts and attention. "Still I am alone with my sweet children," Armstrong confided in her journal. "Their papa is absent." One of them, William Nevins, her first son, died just over a year after his birth. She gave the same name to her second son to take the place of his older brother. "The one a sweet spirit in heaven," she described her dead son, "the other a sweet babe at my breast. The one living has mild blue eyes, & a sweet countenance like his departed brother, is quiet & often reminds of him." Having children sharpened Clarissa's desire to see her parents and to have them embrace her children, their grandchildren. "Two nights in succession this week, I have dreamed that my father was dead. . . . How much I have desired to dream of seeing & conversing [with] my dear parents & other dear friends, but my wishes are vain." And, "O how I should love to step in & cheer them, & show them my little ones."[22]

Richard Armstrong was born in McEwensville, Pennsylvania, in 1805 and was a graduate of Dickinson College in Carlisle, Pennsylvania, where an Indian school, inspired in large part by his son, would be built. He studied at Princeton Theological Seminary and was ordained in 1831. Of his decision to be a missionary, Armstrong wrote: "The work of a missionary, it is true, is self-denying and laborious, but I must remember that he who does not love Christ more than houses or lands, or home or friends, cannot be his disciple."[23] He served as pastor of churches in Hawai'i and briefly in the Marquesas Islands and withdrew from mission work and in 1847 accepted the position of minister of public instruction under the Hawaiian king, Kamehameha III.[24] "No branch of government, seems to me of more vital importance to the welfare, of the Hawaiian race than this," Armstrong declared of his new ministry. "*Here* it is of peculiar importance, where the glory and safety of the nation must depend in so great a degree upon the proper training of the young. If depopulation here is to be arrested; if the vices which are consuming the natives are to be eradicated; if an indolent and thriftless people are to become industrious and thrifty; if Christian institutions are to be perpetuated, the work must be accomplished mainly where it has been so prosperously begun, *in the education of the young.*"[25] His wife Clarissa supported this career change as a chance to render good works and receive wages not beholden to "the charity of the churches."[26]

A history of education in Hawai'i calls Armstrong "the father of American education" in the Islands because, although he was the second holder of that office, he instituted a system of education where none existed before.[27] As chief administrator he was charged with oversight of "private and public morals" in some two hundred schools then in operation. Armstrong's brand of "American education" was based on his conviction that the kingdom faced two major and related problems— education and land utilization. His curriculum thus stressed agriculture ("proper" land use) for boys and homemaking (preparation for motherhood) for girls. This was manual labor training, along with heteronormativity and domesticity, in advance of manual and industrial education in the United States.[28] That variety of education, however, was long favored by missionaries, including the American Board, in their work with American Indians.[29] Although it is difficult to ascertain the influence of that idea of native education on Richard Armstrong, it is clear that missionaries generally saw scant difference in regard to condition and needs between the indigenous inhabitants of the continent and those of the Hawaiian Islands.

For Richard Armstrong, the promotion of "Christian education" was essential for the nurturing of a "mental and moral culture" in which Christianity, civilization, and industry might prosper. Even before becoming the kingdom's chief education officer, Armstrong prescribed manual labor for the moral and physical education of youth. "I think an effort should be made to connect some sort of manual labor, especially agriculture, with all the schools," he wrote in response to a question posed by the Hawaiian king's minister of foreign relations, Robert C. Wyllie, in 1846. "Early habits of industry will supply their wants, make their homes comfortable and remove the temptation to wander about and commit crime in order to get money or fine dress."[30] In addition, the senior Armstrong noted, Hawaiian parents were too poor to pay enough to support teachers, and they were "too ignorant to know the value of education." But if agriculture were stressed in the schools and students were required to produce for their upkeep and that of their teachers, then schools might be economically feasible and flourish.[31] It was this view of native education that Richard Armstrong imparted to his son, Samuel

Chapman Armstrong, who in 1851 toured some of the schools under his father's care and in 1860 worked as chief clerk in the Department of Public Instruction.[32]

The Hawaiian "paradise" crafted and sustained by the Armstrongs and others like them was the playground in which their children frolicked. Some of Samuel Chapman Armstrong's fondest memories involved wading in mountain streams, climbing trees, and riding horses with his fellow mission boys. "As it seems to me now," he reminisced, "the delight of our Hawaiian life was going barefoot, as we did till we were quite grown, Sundays excepted, in the midst of wonderful natural beauty—the health and the joy of it!"[33] Armstrong was born on Maui but spent most of his childhood on Oʻahu, and despite his fond memories of having "gone native" in the tropics he hardly knew native Hawaiians, whom he referred to as "kanakas" and "my kanaka" and "our porter."[34] Despite that distance from the original inhabitants of the Islands he maintained, as "a native," the presumed prerogatives of birth. As a college student at Williams, Armstrong claimed, like other "native" sons and daughters of the U.S. west: "Well, I think seeing our Fathers have done more for poor Hawaii than all others besides, and that we are natives of the soil, the Islands are our *lawful inheritance.*"[35] After two years at Oʻahu College (Punahou School), Armstrong left for Williams College.

HAWAIʻI IN THE SOUTH

In 1862, with the Civil War raging, Samuel Chapman Armstrong joined the Union Army, and in November 1864 he was given charge of a regiment of African American soldiers—the 8th and 9th United States Colored Troops. Just about a year earlier, Armstrong had confided to a friend that he thought African Americans were "worse than Kanakas," and "I am a sort of abolitionist, but I haven't learned to love the Negro."[36] Just before leading his African American regiment into battle, Armstrong explained to his mother the global and heroic significance of his paternal mission: "The Negro troops have not yet entirely proved themselves good soldiers; but if the Negroes can be made to fight well, then is the question of their freedom settled. I tell you the present is the grandest time the world ever saw. The African race is before the world, unexpectedly to all, and all mankind are looking to see whether the African will show himself equal to the opportunity before him." And, he added, "It will yet be a grand thing to have been identified with this Negro movement."[37]

After the war and in his work with the Freedmen's Bureau, established in 1865 by Congress as an Army agency to assist poor whites and the former enslaved, Armstrong strengthened his association with the "Negro movement" by supervising schools in the Bureau's Ninth District of Virginia. "The work is very difficult; there are here, congregated in little villages, some 5,000 colored people, crowded, squalid, poor, and idle," he wrote his mother on June 2, 1866. "It is my work to scatter and renovate them." And in his report to the bureau dated June 30, 1866, he described the newly freed men and women as helpless because of "improvidence, or carelessness, or poverty, or to their not comprehending the fact of restoration," and as a class they were "destitute of ambition," and many clung to the "supremely stupid and pitiable" idea that they were permanently condemned to that status and that white efforts to uplift them were designed to reenslave them. Despite that "ignorant" ingratitude, Armstrong affirmed his determination to "stick with the darkies while there is anything to be done for them."[38]

His education work with the Freedmen's Bureau and particularly his experience in Hawai'i prepared him for founding the Hampton Normal and Agricultural Institute in Virginia in 1868 under the aegis of the American Missionary Association. As put by his daughter, "As he meditated upon the development of the plan [for Hampton], the Hilo Manual Labor School for Native Hawaiians, which he had observed in his boyhood, often occurred to his mind as an example of successful industrial education for an undeveloped race."[39] Armstrong's racialization that lumped Hawaiians with African Americans as a single, dark-skinned, "undeveloped race," or as classified by his daughter and Hampton associate as a race at its "dawn of civilization,"[40] allowed for the educational connection to be made. Students with similar profiles and needs required similar schooling. "It meant something to the Hampton school," observed Armstrong, "and perhaps to the ex-slaves of America, that, from 1820 to 1860, the distinctively missionary period, there was worked out in the Hawaiian Islands the problem of the emancipation, enfranchisement, and Christian civilization of a dark-skinned Polynesian people in many

FIGURE 29. Samuel Chapman Armstrong and dog, with Cora Folsom's class, circa 1885. Courtesy of Hampton University Archives, Hampton University, Hampton, Virginia.

respects like the negro race."[41] More imaginatively, in his recollections of his father, Armstrong mused: "Sometimes, when I stand outside a Negro church, I get precisely the effect of a Hawaiian congregation, the same fullness and heartiness and occasional exquisite voices, and am instantly transplanted ten thousand miles away, to the great Kawaiahao church where Father used to preach to 2500 people, who swarmed in on foot and horseback, from shore, and valley and mountain, for miles around. Outside, it was like an encampment, inside it was a sea of dusky faces."[42]

The Hampton Institute, situated between the York and James rivers on 125 acres known as "Little Scotland," functioned, in Armstrong's words, "to train selected Negro youths who should go out and teach and lead their people, first by example, by getting land and homes; to give them not a dollar that they could earn for themselves; to teach respect for labor, to replace stupid drudgery with skilled hands, and to those ends to build up an industrial system for the sake not only of self-support and intelligent labor, but also for the sake of character."[43] In retro-

FIGURE 30. View of Hampton Institute from the river, circa 1890. Courtesy of Hampton University Archives, Hampton University, Hampton, Virginia.

spect and more critically, according to an account, Armstrong's Hampton aimed ostensibly "to develop habits of industry, build character, and instill a feeling for the dignity of labor," but its primary mission was "to train a cadre of conservative black teachers who were expected to help adjust the Afro-American minority to a subordinate social role in the Southern political economy."[44] Hampton's essential purpose, thus, was not to teach African Americans useful labor or morals, although it sought to promote those values, but to train teachers as a normal school or, in Armstrong's martial words, "an army of black educators," as if preparing for a military campaign. Between 1872 and 1890, accordingly, 604 of Hampton's 723 graduates went on to become teachers. Further, the "Hampton idea," a scholar pointedly declared, was the dismantling of Black Reconstruction—"the effective removal of black voters and politicians from Southern political life, the relegation of black workers to the lowest forms of labor in the Southern economy, and the establishment of a general Southern racial hierarchy."[45]

Hampton as a normal school to train teachers to free or to subjugate the race, depending upon one's perspective, had precedents in Hawai'i, as Armstrong well knew. The first schools established in Hawai'i by missionaries were restricted to the *ali'i* (chiefly class) by order of the king to allow for an assessment of its benefits and liabilities before its spread to the masses.[46] For the missionaries, as was their object for American Indians before foreign missions, schooling was a means for the promotion of Christianity and civilization. Accordingly, they resisted withholding from the commoners learning and literacy, which they saw as a way to fulfill their primary mission, especially after they devised a Hawaiian alphabet, translated the Bible, and published religious tracts in the vernacular. A way to retain royal privilege and enable mass education was to train *ali'i* as teachers who tutored their own students but who remained under missionary control. Missionaries thus set up a system of schools to accomplish that plan during the 1820s and '30s with the key support of Ka'ahumanu, the *kuhina nui* and arguably the most powerful person in the kingdom, who donated funds and supplies for education and ordered district headmen to build schoolhouses and ensure that teachers had shelters and food.

At first directed at adult literacy and the *ali'i,* mission schools shifted during the 1830s to common schools for the education of masses of children, and select schools were established for the best students drawn from the common schools in the district. To train teachers for those schools, the missionaries started the Lahainaluna high school and later seminary in 1831.[47] The resolution establishing the Lahainaluna school outlined its purposes:

> first, to aid the mission in its great work of perpetuating the faith, with all its blessings—civil, literary and religious; second, to disseminate throughout the Islands sound knowledge, embracing general literature and the sciences and whatever would elevate the mass of the people from ignorance and degradation and would cause them to become thinking, enlightened and virtuous people; third, the training up and qualifying of native school teachers . . . ; fourth, the educating of native young men of piety and talent in order to fit them to become preachers of the gospel.[48]

In 1834, the chiefs and therewith the government agreed to erect buildings and support teachers, and in 1840 the kingdom began funding the common schools, which became the public schools separate from the select mission schools.[49]

FIGURE 31. Drawing of Lahainaluna Seminary (1839). Na Momona I kaha. Courtesy of Bishop Museum.

Like the New England missionaries who came as husbands and wives, Hawaiian young men who trained as teachers and preachers required suitable spouses. They were made available by way of the female boarding schools that paralleled the boarding schools for boys. Begun in the 1830s, the Wailuku Female Seminary on Maui and Hilo School for Girls on Hawai'i functioned mainly to provide wives for graduates of the boys' boarding schools.[50] One of the teachers at the Wailuku Female Seminary, Maria Ogden, described her task: "I feel it important as far as our means will allow to root out every vestige of their former manner of living[,] raise them in morals and civilization as high as we can get them. So I am obliged to be wide awake in the school, at the table and in the playground and even follow them into their bed chambers. I am more and more satisfied that nothing but just constant vigil and supervision will accomplish the object we aim at."[51] Hawaiian girls posed a special problem for the missionaries, who sought to control their sexuality, which they saw as unbridled and licentious and hence a cause for surveillance around the clock. Ogden taught her students spinning, knitting, and sewing for two hours each day, and the girls spent two hours in recitation and study and an hour's work in the garden.[52]

"The Hawaiian wife and mother would be targeted as the agent for regeneration; the main reliance, then, would be upon instilling 'moral and religious culture' in the females," a historian summarized the lofty education mission for girls. "The meaning of marriage and chaste sexuality would be made plain; the role of housewife and mother would be elucidated; then the influence of the Hawaiian woman, at the center of her well-regulated family, would ripple outward, redeeming the wayward children, errant husbands, and, finally, the whole kingdom, for godly living."[53] Such was the ambition for women's education. Missionary Sheldon Dibble added:

> The design of the female seminary . . . is to take a class of young females into a boarding-school, away, in a measure, from the continuing influences of heathen society, to train them to habits of industry, neatness, and order, to instruct them in employments suited to their sex, to cultivate the minds, to improve their manners, and to instil the principles of holy religion; to fit them to be suitable companions for the scholars of the Mission Seminary, and examples of propriety among the females of the Sandwich Islands.[54]

The Hilo Boarding School for boys was established in 1836 by missionary David Belden Lyman, who arrived in Hilo in 1832, and it was intended as a select and feeder school for the Lahainaluna school. Having grown up on a Connecticut farm, Lyman maintained an abiding faith in the value of manual labor, especially its capacity to transform a people from barbarism to civilization. He thus made manual labor an integral part of the Hilo Boarding School's curriculum.[55] Further, the idea of a boarding school as opposed to a day school was to separate students from the coarseness of barbarism and to immerse them completely, as in baptism, in the gentle manliness of civilization.[56] Lyman indigenized his reason for boarding students as a necessary corrective to the lax, as he portrayed it, Hawaiian home, where discipline was absent. Regularity in daily and fixed routines was the way to mold character in Hilo's students, he held, and this was much publicized as a distinctive feature of his boarding school.[57]

"The original plan was to fit the Hawaiian boys to become useful, Christian citizens, and this has ever been the first aim," stated a Hilo Boarding School fundraising pamphlet. "From the founding of this school, manual training has always been its strongest feature."[58] A commemorative pamphlet for the school boasted of its manual labor curriculum: "It aimed to take Hawaiian youth in their natural uncultured state and by dint of unsparing painstaking [effort] to impart to them such mental and moral furnishing as they were able to receive and appropriate, in combination with a wholesome physical training in the ways of social and civilized life." Of its founder, Lyman, and his motives for manual training, "nothing could induce him to contribute one jot towards feeding the vanity, and puffing up the infantile and chaotic mind of the Hawaiian as he then was, by imparting to him a shallow smattering of things too high for him."[59] As was widely feared, a little education for "infantile and chaotic" minds might easily delude the "darkies" into thinking themselves the equals of whites.

David Belden Lyman and his wife, Sarah Joiner, were in the same company of missionaries and on the same whaling ship that brought Richard Armstrong and Clarissa Chapman to Hawai'i.[60] That connection served them well in their later work because Lyman, it is reported, consulted regularly with Armstrong about Hawaiian education.[61] Contrary to both celebratory and critical accounts of manual labor at the Hilo Boarding School, Lyman's journals and reports suggest a more situational, practical rather than planned, philosophical explanation for the school's stress on manual training. Simply put, the school was financially strapped, and the students' productive labor was crucial for its continued existence.[62] That manual training imparted "mental and moral furnishing," it seems, providing an abstract and lofty educational justification for a crass, monetary reality.

"Commenced our Boarding School with 7 scholars," Lyman wrote in his journal on October 3, 1836. "The partitions between their sleeping apartments are yet to be put up." Near the month's end, he reported: "Last night received another boy from Olaa. He is very promising in his appearance and probably not over

FIGURE 32. Hilo Boarding School, 1840. Art by Edward Bailey, engraving by Na Kepohonu I kaha. Courtesy of Bishop Museum.

about seven years of age. Have concluded to try the school with 1½ hour's labor in the morning, in other respects continue the same plan as from the beginning."[63] Lyman surely was experimenting with the timing and amounts of manual labor in the curriculum.

More compelling are his annual reports, which reveal an unfolding scenario of dependence upon student labor.[64] Lyman reported nothing on expenses in his first annual report (1837), but the following year he listed the school's expenses as $484.15 and its income as having come from deposits, mission property, and contributions principally from Hawaiians. "The regular hours for prayers, meals, labor, recreation, & school have been the same as during the preceding year," he wrote. In 1839, Lyman noted that expenses totaled about $200 and that student labor paid off $75 of that debt. Manual training fails to appear as a discussion item under either moral or religious instruction or as instruction and study in this third annual report, but it does appear under "Expense of Supporting the Scholars." The school's expenses continued to grow and reached a peak in 1840, when they totaled $900 "in addition to the avails of the scholar's labor," but they receded the next year to about $500 "in addition to the avails of the boys labor in cultivating their own food." The situation was such that the boys cultivated not only their own food but also sugar cane, and only in its third year of growth and harvest, 1841, were profits from that crop realized. As in past years, Lyman's report for 1842 discusses student labor not under "state of morals & religion" or "studies" but under "expenses," indicating his idea for manual training as a means by which to alleviate costs. Accordingly, in his summary of "future wants," Lyman reported: "We have in prospect no means of supporting the school except the funds of the mission & the labor of the boys in cultivating their food." By 1848 and 1849, profits from student labor had grown so substantially that they reduced the ballooning total school expenses to $430 in 1848 and to a mere $250 in 1849.

In his 1851 report, Lyman was able to state: "More time has been devoted to manual labor the last two years than formerly; more of their kalo [taro, the staple] has been brought upon the table in solid form, & more use has been made of animal food. Thus far, our experiments in these respects have been quite satisfactory. The avails in the boys labor during these years have exceeded those of any former time by more than $100 per year." Such was the students' productivity that Lyman observed in his 1852 report: "Manual labor has been continued as formerly. The school buildings having required but slight repairs, & the native teachers having been paid principally by government, the avails of the boys labor with the use of the land & other property devoted to the school have about met the expenses, except the support of the missionary teachers." And his 1856 report summed up this manual labor "experiment": "The manual labor system on which the school is conducted has been very convenient the last year, as it has afforded facilities for procuring native labor required in building the school house & in fencing the school land. From the commencement of the school it has very considerably lessened the expenses, & has tended to promote the health & good morals of the scholars."

Reflecting upon the merits of that education, Titus Coan, a colleague of Lyman's at the Hilo mission, summarized its two virtues: "Under the efficient care of Mr. and Mrs. Lyman the school has been a great success. Its department of manual labor is an important feature in the institution. It has given a very valuable physical training to the boys, imparting to them skill and health, and making the school nearly self-supporting."[65] In 1838, Sarah Joiner Lyman opened a school for girls, and as a consort to her husband's school for boys it was designed to be "self-supporting in part" through the food and labor supplied by the students' parents and friends. It also taught the girls "the rudiments of necessary book knowledge, and of singing, sewing, washing and ironing, gardening, and other things."[66]

In private correspondence, Lyman confessed to "a rigid economy" that involved "a constant effort to obtain as much labor as practicable from the scholars" but "at the same [time] holding out all inducements in my power for their parents to aid in meeting the expenses of their own children."[67] Squeezed for resources, the school's students and parents, the supposed beneficiaries of this brand of education, responded predictably, as indicated in Lyman's 1856 report. Despite the modest economic success of his strategy, he admitted, not surprisingly, "It does not tend directly to promote the popularity of the school either with the pupils or with the native population generally." Hawaiian students and their parents, it seems, may have apprehended a distinction between the life of the mind and that of the hand.

The Hilo Boarding School, according to Samuel Chapman Armstrong, was one of his models for the Hampton Institute, a Hawaiian educational institution transplanted in old Virginia and the American South. In the Hilo school, Armstrong inherited the New England legacy bequeathed by his father, Richard Armstrong, and his father's colleague, David Belden Lyman.[68] It was his racialization of Hawaiians and African Americans as an undifferentiated "race" and people that allowed for, indeed required and justified, this schooling for subservience. "The negro and the Polynesian have many striking similarities," observed Armstrong. "Of both it is true that not mere ignorance, but deficiency of character is the chief difficulty, and that to build up character is the true objective point in education." Further, "morality and industry generally go together. Especially in the weak tropical races, idleness, like ignorance, breeds vice."[69] Complicit with that racialization was a gendering, like the parallel schools in Hawai'i for girls and boys, that consigned men to the field and women to the home. At Hampton, the Women's Labor Department prepared its students for marriage and instructed them in homemaking—cooking, cleaning, washing, and ironing—to teach them the dignity of labor.[70] As conceived by New England missionaries in Hawai'i and one of their sons at Hampton, marriage, procreation, and the home were the bases of civilization, and with them heterosexuality, patriarchy, and women's subjection to men.

The rhetoric claiming the educational value of manual labor and the reality of its economic benefits at both Hilo and Hampton bear examination and comparison. Manual labor at Hilo both "civilized" Hawaiians and sustained the school, and despite Hampton's claim that its manual labor education was for the purpose of building character, it was also understood that the students' productivity enabled their stay at the institute and defrayed the costs of their "education." So while maintaining that work built "accurate habits of thought and deed" among "undisciplined races," a Hampton publication stated that the heavy outlay on machinery in some departments was covered entirely by the output of students' labor, which was considerable, especially when weighed against the hours spent in study. During their stay at Hampton, the report announced, "the students work eight or ten hours daily and study two hours in the evening, an arrangement which, as may be imagined, weeds out effectively the incapable or unwilling."[71] That disparity in emphasis between work and study was given a positive spin and explained as a way "to give the students an opportunity to work out a portion of their boarding expenses" and "to prevent the school from becoming a hothouse for producing students with no power of self-help or independence."[72] Still, two of Hampton's proponents explained what they meant by the manual labor system's "success": "The expenses of the school are reduced to a minimum, while the students, not overburdened with physical labor, come to their books with fresh interest and untired faculties."[73]

Like Lyman and his Hilo Boarding School, Armstrong believed in regimenting the lives of his pupils for a total saturation and complete transformation. "The average Negro student needs a regime which shall control the twenty-four hours of each day; thus only can the old ideas and ways be pushed out and new ones take their place," Armstrong maintained. "The formation of good habits is fundamental in our work. . . . The Negro pupil, like the Negro soldier, is readily transformed under wise control into remarkable tidiness and good conduct generally."[74] Lyman and Armstrong shared a skepticism of the ability of "weak tropical races" to appreciate book learning and achieve the life of the mind. To Lyman, that brand of education would inevitably ring hollow in "infantile" Hawaiian minds and lead only to empty vanity and display; to Armstrong, African American "over-education" produced dysfunctional members of society.[75] Both, thus, preached manual labor for the uplift of the race. "The temporal salvation of the colored race for some time to come is to be won out of the ground," wrote Armstrong. "Skilful agriculturists and mechanics are needed rather than poets and orators." "Too much is expected of mere book-knowledge; too much is expected of one generation. The real upward movement, the leveling up, not of persons but of people, will be, as in all history, almost imperceptible, to be measured only by long periods."[76] Those deferred dreams, that glacial movement for immediate, full equality applied to Hawaiians. "The condition of the Hawaiian people is the product of centuries of barbarism followed by fifty years of civilizing influences," Armstrong told his Hawaiian audience. "Externally modified by the latter to an astonishing degree, they have internally changed as innate ideas and instincts only can change, slowly. Ten rather than two generations are required to overcome the inertia of the past."[77]

Finally, insofar as the Hilo Boarding School sent its top students to Lahainaluna High School, both Hilo and Hampton served as normal schools to train teachers and leaders of their people. From those halls, the "army of black educators" set forth to conquer and subjugate a people. And as the Europeans did with the exotic plants and cash crops they spread throughout their nineteenth-century global empires, Armstrong gloried in his claim that "an idea transplanted from the Pacific ocean has flourished wonderfully in old Virginia."[78]

WHITE AND BLACK

Despite Armstrong's belief that African American students were childlike "in the early stages of civilization" and hence "docile, impressible, imitative and earnest,"[79] some students and their parents, like Lyman's discerning Hawaiian pupils and their parents, were disappointed by Hampton's educational design, which they saw as stifling their ambitions and exploiting their labor. A mother, Roberta Whiting, expressed her concern: "I received a letter from my son and he tells me that he has not attended day school since entering your institution. He also mentioned that his work was hard having to milk, and attend to a number of cows every day and that he has to get up at four A.M. to do this and the only time spent in school was at night." A student, William W. Adams, criticized the rudimentary quality of Hampton's course of study, claiming that he was "not learning anything" but merely "going over what I had learned in a primary school." He quit in disgust and called the program "greatly over-rated." Prominent African American leader Henry M. Turner reported of his 1878 visit to a Hampton classroom, "The teacher knew comparatively nothing about it [astronomy], and the class knew, if possible, less than nothing." Hampton failed to develop its students intellectually, Turner charged, especially in "algebra, geometry, higher mathematics, Greek, Latin, and Science."[80]

Booker T. Washington, Hampton's most illustrious graduate, eulogized his great teacher: "My race in this country can never cease to be grateful to General Armstrong for all that he did for my people and for American civilization. We always felt that many of the ideas and much of the inspiration he used to such good effect in this country, he got in Hawaii."[81] Washington, founder of the Tuskegee Normal and Industrial Institute in Alabama in 1881, was a leading apologist for Armstrong and his manual labor school because of widespread suspicion among African Americans occasioned by southern white support of Hampton and Tuskegee, which was cast from the Hampton die. "The southern white people as a rule approved of industrial education," Washington noted. "This made the colored people all the more suspicious of its value and object." Armstrong disregarded that "misunderstanding," Washington recalled, and pressed forward with his plan "to give the colored people an idea of the dignity, the beauty and civilizing power of intelligent labor with the hand." Through "industrial education," Washington added, Armstrong sought to "bring the two races in the South into closer relations with each other."[82]

Washington and Tuskegee were indebted to Armstrong and Hampton beyond

FIGURE 33. Booker T. Washington as a Hampton student, 1873. *Southern Workman* 31 (May 1902).

what usually comes with a student and teacher relationship. "I hope I may never live to be the student to show ingratitude to, or in any way hinder the progress of the institution whose officers and teachers I love so dearly and to whose parental care I owe all that I am," Washington vowed to Hampton's treasurer and Armstrong confidant, James F. B. Marshall.[83] From Tuskegee's start, Washington dutifully reported the progress of his work to Armstrong, who had recommended him for the post. "As soon as I got here I went to work looking for a suitable place for the building," he wrote to Armstrong. "While doing so I came to this conclusion; that the people in this part of the South are not able to send their children to school and pay $9 or $10 per yr. for their board, so I have decided that the only way to make this a permanent and successful school is to get [?] the labor system as soon as possible."[84] It is striking that at Tuskegee, like Hilo and Hampton, manual labor education was foremost a matter of fiscal necessity and not of curricular or educational reform. Those economic needs, especially during Tuskegee's early years, translated into loans of expertise, labor, and cash from Hampton to Tuskegee as a "parent" to its "child." Washington frequently sought Armstrong's and Marshall's advice, especially about legal and fund-raising questions for the institutionalization of Tuskegee. He also received expert help from Hampton during down times, such as the summer when Hampton's trained staff worked for a period at Tuskegee. Exemplary of that relationship between Hampton and Tuskegee was an 1883 letter sent by Marshall containing a $200 loan to Tuskegee and an expression of concern over Washington's bookkeeping. Washington, in reply, admitted his ignorance of record keeping and asked for a Hampton professional to set up and sort through Tuskegee's financial ledgers.[85]

On Founder's Day in 1909, Booker T. Washington returned to his alma mater to address members of Hampton's family. The "sainted Founder of this institution," he told his audience, "presented the most perfect type of the physical, the mental, the spiritual man that it had ever been my privilege to see; and through all my course of attendance here as a student, and afterwards in all my work away from this institution, it was my privilege to be guided, to be instructed, to be inspired by him and his words, and I have never had occasion to change the first impression which he made upon me."[86] Armstrong's first and great contribution to African Americans, he enumerated, was to impress upon them the realization that their salvation rested in their own hands and not in handouts from others. His next lesson was to teach African Americans the value of the soil, to make them feel that in working the earth they were touching "real things." Instead of more books, costlier books, and books with long titles, Armstrong taught African Americans to throw aside books and instead study "things" in the laboratory, field, and shop. Against much despair among the newly freed African Americans, Washington summarized, Armstrong planted the powerful idea that the salvation of the race came from within, "through himself, in his own community, through his own energy. . . . In changing the outlook of the Negro race, Armstrong did a service for us as a race which we shall never forget."[87]

WHITE, BLACK, AND RED

In addition to blacks and whites, "the two races in the South" according to Washington, Armstrong and Hampton were influential in the lives of another "race"—American Indians. In his popular autobiography, *Up from Slavery* (1901), Washington described his role in the education of Indians at Hampton. Armstrong, he wrote, "secured from the reservations in the Western states over one hundred wild and for the most part perfectly ignorant Indians."[88] He hired Washington to be a sort of "house father" to the young Indian men, to live with them and to discipline and civilize them. Ironically, Washington noted, Indians held African Americans in contempt because, unlike African Americans, Indians had never been enslaved by whites. And yet Washington's paternal oversight of American Indians fell in line with Hampton's racial hierarchy. The school's paper, the *Southern Workman*, in an article titled "Work and Fun in the Geography Class," posed a series of questions about race and their answers, including these: "Which are the first [of humankind's races]? The white people are the strongest. Which are the next? The Mongolians or yellows. The next? The Ethiopians or blacks. Next? The Americans or reds. Tell me something of the white people. The Caucasion [sic] is away head of all the other races. . . . it is God who made the world."[89]

The lesson taught not only white superiority but also the effect of white uplift and benevolence. Although both began in a state of savagery, Africans in the United States, under the regime of slavery, worked their way up the racial ladder toward civilization, whereas the untutored, undisciplined American Indian remained at the bottom. In actualizing that racial ideology, Hampton's African American students helped Indian students with the English language and the acquisition of "civilized habits," according to Washington. Of relations among the three "races," he mused, "I have often wondered if there was a white institution in this country whose students would have welcomed the incoming of more than a hundred com-

FIGURE 34. "Class in American History" (1900). Two museum pieces for student inspection: Louis Firetail (Sioux, Crow Creek) poses with a stuffed American eagle. Courtesy of Hampton University Archives, Hampton University, Hampton, Virginia.

panions of another race in the cordial way that these black students at Hampton welcomed the red ones."[90] Still, Hampton's policy was to segregate Indians from African Americans in academic and social activities.[91] As a Hampton teacher noted about the relations between African American and Indian students, "General social intercourse between the races of opposite sexes is limited and guarded. Trouble might come of it."[92]

Contrary to Washington's claim that Armstrong "secured" Indian students from reservations in the West, Hampton's "experiment" in Indian education began with the final phase of the U.S. war of subjugation waged against "untamed" and resistant Indians. In the process of "winning the West," the government incarcerated Indians, who were in reality prisoners of war from independent nations but whom it considered to be "in rebellion." After the Civil War, Lt. Richard Henry Pratt, a commander of African American troops like Armstrong, was given command of some 150 Arapaho, Cheyenne, Comanche, and Kiowa prisoners who were accused of participating in an uprising in Oklahoma.[93] At his compound in Fort Marion, Florida, Pratt sought to "civilize" his wards by removing their shackles, cutting their hair, and having them wear "the clothing of the white man." He put them to work making curios for tourists, drilled them as in the army, and schooled them in English.[94] In addition, even as he strived to make his wards their own jailors as "Americanized" subjects, he sought their release to absorb them more fully into the United States. "I have the honor to report that the Indian prisoners, confined here under my charge, have made very urgent appeals to have something done in their case," Pratt appealed to the army's adjutant general in 1875. "They are particularly distressed about being separated from their women and children."[95] Finally, in 1877, the army and Indian Commissioner Ezra A. Hayt agreed to release Pratt's Indians for their education in eastern schools. Sarah Mather, teacher of Pratt's prisoners, knew Samuel Chapman Armstrong, and she wrote to him to inquire about his willingness to take in Indian students at Hampton. Armstrong was initially cautious, but when it became clear that Indian education might open the way for additional financial support for Hampton he jumped at this chance to train another of "our darkies."[96] As he confided to his wife about the arrival of Indians at Hampton, "They are a big card for the school & will diminish my grey hairs. There's money in them I tell you."[97]

In admitting the first group of seventeen Indians to Hampton in 1878, Armstrong believed that the African American experience proved instructive for managing Indians. Because of enslavement, he noted, African Americans were disciplined by hard labor, whereas Indians, wild and free, held it "in lofty contempt," an attitude fatal to their development. "The Indian question will never be settled till you make the Indian blister his hands," he declared. "No people ever emerged from barbarism that did not emerge through labor." And insofar as character training was best achieved through labor, he defended the institution of slavery and found wanting the reservation system when he observed: "The severe discipline of slavery strengthened a weak race. Professed friendship for a strong one has weakened it. A cruel semblance of justice has done more harm than direct oppression could have done. The Negro is strong, the Indian weak, because the one is trained to labor and the other is not."[98] As affirmed by Armstrong's second wife and Hampton teacher, "It is, we are convinced, to this labor system closely and faithfully applied from the outset, both to Negroes and Indians, that we owe to a great extent the character of our graduates."[99]

After visits by President Rutherford B. Hayes and Secretary of the Interior Carl Schurz, the government approved a program of 120 Indian students for Hampton at $167 a year for each student.[100] Pratt, who remained at Hampton to ensure the smooth transfer of his charges, arranged for what became known as the "outing system" based on his belief that all Indians should become farmers. This labor system involved the loaning of students during their vacations to farmers who provided room and board in return for the students' work. Notwithstanding the possibility for exploitation, the outing system, Pratt maintained, reduced racial prejudice by promoting cultural contact, which was "the best of all education."[101] And the assimilation of the Indian was to be gained through his total immersion in white American culture to saturate and swamp him and thereby remake him into a new man. "A great general has said that the only good Indian is a dead one, and that high sanction of his destruction has been an enormous factor in promoting Indian massacres," Pratt conceded. "In a sense, I agree with the sentiment, but only in this; that all the Indian there is in the race should be dead. Kill the Indian in him, and save the man."[102] Armstrong argued more practically. "The alternative is civilization or extermination," he reasoned. To civilize Indians would require wisdom and energy; to exterminate them would cost at least one white for each Indian life, along with "untold suffering and expense; it can be done, but it will hurt us as much as the Indian."[103]

Like Armstrong, Pratt held that the African American experience taught lessons for the regeneration of Indians. Despite the "irregularities" of slavery amid promises of freedom, Pratt offered a triumphalist reading of that history: "For many years we greatly oppressed the black man," he began, "but the germ of human lib-

FIGURE 35. Fifteen-year-old Zie-wie Davis (Lakota, Crow Creek Agency), one of the first Indian girls at Hampton, stares directly into the camera in 1878 upon her arrival (left) and averts her eyes from the camera's lens after a year at the institute (right), seemingly taking her cue from the photographer. Courtesy of Hampton University Archives, Hampton University, Hampton, Virginia.

erty remained among us and grew, until, in spite of our irregularities, there came from the lowest savagery into intelligent manhood and freedom among us more than seven millions of our population, who are to-day an element of industrial value with which we could not well dispense." Without that gift of civilization, "the greatest blessing that ever came to the Negro race," Pratt continued, African Americans would remain mired in "cannibalism in darkest Africa" instead of their present elevation to "citizenship in free and enlightened America." Through white intervention, Pratt concluded, "under the care and authority of individuals of the higher race," African Americans moved from savagery to civility and citizenship and were made healthy, prosperous, and beneficial to society. Likewise, he declared, "When we cease to teach the Indian that he is less than a man; when we recognize fully that he is capable in all respects as we are, and that he only needs the opportunities and privileges which we possess to enable him to assert his humanity and manhood; when we act consistently towards him in accordance with that recognition; when we cease to fetter him to conditions which keep him in bondage, surrounded by retrogressive influences; when we allow him the freedom of association and the developing influences of social contact," Pratt predicted, "then the Indian will quickly demonstrate that he can be truly civilized, and he himself will solve the question of what to do with the Indian."[104]

Secretary of War George W. McCrary directed Pratt to secure for Hampton, with "tribal and parental consent," fifty boys and girls from the Nez Perce of Chief Joseph, who was at the time being held as a prisoner. In 1877, Joseph had led a band of about 550 men, women, and children on a remarkable 1,321-mile flight of seventy-five days from pursuing U.S. soldiers. His Nez Perce had killed four white settlers after having been forcibly removed by the government from their homes in Oregon to a reservation in Idaho. Eluding capture, they were finally caught short of the Canadian border, although some managed to reach Canada. Joseph, tired, sick, and sad, surrendered on the promise that his Nez Perce would be allowed to return to Idaho. The government reneged on that agreement and moved the Nez Perce from one place to another for several years.

The "recruitment" of their children was, no doubt, the government's attempt to punish them for their rebellion and to maintain a hold over them. Joseph and others of his band saw through the government's deception couched as liberality and generosity in the proposed "education" of their children. At a meeting with Joseph and other leaders, Pratt reported, "They all persisted in refusing their children until they knew their own fate. Chief Joseph was noted as an orator, and his long speech was full of impressive arraignment of our government and people for mistreatment of his people."[105] Leaders of other tribes similarly refused the government's effort to kidnap their children, notably an 1884 Sioux council, which told recruiters, "They have taken away our tobacco and we will give up our rations; but we will *not* give up our children."[106] Suspicion of white benevolence was, of course, well established on the long trail of violence and expulsions and broken treaties and unfulfilled promises. Pratt knowingly participated in another of his government's acts of treachery. When he visited two Pawnee bands who had recently resisted government efforts to remove and resettle them, the commissioner of Indian affairs told Pratt of his particular desire to seize children from the rebels, "saying that the children, if brought east, would become hostages for tribal good behavior."[107]

Perhaps as a result of his conflation of African Americans with Indians, Pratt was determined to create distances between them, apparently because he knew that whites associated Indians with blacks and thereby "lowered" and "darkened" the objects of his benevolence.[108] As told by Pratt, Carlisle Indian Industrial School, begun in 1879, came about through individual meetings with Schurz, the secretary of the interior, Hayt, the Indian commissioner, and McCrary, the secretary of war. Congress approved the transfer of Carlisle Barracks from the War Department to the Interior Department, and Schurz and Hayt agreed to put Pratt in charge of the Indian school and promised to find money to support 100–125 students. "Being ignorant of the methods and ways of legislating in Washington," Pratt admitted, "I was elated to find that things could be so easily and quickly attended to if you only had best help and directions."[109]

As with his "recruitment" of Indian students for Hampton, Pratt endorsed and was guided by "the hostage idea" when selecting tribes from which to pluck children for Carlisle. Also important were children of chiefs not only because of the example they would set for their people but also because of the government's desire to subjugate them and, through them, their followers. In 1880, two-thirds of Carlisle's students were children of chiefs and headmen.[110] "I am your friend," Pratt told Spotted Tail, the renowned leader of the Brule Sioux during his first recruitment trip for the Carlisle School in 1878. All the while he knew that Indian Commissioner Hayt had directed him to Spotted Tail's Sioux "because the children would be hostages for the good behavior of their people." Instead, Pratt piously announced that the government's interest in Indian education was motivated by the desire to treat Indians as equals, "as competent as white children," and to see them advance in language and industry for their self-interest and independence. "The

FIGURE 36. At the grave of Lucy Pretty Eagle, a Sioux child who died on May 9, 1884, someone had placed, among other essentials, a pair of shoes, as if to summon her spirit to flee Carlisle for the warmth of home. Carlisle Indian School cemetery, Carlisle, Pennsylvania, 2003. Gary Y. Okihiro photograph.

white people are all thieves and liars," Spotted Tail retorted. "We do not want our children to learn such things." "Spotted Tail," Pratt persisted, "I hear you have a dozen children. Give me four or five and let me take them to Carlisle and show you what the right kind of education will do for them." Then, "I asked the interpreter in an undertone, 'Who else has children?' He said, 'Two Strike has two fine boys.' I said, 'Two Strike, give me your two boys to take to Carlisle and I will make useful men of them.' I again asked the interpreter, and he said, 'Milk has a boy and a girl.' I said, 'Milk, give me your boy and girl for Carlisle and let me show you what I can do with them.'" In the end, Spotted Tail, Two Strike, Milk, and others gave their children up to Pratt. "I was elated and told them so," he wrote.[111]

Whether at Hampton or Carlisle, too many of the Indian children fell ill and died. Highly susceptible to diseases for which they had little immunity, the hostages

FIGURE 37. The son of Elk Feather, Cracking Wing (Sutateish) was, according to his captors, "an exceptionally bright, industrious boy" who had a gift for languages. Courtesy of Hampton University Archives, Hampton University, Hampton, Virginia.

were further weakened by the arduous journey east, a change in climate, unfamiliar foods and diet, and psychological distress and feelings of alienation. But Hampton's resident physician, writing of the thirty-one Indians who died at the institute during the first ten years, attributed their deaths only to "constitutional weakness in certain cases, and general race tendencies." Aside from those deaths, 111 Indian students returned to their homes because of poor health. Hampton during that first decade admitted a total of 467 Indian students, 320 boys and 147 girls.[112] One student, Cracking Wing, arrived at Hampton in October 1881 from Dakota Territory. In January 1884 he inquired: "And I myself sick two days now my breast is hurt, & coughs all the time. Can you give me some medicine that you told me to take . . . when first I came up here." Some three months later Cracking Wing was dead; he was seventeen years old.[113]

WHITE, BLACK, RED, AND BROWN

Even as Hampton sired Tuskegee, Booker T. Washington's institution inspired the education of Indians by others, like the superintendent of Indian schools, Estelle Reel, the first woman in U.S. history appointed to a position requiring Senate confirmation. In that office from 1898 to 1910, Reel toured some 250 Indian schools under her jurisdiction across the continent, beginning at Carlisle, and she published the *Uniform Course of Study* in 1901 to standardize the schools' curriculum. It is reported that three thousand copies of the *Course of Study* found their way to Indian schools, and twice that number were sent to U.S. colonies in Puerto Rico and the Philippines. Tuskegee framed Reel's course of study in that, according to a press release, Reel "does not believe in making a white man of the Indian but thinks it best to educate him and let him remain an Indian. . . . She believes in what Booker T. Washington is doing for the negro, and has adopted many of the Tuskegee methods for Indian schools."[114]

Like Washington and his mentor, Samuel Chapman Armstrong, Reel advocated a practical course of study for the darker races, involving the "correct" minutiae of manual labor, involving agriculture and trades for boys and domestic life for girls. Her attention to detail in the process as well as the nature of manual labor drew from her notions of the presumed connection between the racialized body and the mind. Accordingly, her instruction "See to it that all sit in an erect position, never resting any part of the arm on the desk" bore direct relevance to the "fact" that "the Indian child is of lower physical organization than the white child" in that "his forearms are smaller and his fingers and hands less flexible; the very structure of his bones and muscles will not permit so wide a variety of manual movements as are customary among Caucasian children, and his very instincts and modes of thought are adjusted to this imperfect manual development."[115] Exercising and regenerating the mind for civilization thus required bodily breathing, marching, calisthenics, and games, and because of physical differences there were correct and incorrect postures, gestures, and movements.

Reel's reach extended to U.S. colonial possessions insofar as her *Course of Study* was followed, marking a trail that began with Hawaiian landings in New England, white New England's domestic mission to American Indians and foreign mission to Hawai'i, and Hawaiian education's refashioning for African Americans in the South, its adaptation for American Indians in the East and West, its exportation to Puerto Ricans and Filipinos in U.S. colonies in the tropics, and finally its return to Hawaiians in the Islands. In light of the generalizing nature of white racializations, it is unremarkable that this brand of education embraced a constellation of darker races. Chinese, Malays, a Portuguese from the Azores, and a "Jew of England" studied with Hawaiians and American Indians at Cornwall's Foreign Mission School; Japanese received instruction along with African Americans and American Indians at Hampton in Virginia;[116] Booker T. Washington recruited Cubans and Puerto Ricans for his Tuskegee; and U.S. colonial officials apparently sent Puerto Ricans to both Hampton and the Carlisle Indian School for an education.[117]

MIS-EDUCATION

Slavery's end failed to extinguish the white supremacist ideology that was crucial for its defense within the parameters of freedom and democracy. The ideas and practices of racial hierarchies and with them the privileges and poverties that accrue to the blessed and wretched of the earth continued to flourish in the nation through its institutions and peoples. The schools were powerful instruments in both the shackling and liberating of students' minds, from one point of view, in the historical transition from the total institution of slavery to the era of segregation. "Mis-education," African American educator Carter G. Woodson explained during the Jim Crow era, was designed to maintain the relations of white dominance on the one hand and black subservience on the other.

> The same educational process which inspires and stimulates the oppressor with the thought that he is everything and has accomplished everything worth while depresses and crushes at the same time the spark of genius in the Negro by making him feel that his race does not amount to much and never will measure up to the

standards of other peoples. . . . When you control a man's thinking you do not have to worry about his action. . . . You do not need to send him to the back door. He will go without being told. In fact, if there is no back door, he will cut one for his special benefit. His education makes it necessary.[118]

The idea of repudiating the nakedness of paganism and barbarism for the garb of Christianity and civilization has antecedents, of course, in this story of Hawai'i and the United States. Nineteenth-century New England missionaries of the Second Great Awakening, filled with religious zeal to expand and conquer, saw the schools as instruments of divine mediation in the conversion of the pagan and uncivilized. Cornwall's Foreign Mission School, established for "heathen youth," served that purpose in the pieties of duty and benevolence by the elect at home. The arrival of strangers to these shores, especially the marooned Hawaiians, catalyzed the movement for foreign missions, which sired missionaries like Richard and Clarissa Armstrong and sent them abroad to the islands of the sea. And from that Christian empire, that sea of islands, returned its sons and daughters and their notions of selves and others, derivative of New England stock but differentiated and adapted in tropical islands, a new generation who helped direct the course of social relations on the temperate continent.

The Hampton idea faced challenges from the objects of that brand of education. During the late nineteenth century, black colleges, many of which were sponsored by mission societies, generally relegated industrial training to subordinate positions in their curricula and instead adhered to a classical education. African Americans widely regarded the Hampton model with suspicion, such that an advocate admitted, "Our trustees have felt strongly that it is important to stir up the colored people to an interest in industrial education," because "there is a perhaps natural feeling among them against this form of instruction."[119] But some northern philanthropists and southern whites kept the Hampton idea alive, setting the stage for the debate and struggle over the education of African Americans in the early twentieth century.

Meanwhile, the originator of the Hampton idea, Samuel Chapman Armstrong, died quietly in his sleep on May 11, 1893. "I wish to be buried in the School grave-

FIGURE 38. In death as in life, "the Great Teacher" is surrounded by his pupils. Cemetery at Hampton University, Hampton, Virginia, 2003. Gary Y. Okihiro photograph.

yard," he wrote, "among the students, where one of them would have been put had he died next. I wish no monument or fuss whatever over my grave; only a simple headstone. . . . I wish the simplest funeral services, without sermon or attempt at oratory—a soldier's funeral."[120] An honor guard of five African Americans and five American Indians carried Armstrong's coffin, and his gravesite, when finished, was marked by a granite stone from Williamstown and a piece of lava from Hawai'i.

Hampton sired Carlisle, and both influenced Indian education in the United States and its island possessions for generations thereafter. Although the education of American Indians by whites long predated Hampton, the school's educational system was influential in the industrial boarding and training schools that typified the government's efforts to educate Indian youth after the end of Indian sovereignty and the installation of reservations in the late nineteenth century. Likewise, Hampton's rigid, military discipline that sought to order the lives of its students twenty-four hours each day was characteristic of Indian boarding schools established during the 1880s and 1890s.[121]

Prevalent was the idea of parallel tracks for boys and girls to fit them for labor but also for heterosexual unions upon which civilized society would be built. Girls, lifted allegedly from men's exploitation and lusts as mere slaves and squaws, bore a special burden as future mothers of families and the race and nation and were groomed for roles within the home.[122] Boys, through cultivation and industry in the public sphere, supplied the material wants and needs of the family and society, something they did not do in their presumed natural state of indolence and degradation. "The Carlisle Indian Industrial School," the historical marker dedicated on August 31, 2003, reads, "was the model for a nation-wide system of boarding schools intended to assimilate American Indians into mainstream culture. Over 10,000 indigenous children attended the school between 1879 and 1918. Despite idealistic beginnings, the school left a mixed and lasting legacy, creating opportunity for some students and conflicted identities for others."[123]

Armstrong and Hampton, in truth, inspired not only Tuskegee and Carlisle but also a strand of missionary education that influenced scores of students of color on the continent and, in return, in the Islands. The Kauai Industrial School begun in 1889 by children of missionaries, Juliette Smith and her brother, Jared Smith, was modeled on the Hilo Boarding School and Hampton and was conceived as an act of "charity" to train that island's Hawaiian children for "agricultural work especially." A statement on coeducation published by this school traced its debt to Hampton: "The founders of this school, and other friends of the race believe that for Hawaiians far better results can be obtained by industrial co-education, properly managed, in morals, manners and preparation for civilized homes, than can be obtained by educating the sexes in separate schools. The great success of co-education among the Negroes and Indians in the United States leads us to believe that it will be equally successful with Hawaiians."[124] Not only was Armstrong's counsel sought in establishing the Kauai Industrial School ("make Kauai bloom with enlightened kanakas," Armstrong had urged Jared Smith), but two key staff members, Margaret Kenwill, the school's principal, and Bernette(?) Bacheler, her assistant, were Hampton veterans.[125]

In 1882, Hawaiʻi's Bureau of Immigration inquired of native son Armstrong whether "negroes from those of the Southern States where labor rates are low . . . would not much mind emigrating." The Islands' planters had considered African American labor as early as 1870, although no action was taken. Armstrong's presence in Virginia and his well-known advocacy of industrial education seemed an opportune moment for an infusion of plantation workers from the South. The Hawaiian legislature, however, in an act of racism opposed the immigration of blacks, and thus the attempt to recruit African American labor ended.[126] Still, the ideas of native education and servile labor for the ostensible uplift of subject races migrated between island and continent, and a seed first cultivated in Hawaiʻi and transplanted in the American South had found its way back, full circle, to the Islands.

5

Hawaiian Diaspora

The steering stars, moving quietly in arcs across the night sky, guided Polynesian navigators who were the children of the original Pacific dispersal—peoples who sailed eastward and then northward from Southeast Asia and Polynesia to map and settle Oceania's immense and fecund "sea of islands." Voyaging was a means of livelihood and production in that it generated resources from both sea and land and enabled the creation, accumulation, and distribution of social and material capital. Those Polynesians of expeditions that transported them to Hawai'i would, as Hawaiians, in the late eighteenth century "discover" strangers from Europe and the United States who charted and transgressed the Pacific for science, profit, and dominion. That chance encounter gave rise to yet another Hawaiian diaspora, one that hurtled along the churning currents of empire and scattered those island peoples across continents—Asia, but also the exotic coasts and interiors of Africa, Europe, and America.

Captain James Cook's arrival in Hawai'i was an accident, quite unlike the landfall of Polynesian navigators who were searching for islands in this part of their Oceania. Rather than searching for islands, the British Royal Society and Admiralty sent Cook, on his third and final Pacific expedition, to find the fabled Northwest Passage, the imaginary channel that joined the Atlantic with the Pacific, and thereby shorten considerably the distance between Europe and Asia. Having failed to find it on North America's eastern flank, the British shifted their attention to the continent's western edge.

On July 12, 1776, Cook's ship, the *Resolution,* outfitted for a scientific mission, slipped out of Plymouth harbor on the English coast eight days after the American Continental Congress adopted the declaration resolving: "That these United Colonies are, and, of right, ought to be, free and independent states; that they are absolved from all allegiance to the British crown." *Resolution*'s companion, the *Discovery,* left about a fortnight later for a rendezvous at the Dutch colony at southern Africa's Cape of Good Hope. After stops in New Zealand, Tonga, and Tahiti, the expedition sailed north through waters uncharted on British maps. Some 3,000 miles northwest of Tahiti, at dawn on January 18, 1778, Hawaiians on the island of Kaua'i spotted the *Resolution* and *Discovery* on their ocean. That Hawaiian discovery and the subsequent failure by Cook to find the Northwest Passage but success in locating natural resources valuable for the Pacific trade tied the islands of Hawai'i with that corner of the continent referred to as America's Pacific Northwest.

PACIFIC NORTHWEST

In 1899, while excavating on Newcastle Island in British Columbia, workmen uncovered a coffin that, according to those who could remember, contained the remains of "Kanaka Pete," a Hawaiian who had been hanged for murder on March 10, 1869.[1] Honolulu resident Peter Kakua, or "Kanaka Pete," left the Islands in 1853 for employment in Canada's Southwest and served for a time with the Hudson's Bay Company and later worked for the governor of Vancouver Island and British Columbia. When he was arrested for the murder of his Canadian Indian wife, Que-en, his infant daughter, and his in-laws, Squash-e-lik and Shil-at-ti-Nord, Kakua had been working for the Vancouver Coal Company at Nanaimo near Newcastle Island.

At the coroner's inquest, Kakua testified that his wife had left him, promising never to return, but after a night of drinking he went home to find Que-en and her parents sitting around a fire. He left them for more drinks, and when he came back he discovered his wife "lying on the bed and her father lying on her. They were in the act of adultery." "I thought this too bad," testified Kakua,

> and took hold of him to drag him out. He caught hold of my hair and pulled me down on the bed and got my finger into his mouth and called out to the old

woman to come and beat me. The old woman rushed at me and began striking me on the head and body with a stick, my wife also striking me. Being considerably intoxicated at the time, and owing to the pain I was suffering I became almost mad and laid hold of the first thing I could reach which was an axe . . . and laid about me indiscriminately. After a time I fell down and remember nothing more until I awoke at daylight . . . when I saw my Father-in-law, Mother-in-law, my wife and child all dead.[2]

When he came to, apparently, Kakua closed the house, drank all day, and in the evening bumped into his African Canadian friend Adam Stepney on the street, and the pair drank whiskey throughout the night under the wharf. The next morning Kakua, with a still sleeping Stepney in his canoe, pushed off for the mainland, but Stepney, after awakening, persuaded Kakua to put him ashore instead on New-castle Island, where a pursuing search party captured them. The inquest found Kakua guilty of "wilful murder" and ordered him to prison to await his trial. The Indian nation to which the victims belonged pressed for Kakua's execution and made clear that future relations between them and the colonial authorities depended upon the results of the trial. Despite petitions from Kakua's attorneys for a delay because they had insufficient time to present an adequate defense, the trial proceeded as scheduled with an all-white jury, despite the six Hawaiians who were on the jury list, and the proceedings were conducted in English, a language imperfectly understood by the defendant.

The jurors found Kakua guilty of murdering his wife but recommended mercy on the curious, cross-cultural ground that "Kanakas are not Christians and killing men may not be such an offense in their eyes." In the matter of his in-laws, however, the jury found Kakua guilty of murder without a recommendation of clemency, and the court in agreement ordered that Kakua be hanged. The Hawaiian consul, Henry Rhodes, urged the governor to commute the sentence because Kakua's confession, on which rested his conviction, was made in English, and his allegation of his wife and father-in-law's incest and adultery, given in Hawaiian, was disallowed from jury consideration. The appeal was rejected, so at 7 A.M. on March 10, 1869, Peter Kakua "ascended the scaffold unflinchingly, made no remarks, and struggled but slightly after the drop fell. His neck was evidently broken," according to the Victoria *Daily Colonist*.[3]

As intimated by the six unselected Hawaiian jurors, Peter Kakua's presence in the Pacific Northwest was not exceptional. Hawaiians regularly visited the area and were key figures in the trade that was forecast by American John Ledyard (as a member of Cook's last voyage) involving North America's furs and skins and China's teas, spices, and other desired goods. Those who preceded Kakua included the remarkable Ka'iana, a warrior chief who moved among the most powerful rulers of his time, including Kamehameha I and Ka'ahumanu, his favored wife, and who was well known among European traders involved in commerce in the Pacific.[4] Ka'iana, from 1787 to 1788, visited China, the Philippines, Alaska, and the western shores of North America and was featured in the accounts of several travel narratives by British authors. Over six feet tall, Ka'iana, in his colorful feathered cloak and high helmet, was a sensation in the streets of Canton. Upon his return to Hawai'i his worldliness enabled his intermediary role between Hawaiians and foreigners, and his death at the age of forty in the pivotal battle of Nu'uanu in 1795 on the losing side against his distant cousin and former ally, Kamehameha I, reflected his mercurial political career. In his collection of stories, King Kalākaua wrote of Ka'iana and his tragic and fatal break with Kamehameha: "After giving to the conqueror his best energies for years, and faithfully assisting in cementing the foundations of his greatness, he turned against him on the very eve of final triumph, and perished in attempting to destroy by a single blow the power he had helped to create."[5]

Born of the ruling line on the island of Hawai'i on his father's side and of royal blood from Maui and O'ahu chiefs on his mother's side, Ka'iana joined his cousin, the powerful King Kahekili of Maui, in the 1783 invasion and conquest of O'ahu. But two years later, when the O'ahu chiefs rose up against Kahekili's occupation, Ka'iana allied himself with the rebels and had to flee the island when the Maui king smashed the rebellion. Taking refuge on Kaua'i under King Ka'eo, his cousin, Ka'iana built his wealth and power as the king's deputy. It is unclear why, in 1787, Ka'iana sailed away from Kaua'i on the *Nootka,* under the command of John Meares, with its cargo of otter and beaver skins from North America bound for the goods of China. Despite storm damage, the *Nootka* reached Macao six weeks later and, still later, Canton. Among the polyglot of Chinese and other Asian seamen and traders, along with their counterparts from Britain, Portugal, Denmark, France, Holland, Italy, and Sweden, Ka'iana stood out in the streets with his *malo* (loincloth), feathered cape and helmet, and spear. According to reports, he engaged in trade, expressed "great concern" for beggars, and posed for a portrait by a celebrated Chinese artist.[6]

In January 1788, Meares and two ships newly acquired in China left Canton for the Pacific Northwest. Of the ninety crew members of both ships, about half were Chinese and the remaining half Europeans. But there were also four Hawaiians on board: Ka'iana, a woman, Winee, and a man and boy from Maui. The latter two had been taken from Hawai'i to China as "objects of curiosity," presumably to be exhibited there, along with an Indian from North America. Winee had left O'ahu in May 1787 to serve the wife of the British captain of the fur-trading vessel *Imperial Eagle.* Meares described Winee as having "virtues that are seldom to be found in the class of her countrywomen to which she belonged; and a portion of understanding that was not to be expected in a rude and uncultivated mind," revealing his assumptions of both Europeans and Hawaiians. Winee must have been extraordinary, not for the reasons given by Meares but because she may have been the first Hawaiian to leave the Islands on a European ship, and by the fact of her early presence in China and her death and burial at sea somewhere off the China coast. Before Winee died, in an act of generosity and reciprocity (Ka'iana had cared for her during her illness), she gave to Ka'iana a mirror, a basin and bottle, and a gown, hoop, petticoat, and cap as gifts for his wife. She entrusted the remainder of her belongings to him to deliver to her parents in Hawai'i. Ka'iana, Meares noted, was "so terribly affected by the death of Winee."[7]

The estimated fifty Chinese on board Meares's vessels served as seamen during the long passage from China to the Philippines and the islands of Melanesia and the Aleutian chain, and as shipbuilders upon their arrival on Vancouver Island, British Columbia, in 1788. They helped to build a forty-ton schooner, the *North West America,* the first ship of European design built in that part of the continent; when it slid down from its platform to the waters of the Nootka Sound, Ka'iana

TYAANA

Published June 27, 1789 by J. Stockdale for L. Godliving.

FIGURE 39. Idealized lithograph of Ka'iana ostensibly based upon the Chinese portrait of him and which, according to a traveling companion, "bears a striking likeness of him." From Nathaniel Portlock, *A Voyage Round the World* (London: John Stockdale, 1789). Courtesy of Rare Book and Manuscript Library, Columbia University.

Wynee, a Native of Owyhee,
One of the Sandwich Islands.

Publish'd Aug'st 1790. by J.Walter,No.169.Piccadilly.

FIGURE 40. Winee, from John Meares, *Voyages Made in the Years 1788 and 1789, from China to the North West Coast of America* (London: Logographic Press, 1790). Courtesy of Rare Book and Manuscript Library, Columbia University.

stood on its deck "capering about, clapping his hands."[8] The "experiment" with Chinese smiths and carpenters a success, about a year later Meares recruited and dispatched a group of Chinese, including a cook, carpenters, blacksmiths, bricklayers, tailors, and shoemakers, to establish Fort Pitt at Nootka. He planned "to get each Chinaman a Kanaka wife" from Hawai'i, but his colony failed when the Spaniards from New Spain, with interests in the area, seized his vessels.[9] Meares claimed to have sent seventy Chinese to Vancouver Island in that venture, but the Spaniards counted twenty-nine.[10]

On December 6, 1788, Ka'iana returned home to Maui; four days later, he arrived at Kealakekua Bay on the island of Hawai'i, where Kamehameha I greeted him warmly. That friendship served Kamehameha well in that Ka'iana facilitated trade with visiting ships involved in the China trade and thereby helped Kamehameha acquire the cannons and guns that were essential for realizing his expansionist ambitions.[11] Under Kamehameha, Ka'iana fought against his kinsmen and former patrons, Kahekili of Maui and O'ahu and Ka'eo of Kaua'i, and on the island of Hawai'i he led Kamehameha's army in the campaign against his rivals. In 1795, after the deaths of Kahekili and Ka'eo, Kamehameha set forth with his fleet to conquer Maui, Moloka'i, and O'ahu. Before the landing on O'ahu, Ka'iana, suspicious of the intentions of some of the Hawai'i chiefs, resolved to join his cousin Kalanikūpule in O'ahu's defense.[12] His wife, Kekupuohi, perhaps in anticipation of the outcome, bid Ka'iana farewell but told him her loyalty remained with Kamehameha. Ka'iana and his warriors diverted from the main force and made landfall at Kailua, near his former home during the 1780s occupation of O'ahu by Maui chiefs. There they climbed the Nu'uanu Pali and joined the O'ahu army for the bloody and decisive battle that established the kingdom that lasted for nearly one hundred years.

Winee and Ka'iana were pioneers in a Hawaiian diaspora that encircled the globe mainly along the trails of the east-west, trans-Pacific trade and engagements with the emergent, transnational U.S. Northeast. In that caravan of primarily laborers, Hawai'i figured prominently in the histories of both coasts. And that role of the Islands and its peoples was not inert and passive or determined solely by the geographical accident of Hawai'i's mid-Pacific location; additionally, its valuable natural resources on land and water and its workers' skills and energies facilitated, and in the instance of foreign missions instigated, exchanges that influenced life in the Islands and on the continent. "During the three years 1845–1847," wrote historian Ralph Kuykendall, "nearly two thousand Hawaiians enlisted as seamen on foreign ships, and during those years there was some discussion of the subject. It was pointed out that many of these native seamen never returned to live in Hawaii and the population was thereby reduced, both absolutely and potentially."[13] As one historical demographer pointed out, a loss of 4,000 in 1850 represented almost 5 percent of the total Hawaiian population and 12 percent of all Hawaiian males of working age eighteen and older.[14] To profit from but also to compensate for those losses, the kingdom initiated a poll tax in the 1840s that allowed a Hawaiian to go abroad only after "his employer has paid an equivalent for the statutory labour likely to be lost to the community during the whole term of his engagement."[15] And in 1846, to protect the interests of Hawaiians on North America's west coast, the government commissioned John Paty of Honolulu to sail to the continent and act on behalf of Hawaiian subjects there.[16]

By that time, Hawaiian seamen and laborers were at Papeete, Tahiti, and Peru to the south and on the Columbia River and the Aleutian Islands to the north. Such was their spread and influence that the Hawaiian minister of interior declared in 1846: "We have heard that there is no port in this ocean [Pacific] untrodden by Hawaiians; and they are also in Nantucket, New Bedford, Sag Harbor, New London [i.e., the Atlantic] and other places in the United States."[17] When Commissioner Paty arrived in Mexico, he found Hawaiians, some of whom had served in the Mexican navy, in Acapulco.[18] A report of the Russian-American Trade Association for 1850/51 showed that there were more Hawaiians than Russians in the Russian-American Company's holdings, which extended along the continent's Pacific shore from the Aleutians to northern California. The company employed only 686 of a total population of 9,273 in its domain, which included 1,070 Hawaiians, 505 Russians, 1,703 "creoles," and 4,051 Aleuts.[19]

As early as 1788, U.S. ship captains knew the advantages of employing Hawaiian seamen: their utility and low cost. Many Hawaiians were excellent sailors and swimmers, skilled builders, and reliable soldiers and guards, attributes that ren-

dered them valuable to their employers in sailing the vessels to the western coast
of North America, establishing forts and trade outposts on the continent, and
securing the invasive venture on American Indian lands.[20] At first Hawaiians sup-
plemented American crews and worked the eastern segment of the trans-Pacific
trade between Hawai'i and the North American west coast, as revealed in instructions to a U.S. ship captain in 1820: "You must Ship good Stout natives enough to
make your complement twenty-two *all told* on board. . . . We hope you will not
bring home more men than you carry out, provided you can discharge them with
their consent, as the present crew is quite large enough to go to Canton with."[21]
Generally, the American crew managed the Hawai'i–China leg and westward from
Canton to the Indian and Atlantic oceans and their homeports in the Northeast,
but Hawaiians also sailed from Hawai'i to China as crew members.[22] So regular was
that dependence upon Hawai'i that one historian, citing contemporary accounts
of Massachusetts ship captains, declared that "practically every vessel that visited the
North Pacific in the closing years of the 18th century stopped at Hawaii for re-
freshment and recreation."[23] Another historian has claimed that, by 1830, U.S. fur-
trading ships along the West Coast were manned primarily by Hawaiians, and in
1842 a contemporary traveler reported that "South Sea" islanders, mainly from
Hawai'i but also from Tahiti and New Zealand, "have become almost indispensable for the ships along the coast of California."[24]

The transition from supplementary to mainstay crew was accompanied by wage
increases that mirrored their labor's value. At first, during the late eighteenth century, ship captains routinely employed Hawaiians merely for food and shelter. Some
of those Hawaiians may have been kidnapped and served terms of involuntary
servitude.[25] Later, as they formed reserve pockets of skilled and scarce labor, however, Hawaiian seamen drove their salaries upward, especially with the increase in
ships competing for their services. Ship captains offered Hawaiians trade objects
like cloth and Chinese goods, and in the early nineteenth century they earned
money and trade items that approximated "regular wages" less the debt they incurred for clothes and other supplies provided by the company.[26] In 1811, twenty-
four Hawaiians hired to establish a trading post at the mouth of the Columbia
River were offered food, clothing, and merchandise worth $100 upon the comple-

tion of their three-year term of service.[27] A year later, twenty-six Hawaiians bound for Astoria agreed to wages that involved a suit of clothes and $10 per month, and their Hawaiian supervisor, "Boatswain Tom," received a monthly salary of $15.[28]

One of the Hawaiians among the 1811 Columbia River crew was Naukane, who might have later been known as John Coxe.[29] Naukane was of royal birth from the island of Hawai'i and was selected by Kamehameha I to supervise this first group of Hawaiian migrant laborers bound for the continent on John Jacob Astor's *Tonquin* to establish his Pacific Fur Company's factory, named Astoria. In the summer of that year, with Astoria secured, Naukane accompanied an expedition to set up a string of fur-trading posts farther inland up the Columbia River.[30] Along the way, the American group met a surveying team from the rival British Northwest Company, whose leader, David Thompson, traded one of his men for the Hawaiian. Under the British flag, Naukane and his companions canoed and portaged across the inland waterways until 1812, when they reached Fort William, the Northwest Company's interior hub, on the shore of Lake Superior.

With war declared between the United States and Britain, the Northwest Company decided to send a ship from England to seize its American rival's factory at Astoria and thereby control the North American fur trade.[31] Naukane, because of his knowledge of Astoria and the turbulent tides of the Columbia River, was selected to join that expedition and so left with a team from Fort William to Montreal, Quebec, and Portsmouth, England. In his service during the War of 1812, albeit on the British side, Naukane joined fellow Hawaiians Thomas Hopu, William Kanui, and Kanui's brother, who fought on the American side. On March 25, 1813, the Northwest Company's *Isaac Todd* departed England and headed south to Rio de Janeiro, around Cape Horn into the Pacific, and northward for the Columbia River. There they found that an overland party had already convinced Astor's employees to sell the fur factory to their rivals, and the Northwest Company renamed the post Fort George.[32] Naukane worked there until August 1814, when all thirty-two Hawaiians, former employees of the absorbed Pacific Fur Company, returned to the Islands on the *Isaac Todd,* manned fittingly by Hawaiians.[33]

In Honolulu, Naukane likely resumed his former position in the retinue of Prince Liholiho. After Kamehameha I's death in 1819 and Liholiho's assumption of the throne as Kamehameha II, Naukane's stature must have risen with that of his patron. When Liholiho sailed with his queen, Kamāmalu, to England on board a whaling ship seeking an alliance with Britain in 1823, he selected Naukane, probably because of his travel experience, to join the Hawaiian diplomatic party. Within a year, the king and queen succumbed to measles in London and died. Naukane accompanied their bodies back to Hawai'i, where rumors floated about a failed mission and money missing from Liholiho's possession. Under those unsavory circumstances, Naukane probably felt compelled to leave the Islands for the familiar grounds of the Pacific Northwest. There, at Fort Vancouver, where the British Hudson's Bay Company, the Northwest Company's successor, maintained its base of operations, Naukane took up employment. A few years later, he retired from the company to raise pigs until his death of tuberculosis sometime between 1836 and 1838. The grasslands on which his cabin stood and his pigs grazed, between Fort Vancouver and the Columbia River, was named Coxe's Plain by the company in his honor.[34]

Accordingly, when in 1817 the Northwest Company's *Columbia* took on board sixty Hawaiians for work on the Columbia River,[35] their value as migrant workers had already been established and the practice had become a pattern. The company's Fort Walla Walla, established in July 1818, consisted of twenty-five Canadians, thirty-eight Iroquois, and thirty-two Hawaiians, such was their significance. And in 1821, when the British government forced the merger of the Northwest Company under the banner of its rival, the Hudson's Bay Company, Hawaiians continued to supply important labor for the latter. They built ships, conveyed passengers and goods between visiting ships and the shore, and as early as 1811 sailed the coastal vessels that plied the north-south waters along North America's hazardous west coast with its offshore rocks, dangerous tides, and blanketing, thick fog.[36] On land, they served as soldiers on the punitive 1828 expedition against the Clallam tribe, erected buildings and forts, operated sawmills, and cleared forests and cultivated the crops consumed by the invaders. Further, Hawai'i as a market outlet, in addition to its value as a labor pool, contributed to the Hudson's Bay Company's fortunes. In 1834 the company opened an agency in Honolulu, which served as a market for its products, mainly lumber and salmon, and a magnet for the company's recruitment of Hawaiian labor for posts in Canada's Southwest.[37]

For the United States, the Pacific Northwest fur trade and the vital place of Hawaiians and Hawai'i in that extractive commerce were key to the development of the other shore, the Atlantic Northeast, where banks financed the undertaking, shipyards launched the ships, suppliers outfitted the expeditions, factories manufactured the glass, cloth, and metal items exchanged for the furs and pelts of North America's west coast, and investors received the final products from Asia along with their profits. The Pacific Northwest's natural resources also alleviated the need for specie, hard cash in the China trade, when gold and silver were in short supply in the Atlantic Northeast. Meanwhile, rapacious hunting led to the virtual extermination of sea otters in the Pacific Northwest around Nootka Sound, and reckless cutting of the fragrant sandalwood tree, valuable in China, resulted in its near extinction in Hawai'i.[38] Prominent among American fur men was William Sturgis of Boston, whose single venture, to illustrate the trade's draw and potential, netted a $284,000 return on a $50,000 investment, and in 1811 fifteen American ships gathered and transported to Canton 18,000 sea otter pelts valued at more than half a million dollars.[39] Hawai'i's assets of sea, land, and labor were central to that expanding and ensnaring grid, encompassing the Pacific Northwest, Hawai'i, and the Atlantic Northeast, and its relationships and reciprocals of extraction and production, underdevelopment and development, which lay the foundations of U.S. dominance in the Pacific and the world.[40]

With given names not of their own language or, likely, choosing, Hawaiians are difficult to locate, trace, or depict.[41] Others referred to them as Bill King, Charley, John Bull, Negro, Honolulu, Maui, Rice, and Pig,[42] they who left the Islands for the continent with ambitions, no doubt, and dreams, possibly. They settled on Vancouver's edge along a road that led from the wharf to the town at a place called "Kanaka Village." There, Hawaiians, Indians, whites, and biracials lived as Hudson's Bay Company employees. Others, led by William Naukana, built homes on Saltspring Island; still others settled in Nanaimo where Peter Kakua, or "Kanaka Pete," lived; and still others inhabited "Kanaka Row" on Victoria's waterfront.[43] In all, according to an 1844 report, there were "from 300 to 400 [Hawaiians] employed on the Columbia River, in the service and vessels of the *Hon. Hudson's Bay Co.* on that coast," and they were hired for three-year contracts and monthly wages

FIGURE 41. William Naukane (circa 1813–1909) fathered six daughters by Indian women. Used with permission of Rosemary Tahouney Unger.

of $10.[44] They split rails for fences and animal pens, repaired canoes and salmon barrels, tilled acres of wheat, oats, barley, and potatoes, herded sheep and cattle, and worked as domestics in the homes of the wealthy. Alone on isolated farms and with no one to talk to in Hawaiian, some of them must have felt lonely and homesick. A few in the 1840s had Hawaiian wives, like Kanaka William, a Christian missionary, and William R. Kaulehelehe, a Hudson's Bay employee, whose wives were Mary Kaai and Mary, respectively.[45]

White missionaries, many of whom relied upon their connections with Hawai'i and Hawaiian labor to build their mission stations, complained that the Hudson's Bay Company treated their Hawaiian employees little better than slaves, frequently whipping and imprisoning them and overcharging them for food and clothing. A

Hawaiian, an Anglican missionary reported to the Aborigines' Protection Society of London, was "confined in irons for the space of five months and four days" for slacking and was later cleared of the charge.[46] Little wonder that Hawaiian employees ran away, and with the discovery of gold in California many of them, like other Hudson's Bay employees, headed south for the mirage of quick fortunes to be had in that fabled land's rivers and mines.[47] In 1859 the company terminated its interests in Hawai'i, and a year later the U.S. Army began dismantling Kanaka Village to replace it with an artillery range.[48]

CALIFORNIA AND THE WEST

Hawaiian prospectors were already in California when whites discovered gold on John Augustus Sutter's land in 1848, and in fact some ten years earlier when Sutter first claimed New Helvetia he had with him eight Hawaiian workers and a bulldog from O'ahu.[49] A migrant, Sutter had left his wife and four children in Germany and crossed the Atlantic Ocean and American continent to Vancouver, where he met that island's governor, James Douglas, an ardent proponent of exporting British Columbia's products to Hawai'i. In 1838, Sutter, carrying an introductory letter from Douglas, sailed from the Pacific Northwest for California via Hawai'i, a long detour but one that traced the flow of commercial traffic. In Honolulu he met William French, who represented Boston merchant William Sturgis, and another financier from the United States, William Coffin Jones Jr., who wrote a letter introducing Sutter to the Mexican commandant general of Alta California, Mariano G. Vallejo.[50] That web involving Hawai'i, the Atlantic Northeast, the Pacific Northwest, and California followed well-trod paths over which labor, capital, and goods traversed.

After about five months, Sutter left Honolulu for California and took with him the Hawaiians he had contracted to serve for three years at $10 per month. On his return, another Hawaiian, William Heath Davis, captained the riverboat that took Sutter and his Hawaiian workers up the Sacramento River to his farm and tannery.[51] American merchants in Hawai'i invested in Sutter's venture, and he de-

FIGURE 42. William Kanui died in Honolulu on January 11, 1861, and was buried among missionaries and their descendants in the plot behind Kawaiahaʻo Church. His grave marker reads, in part: "In the life and death of Kanui, God's Providence and Grace were wonderfully manifested." Honolulu, 2006. Gary Y. Okihiro photograph.

pended upon those funds from Honolulu and Hawaiian labor to build his fort and houses.[52] Later those Hawaiians and their offspring would become gold miners, river boatmen, fishermen, and farmers in the West.

By the mid-nineteenth century, Hawaiians knew California's coastal waters, had settled in San Francisco, and flocked to the gold mining districts from Hawaiʻi and the Pacific Northwest. In 1847, San Francisco's forty Hawaiians, thirty-nine men and one woman, most of whom worked on boats that navigated the bay, constituted nearly 10 percent of that town's total population.[53] Other migrating Hawaiians included the remarkable Thomas Hopu and William Kanui, veterans of the War of 1812 and former students at Cornwall's Foreign Mission School, who had returned to the Islands in 1820 with the first missionary company and about thirty years later were swept back to the continent in California's gold rush. After some success in the gold fields, Kanui settled for a time in San Francisco, Hopu in Sacramento.[54]

As early as 1852, some of California's political leaders imagined an exaggerated gathering threat from "the concentration, within our State limits, of vast numbers of the Asiatic races, and of the inhabitants of the Pacific Islands, and of many others dissimilar from ourselves in customs, language and education."[55] Thus in that year both Hawaiians and Chinese, although less than 10 percent of California's population, came under legislative scrutiny and censure for their alleged "vast numbers" and unfair labor practices when the senate resolved the exclusion from the state of "Chinese or Kanaka carpenters, masons, or blacksmiths, in swarms under contract to compete with our own mechanics."[56] Those skilled Chinese and Hawaiians may have been the shipbuilders of the Pacific Northwest who had produced vessels for the coastal carrying and trans-Pacific trades. Two years earlier, in 1850, European Americans, themselves immigrants, slapped Hawaiians and other miners, notably Chinese, Californios, and Chilenos, with the Foreign Miners' Tax, which levied charges on "foreigners" for the privilege of mining in the state.[57] Under the pretext of enforcing the law, whites, including state employees, exacted payments beyond the law's requirement and drove off nonwhite miners from their legitimate claims, such as the Hawaiians at "Kanaka Dam" in 1850.[58]

Hawaiians, perhaps out of preference but surely also out of necessity to protect themselves against anti-Hawaiian violence, appear to have settled and worked in groups. Some of the men arrived in California with Hawaiian wives, but probably more of them married Indian women. As reported by a newspaper correspondent in 1863 of Hawaiians in California and their relations with Indians, they had "settled near them, intermarried with them, and taught them the way of life."[59] Kenao's village, consisting of twenty-four Hawaiians, including two Hawaiian and three Indian women and four *hapa* ("half," or biracial) children, was located along Indian Creek in El Dorado County. At John Kapu'u's fishing settlement named

Puu Hawaii (Hawaiian Haven) at Vernon on the Sacramento River, eight Hawaiian men, one woman, and three children, along with an Indian wife of one of the Hawaiian men, caught pike and sturgeon, which they sold in the markets of Sacramento.[60] And in Colfax, John Makani, a California Indian educated and trained in Hawai'i, ministered in a school for Indian children. Like many of the Indian wives and children of Hawaiian men, Makani spoke Hawaiian.[61]

"The way of life" introduced to North America's west coast by Hawaiian settlers included language but also food and celebrations. The Hawaiian feast, or *lu'au,* was formerly laden with class and gender meanings, containing restrictions *(kapu)* for commoners and women. Before 1819, when Ka'ahumanu and Keōpūolani, Liholiho's mother, prevailed upon the Hawaiian king to eat at a *lu'au* with them, men and women ate separately and women were restricted from eating certain foods, like pork, which was a feature of the feast. After that breaking of the *kapu,* however, dietary proscriptions fell, along with the religious order that maintained the *kapu* system, although the *lu'au* was still likely limited to the wealthy. As a nineteenth-century account noted, "The poor did not often make a feast; very few could afford one."[62] On the American continent, Hawaiians melded their food ways with those they encountered. On August 23, 1865, John Kao'o and his wife, Mary Pau, celebrated their son's birthday in British Columbia. For the *lu'au,* they had taro poi from Honolulu, local pig and fish, and *haole* (Anglo) food like tea, coffee, and bread.[63] They placed the food on an eating mat laid out on a porch, which they covered with white linen cloth, and instead of bowls and fingers they ate with plates, knives, spoons, and forks. The celebration lasted all day, and the recorder of the event, L. Naukana, declared, "Let it be continued so all from Hawai'i to Ni'ihau will know."[64] In a return migration, *lomi lomi* (massaged or rubbed) salmon from the Pacific Northwest, preserved with salt manufactured in the Islands,[65] became a feature of the *lu'au* in Hawai'i.

In California and the Pacific Northwest, Hawaiians faced a racism that equated them with Indians, "Negroes," and mulattos or "nonwhites" and hence ranked them as inferior to whites, despite their signal contribution as "common labor not easily secured elsewhere and so necessary to the exploitation of virgin territory."[66] When California forced the relocation of the Maidu near Sacramento to Round

FIGURE 43. John Kapuʻu and Pamela Clenso, his Maidu wife. Kapuʻu was the son of two of John Sutter's Hawaiian workers, Sam Kapuʻu and his wife. Richard Coke Wood (ed.), *Proceedings of the Second Annual Meeting of the Conference of California Historical Societies* (Stockton, Calif.: College of the Pacific, 1956), 89. Used with permission of Conference of California Historical Societies.

Valley Reservation during the 1850s, Ioane Keʻaʻala O Kaʻiana, grandson of famed traveler and chief Kaʻiana and one of Sutter's original Hawaiians married to a Maidu, shared his wife's status and made the journey on foot with her and her tribe.[67] Oregon's provisional government deliberated in 1845 an act to impose a $5 tax on anyone introducing Hawaiians to the territory and an additional $3 levy on employers of Hawaiians who failed to return them to the Islands. Four years later, when Congress created Oregon Territory, Hawaiians petitioned to vote in the June elections but were excluded from the franchise, apparently because they were considered "nonwhite."[68]

In 1850, Oregon Territory's delegate to Congress, Samuel R. Thurston, opposed giving public lands to Hawaiians because, in appeals to xenophobia and racism, it would benefit their employer, the British Hudson's Bay Company, and because they were "a race of men as black as your negroes of the South, and a race, too, that we do not desire to settle in Oregon."[69] Although Thurston sought the expulsion of Hawaiians from Oregon, he advocated U.S. control of Hawai'i, seeing in that seizure the hand of divinely ordained "fate" and "destiny." "The North American continent, with the Islands of the seas," Thurston wrote, "is ours by the gift of God."[70] That sentiment resonated well in an age of North American "manifest destiny" that culminated with the U.S. war on Mexico, which wrested away the latter's northern territories sealed by the 1848 Treaty of Guadalupe Hidalgo and also extended the nation's reach beyond its continental limits to the islands of the seas.

ATLANTIC NORTHEAST

Thurston's desire to expel Hawaiians from Oregon Territory and to impose U.S. control over Hawai'i was not a contradiction. Although repelled by the specter of race and possibly racial mixing, Thurston and others like him recognized the economic and political gains to be had through the acquisition of Hawaiian land, labor, and markets. Perhaps the majority of the workforce in the U.S. trans-Pacific fur trade in the 1830s, and "indispensable" for ships involved in the West Coast carrying trade during the 1840s, Hawaiians constituted as much as 20 percent of the sailors on U.S. whaling vessels at the industry's peak, around the mid-nineteenth century. At the time, possibly half to three-fourths of American whale men were foreign born, perhaps because of the foul conditions on board the ships and the rough treatment given them. "There is no class of men in the world who are so unfairly dealt with, so oppressed, so degraded, as the seamen who man the vessels engaged in the American whale fishery," wrote a contemporary reporter.[71] Among the Pacific whaling fleet, according to one claim, Hawaiians formed a third of the crew members during the 1840s, and half during the 1860s.[72]

Hawaiian whale men signed contracts that promised voyages of a year or less and required them to "perform [their] duty faithfully, whether on board said ship or in her boats, whether by night or day, as good and obedient seamen."[73] They were paid variously, in cash or in lays, a percentage of the gross profits of the voyage. Whereas ordinary white seamen might have received 1/175 lays, Hawaiians got more lucrative cuts at 1/140. At the same time, Hawaiians were usually employed for only the Pacific segment of the ship's tour, whereas whites generally got percentages for the entire voyage from and back to New England and hence received larger totals.[74] Further, for Hawaiians and whites, expenses incurred during the voyage reduced their actual incomes, as in the example of the *Minerva* in 1853 and its Hawaiian crew: Kahoau (Jim Maui) earned a 1/150 lay, or $90.56, but with expenses of $53.25 netted a total of $37.31; Pai (Bill Maui) earned a 1/160 lay, or $84.90, was billed $69.72, and received $15.18.[75] On board the *Elizabeth Swift* from 1868 to 1869, Kapuahiloa (Isaac) purchased a chest, knife, shirts, pants, socks, mittens, and boots totaling $131.10. His share of the profits was $139.88, and his returns for the entire, one-year voyage, accordingly, were $8.78. Less successful was Kakaie (Sam), who sailed on the *Elizabeth Swift* the following year and accumulated a bill of $134.83 for tobacco, a knife, socks, ten yards of calico cloth, mittens, pants, boots, blanket, shirts, and medicine while earning $139.88, leaving him $5.05 for the year's service. The returns for the ten Hawaiians who worked on the *Elizabeth Swift* during two tours ranged from a low of $2.63 to a high of $128.11.[76]

In 1845, New Bedford was the nation's fourth-leading port, behind only New York City, Boston, and New Orleans. Its 736 whaling vessels brought in 158,000 barrels of sperm oil, the finest grade of whale oil, 272,000 barrels of other whale oil, and 3 million pounds of whale bone. To outfit the fleet generated income of more than $10.5 million, and income from whale products in 1841 totaled more than $7 million. The size of the industry was such that "the whaleships owned in New Bedford would have made a line ten miles in length. The whaleboats which they carried would have extended six miles if strung out in a line, and there were 10,000 strong sailors to man them."[77] Like the fur trade, whaling supported industries and their owners and workers beyond those directly involved in the depletion of the ocean's resources. The workforce employed in building, equipping, and repairing whale ships and those involved in provisioning them totaled 50,000 according to one estimate; the business of whales thus made "an immensely valuable contribution to the nineteenth-century American economy."[78] And New Bedford's wealth was drawn quite literally from the oceans of the world. As Herman Melville put it, "Nowhere in all America will you find more patrician-like houses; parks and gardens more opulent, than in New Bedford. . . . Yes, all these brave houses and flowery gardens came from the Atlantic, Pacific, and Indian oceans. One and all, they were harpooned and dragged up hither from the bottom of the sea."[79]

Although New Bedford may have been the whaling capital of the world during the 1840s and '50s, Hawai'i and its ports, Honolulu and Lahaina, were "the principal base of the industry in the Pacific, where six-sevenths of the whaling fleet was operating." In fact, Hawai'i was so central to this enterprise that "New England owners of whaling ships felt that Hawaii was getting more than its share of the profits."[80] The first whaling vessel arrived in Hawaiian waters in 1819, and thereafter, with the opening of hunting grounds off the coast of Japan and in the Arctic Ocean,[81] visits by whalers increased rapidly, from an annual average of 104 during the period 1824–27 to a high of 419 during 1843–54.[82] Even before the boom in October 1829, the U.S. agent for commerce, John C. Jones, calculated that U.S. trade in the Islands amounted to "one hundred and twenty-five vessels, estimated at forty thousand tons, and valued at five millions two hundred and seventy thousand dollars. This estimate is made from the average number of vessels, which have visited these islands during the last three years; and will, I believe, be found to be very near the extent and value of our commerce here."[83]

Even as many U.S. vessels relied upon Hawaiian labor and supplies, Hawai'i's rulers came to depend upon the arrival of foreign ships, and during the 1830s through the 1850s upon the whaling fleet. As Hawaiian interior minister Keoni Ana confessed, "The whaling ships lay the foundation of nearly all our foreign commerce, and it is from them we receive our money."[84] In 1844, Robert Crichton Wyllie, at the time a British government representative and later Hawaiian minister of foreign affairs, observed: "The prosperity of these islands has depended, and does depend, *mainly* upon the whaleships that annually flock to their ports. . . . Were the whale fishery to fall off," Wyllie noted as an outsider, "the Sandwich Islands would relapse into their primitive insignificance."[85] The whaling industry was thus a transnational traffic that sustained Hawai'i but also New England while depleting a precious resource of the Pacific and enriching, albeit in precarious fluctuations, the Hawaiian elite and merchants in the U.S. Northeast.

That reciprocity was apparent in the bodily presence of New England in Hawai'i, and of Hawai'i in New England. Port cities like Honolulu, Lahaina, and Hilo were built in the image of New England towns, with their frame houses, stores, and taverns. "Could I have forgotten the circumstances of my visit," wrote a Hawai'i visitor, "I should have fancied myself in New England."[86] During the off-season, in the spring and fall each year, thousands of foreign seamen crammed the streets of Lahaina and Honolulu, and deserters and the discharged sick and disabled became long-term Island residents. The U.S. consul, as a custodian of capital, disciplined unruly sailors contracted with American ships. In 1840 some crew members of the Nantucket whaler *Catharine* tried to desert the ship after its captain died. The consul assembled and addressed the crew, "stating clearly to them what the laws of the United States required in similar cases, respecting the power of the officers, and the obedience of the crew," and he confined four of the "mutineers" to the fort in Honolulu.[87] Despite those attempts at policing by the state and missionary efforts to control liquor and prostitution, some sailors whose tastes, allegedly, "rose no higher than the grogshop and the brothel" engaged in public disorder. In 1825 the crew of the British whale ship *Daniel* tormented Lahaina's population for three days in reprisal for a missionary-inspired ban on Hawaiian women visiting ships anchored offshore, and in 1852 seamen rioted for more than twenty-four hours and set fire to Honolulu's police station.[88]

In contrast, New Bedford seemed a sober port, where the temperance movement was persistent and influential, although certain sections of the town were "infested with a dangerous class of citizens" and saw riots in 1826, 1829, and 1856. The town's eastern section was "a noted resort for drunken sailors and evil disposed persons" where the streets "abounded in dance-halls, saloons, gambling dens, and brothels" that catered to seamen.[89] A brief resident of New Bedford before shipping out in January 1841, Herman Melville painted the town as an ominous place where "actual cannibals stand chatting at street corners; savages outright; many of whom yet carry on their bones holy flesh." And, "Such dreary streets! blocks of blackness, not houses, on either hand, and here and there a candle, like a candle moving about in a tomb."[90] In a similar vein, a letter purportedly from Nantucket published in the *Boston Recorder* reported that Hawaiian and Society Islanders "on stated evenings when it was clear, assembled in the streets, erected ensigns of idolatry, and [engaged] in frantick orgies" while townspeople, innocent of their religious meaning, witnessed their "innocent frolics."[91] At the whaling port of Cold Spring Harbor on Long Island, Hawaiians settled on "Bedlam Street."[92] Behind these fantastic images of Hawaiians lies the obscenity of racializations that, on the bases of color and culture, commonly merged them with African Americans as dark, savage, and inferior peoples.

African Americans had long settled in New Bedford, and, especially after 1716 when the Quaker majority expressed their opposition to slavery, the town attracted freed slaves and runaways. Blacks, including African Americans, West Africans, Cape Verdeans, and West Indians, manned New Bedford's whale ships mainly as crew but occasionally as captains, like Absalom Boston, Pardon Cook, and Paul Cuffe.[93] For twenty years, Crispus Attucks, an African American patriot killed by the British in the 1775 Boston Massacre, worked as a New Bedford whaler and merchant seaman. In all, more than 3,000 African Americans sailed on New Bedford whalers between 1803 and 1860, and an African American blacksmith, Lewis Temple, developed in 1848 the toggle harpoon head that was the most successful of all such designs. As crew members of whaling vessels, Africans and African Americans sailed the Atlantic and Pacific, and some landed and settled in Hawai'i.[94] Although ostensibly egalitarian, the whaling industry replaced blacks with whites as white migrants—especially the Portuguese, who were racialized variously from white to black—increased during the first half of the nineteenth century.[95]

On board whaling vessels, crews carried racializations, indicated as skin color, as shown in crew lists that identified members by name, birthplace, residence, citizenship, age, height, complexion, and hair and eye color. Something rarely seen, the crew of the *John Garner* out of New Bedford were classed by complexion with descriptors that included "light," "mulatto," "dark," and "black." Thus, Charles Leland of Syracuse, New York, bore a "light" complexion with brown hair and blue eyes; Christian Augon from Guam had a "mulatto" skin color and black hair and eyes; and Mauritian Ben Brown a "black" complexion with black hair and eyes. Portuguese crew members varied from "dark" to "black" in color, and most U.S. citizens were "light."[96] Hawaiian whale men were given skin colors that included "Indian," "native," "copper," "colored," "dark," and "black."[97]

Similarly, the U.S. Census classed Hawaiians and Asians as colored. Beginning with the 1860 U.S. Census, in which the birthplace of the enumerated appears along with their "race," we find in New Bedford Hawaiian seamen such as George Adams, William Grey, Henry Jones, John Maroin, and William Mohee, all bearing the racialization "black," and John P. Booth and John Swain, "mulatto." Also listed in the 1860 census are two Chinese, fourteen-year-old Sit Afoo and a twenty-eight-year-old seaman, John Apho, both classified as "mulatto," and possibly a Hawaiian woman. At a time when there were few Hawaiian women in the United States, the census found thirty-five-year-old Mary E. Hardwick, Hawaiian born but with no racial classification, usually a sign of whiteness. Hardwick was married to master mariner William H. Hardwick of New York and resided in New Bedford's Ward 2, along with Hawaiian John Swain.[98] Although it is possible that Hardwick was a white American born in Hawai'i, she raises the possibility of at least one Hawaiian woman in 1860 New Bedford.

The 1870 census lists seamen Domingo Carder and George Nichols, both from Guam and racialized as "black." Carder lived with his African American wife, Elizabeth, a Massachusetts native, and their six-year-old son, Willie, and two-year-old daughter, Lillee. The census also enumerates Hawaiian-born Mary Chockley, a twenty-one-year-old wife and mother, and sixteen-year-old Herbert L. Walker, both racialized as "white," showing the possible "return" to the continent of white Americans, like Samuel Chapman Armstrong, who were born in the Islands.[99] Likewise, in the 1880 census we find whites such as Ernest, who was born in India, Frances, born in Japan, and Phebe, born in China, all of whom were children of itinerant Peter and Caroline M. Hussey. Peter Hussey was an American merchant whose children were born in Asia, with the exception of his daughter Mary, who was born in New York. In following a pattern found in New York City of marriages of Chinese men and Irish women, we find in New Bedford thirty-six-year-old Chinese tea merchant George Jones and his thirty-six-year-old Irish wife, Annie, and twenty-nine-year-old Chinese baker Joseph Gardner and his two "daughters," six-teen-year-old Annie and fourteen-year-old Lizzie, both of whom were born in Ire-land and worked in a cotton mill.[100] Gardner's wife fails to appear in the census, although he is listed as married.[101]

Nantucket, like neighboring New Bedford, drew Hawaiian seamen.[102] The is-land and town lay just offshore of New Bedford and Cape Cod, and in its reliance upon the sea and the world Nantucket resembled New Bedford, Fairhaven, and a host of other port cities that dotted the New England coastline. As early as 1825, the *Nantucket Inquirer* estimated that there were "more than fifty natives of the South Sea Islands" employed on board Nantucket whale ships, and "many" of them lived on the island. Perhaps some of them stayed at New Zealand–born William Whippey's "Canacka Boarding-House" while on the island, although as "black" men, they probably lived in New Guinea, a segregated enclave reserved for African Americans. And when they died on the island, as did a Hawaiian whale man whose body was found under a barn on the north shore in 1832 or twenty-four-year-old Hawaiian seaman Joseph Dix, who died of tuberculosis in 1843, their final desti-nation, having traversed the Pacific and Atlantic, was almost certainly the island's "Colored Cemetery."[103]

ATLANTIC SOUTH

The Anti-Slavery Society was formed in New Bedford at Lyceum Hall on June 25, 1834, followed two years later by the Young Men's Anti-Slavery Society, which held in 1838 a commemoration of slavery's end in the British West Indies.[104] Together with temperance, the abolitionist movement gripped the town, especially during the 1840s, when William Lloyd Garrison, Wendell Phillips, Frederick Douglass, and Henry Ward Beecher lectured to packed audiences at Liberty Hall. Douglass lived in New Bedford from 1837 to 1841 and worked for a time along the wharves before becoming a renowned orator, author, and abolitionist.[105] Passage by Con-gress of the Fugitive Slave Act in 1850, which allowed the pursuit of alleged run-aways, was a source of considerable anxiety, especially among New Bedford's African American community, and several false alarms of federal raids spread the feeling that "real danger was at hand." In defiance of the new law, New Bedford was a noted stop on the underground railroad that conducted African Americans from slavery to freedom. That involvement was a source of civic pride. "We are pleased to announce," reported the *Mercury* on April 21, 1851, "that a very large number of fugitive slaves, aided by many of our most wealthy and respectable citizens, have left for Canada and parts unknown, and that more are in the way of departure." The paper spoke for many of New Bedford's whites when it declared, "The utmost sympathy and liberality prevails toward this class of our inhabitants."[106]

In January 1861, four days after the first shots were fired at Fort Sumter on an island in the Charleston, South Carolina, harbor, men of the New Bedford Guards, Company L, 3rd Regiment, Massachusetts Volunteer Infantry, in response to President Abraham Lincoln's call to arms, stood in formation in front of city hall. They, along with "an immense throng of citizens, who crowded the square and adjoining streets," heard former governor John H. Clifford salute and assure them: "Go in peace about your families; your fellow citizens will see to it that those you leave behind shall want for nothing while you are gone. We shall hear from you on the field of duty. . . . God keep you safe under His care, and bring you back with untarnished glory, to be received by your fellow citizens with hearty joy and honor."[107] Among the mustered for the Union cause was the 54th Regiment, the first contingent of African American soldiers raised in the state and the North; Company C of the 54th consisted of men from New Bedford. Sent to the front in May 1863, the 54th distinguished itself on July 17, 1863, at the siege of Fort Wagner, where, in the words of Sgt. William H. Carney, an African American from New Bedford and Congressional Medal of Honor recipient, "the truest courage and determination were manifested on both sides on that day," and "there was no longer a question as to the valor of northern negroes," who, despite unequal salaries, "continued to fight for the freedom of the enslaved, and for the restoration of our country."[108]

Hawaiians were among those African American units on the Union side during the Civil War. Although it is difficult to trace their entry into those ranks and their possible motivations for enlisting, records show that Hawaiians served in both the Union army and navy. These were the descendants of Hawaiians like Thomas Hopu, William Kanui, and Kanui's brother, who fought on the American side during the War of 1812, and Naukane, who served with the British. Were these Hawaiians, citizens of the Hawaiian kingdom and unemployed aliens in Northeast port cities like New Bedford, Boston, and New York City, enticed by the prospect of bounties and steady wages? Were they caught up in the cause of the enslaved? Were they making common cause with fellow "blacks," racialized as they were? One can only imagine New Bedford's Hawaiians assembling with African Americans in Liberty Hall to hear Colonel Maggi's "stirring speech" and, a few days later, going down to the recruiting office "on William street, in the building that was for many years occupied by Toby & Coggeshall . . . where the recruiting was begun, with James W. Grace as recruiting officer, and Dr. John H. Mackie as examining surgeon."[109] Whatever their motivations and means of enlistment, Hawaiians were found among the ranks of African Americans who fought, were wounded, and died for "the freedom of the enslaved" and "the restoration of our country."

Fleeting are the glimpses of Hawaiian soldiers and sailors during the Civil War. Samuel Chapman Armstrong reported that he encountered Hawaiians as a commander of African American troops. "I found several of them among the Negro regiments," he recalled. "During the bombardment of Fort Harrison, north of the James River, while commanding a supporting brigade, I heard my Hawaiian name, Kamuela, called from a color-guard, and looking down saw a grinning Kanaka, a corporal, who had recognized me—as cool as a cucumber. Another turned up as a headquarter orderly—holding my horse. I read, in an account of the naval land attack on Fort Fisher, that among the first seamen to volunteer for the deadly work were two Hawaiian sailors." And, he added, as a father might of children, "They were all good soldiers; like the Negro, they are noble under leadership, often wonderful in emergencies."[110]

Given the skin colors "mulatto," "black," "Negro," "copper," and "yellow," Peter Adams, Johnny Boy, Mariano Flores, George High, John Ourai, Antonio Perez, Prince Romerson, John Smith, and Henry Williams served as mariners, sailors, seaman, barber, cook, and laborer in the Union navy. They ranged in age from eighteen to thirty-seven and hailed from Honolulu, Oʻahu, and the Sandwich Islands. Peter Adams enlisted in Boston, Johnny Boy in Portsmouth, Mariano Flores in New London, George High in Providence, John Ourai in New York, and Henry Williams in New Bedford. My search through one Civil War sailors database yielded twenty-six who were born in Hawai'i and who were almost certainly Hawaiians and not whites, as indicated by their racializations. They were among some 18,000 "African American" men and more than a dozen women in the Union navy.[111]

About 179,000 "African Americans" served in the Union army, and overall they were about 10 percent of all who enlisted in the armed forces of the North.[112] Not all of the U.S. Colored Troops (U.S.C.T.) were African Americans, because they included Chinese, Hawaiians, Mexicans, Puerto Ricans, and South Asians, all of whom were designated as "black" in complexion.[113] Among the Hawaiians in the Union army's infantry was twenty-one-year-old Samuel M. Watt, a sailor by trade who served in the U.S.C.T. 20th Regiment, Company A. Watt enlisted on October 11, 1864, in Kingston, New York, for a one-year term and was discharged in New Orleans on August 17, 1865, by reason of a disability, possibly from a wound suffered during the war. In the 29th Regiment, Company F, Connecticut Colored Infantry was Bebir(?) Johnson, a twenty-five-year-old seaman who was born in Honolulu. Johnson enlisted on April 11, 1842, in Bridgeport, Connecticut, for a three-year term but died less than a year later on January 9, 1843.[114] Because Hawaiians (and Asians and Latinos) were classified as "colored," their deeds remain folded within the archives, conditions, and achievements of African America.

Hawaiians must have shared the African American military experience of lower wages, inferior rations and medical care, inadequate training and weapons, the prospect of being enslaved or executed if captured, racism from white fellow soldiers, demeaning tasks and assignments, and slavelike discipline and punishments.[115] Having to prove themselves, as men and as soldiers, African Americans (and Hawaiians) fought bravely and against great odds. "They charged and re-charged and didn't know what retreat meant," remembered a white New Yorker. "They lost in their two regiments some four hundred men."[116] But African Americans, and possibly Hawaiians, challenged discrimination in the military and pointed to the hypocrisy of fighting a war for freedom while maintaining racial distinctions in the army. As noted by James Henry Gooding, a corporal in the 54th Massachusetts Infantry, in a letter to the president before his death at Andersonville in July 1864, "We have done a Soldiers Duty. Why cant we have a Soldiers pay?" Though "the United States exacts uniformity of treatment of her Soldiers, from the Insurgents, would it not be well, and consistent, to set the example herself, by paying all her *Soldiers* alike?" In the end, "We appeal to You, Sir: as the Executive of the Nation, to have us Justly Dealt with."[117]

Lincoln's Emancipation Proclamation of 1863 quietly transformed a conflict over union into a war for black liberation and enabled African American freedom and service in the military, which in turn loosened the grip of the slaveholding class, reorganized the U.S. armed forces, and established African American claims for equality.[118] As foretold by Frederick Douglass, "Never since the world began was a better chance offered to a long enslaved and oppressed people. The opportunity is given to us to be men. . . . Once let the black man get upon his person the brass letters U.S.; let him get an eagle on his button, and a musket on his shoulder, and bullets in his pocket, and there is no power on the earth or under the earth which can deny that he has earned the right of citizenship in the United States."[119] Hawaiians, as Union soldiers and sailors, contributed toward those momentous and profound changes in the lives of blacks and whites, and with those gifts Hawaiians helped to transform the nation.

As in the Revolutionary War and the War of 1812, New Bedford's maritime industry suffered during the Civil War. Rebel cruisers, particularly the *Alabama,* swept the seas for Yankee whalers and other vessels, and New Bedford lost more than $1 million in whale ships and $500,000 in whale oil.[120] In the Pacific, with word of a Confederate privateer bent on wreaking havoc on Yankee shipping in June 1861 and with no navy or means to protect the millions of dollars' worth of American whale investments and products in Hawaiian waters, the kingdom declared its neutrality in the War between the States on August 26, 1861.[121] Still, Hawaiians were caught up in the conflict when the Confederate vessel *Shenandoah* entered the Pacific to prey upon Union merchant vessels and whalers as far north as the Arctic and west to the Marianas Islands, where in 1865 it destroyed the Hawaiian ship *Harvest,* which belonged to the Honolulu firm of H. Hackfeld and

FIGURE 44. The Confederate raider *Shenandoah* attacking Yankee whaling ships in June 1865. Courtesy of New Bedford Whaling Museum, New Bedford, Massachusetts, Image No. 1968.52.

Co. Manning those ships, including the *Harvest,* were many Hawaiians who were left destitute as a result of the *Shenandoah*'s predations, which included the destruction of thirty-eight Union whaling and trading vessels. Despite its neutrality, after the attack on the *Harvest* the Hawaiian government declared the *Shenandoah* a pirate ship and demanded its surrender.[122] James Waddell, the *Shenandoah*'s commander, eluded capture and after the war's end returned to England, where the ship had been built.[123]

On the Fourth of July, 1876, with the "war of the rebellion" over, William W. Crapo addressed New Bedford's citizens at Liberty Hall at noon during a day packed with activities, including a parade, a regatta, baseball games, balloon lifts, and a fireworks display. "Beautiful, indeed, for situation, is this city of New Bedford," Crapo declared. "Few places are there on this continent, or elsewhere, which so unite the institutions, benefits and advantages of the city with the freshness and simplicity of rural life." He went on to describe New Bedford's well-made and -kept avenues and homes, its latest conveniences, like clean water, gas lighting, and a fire department, and its churches, hospital, and orphanage. On the centennial birthday of the nation, Crapo continued, the republic had survived its violent birth in the Revolutionary War and its tragic, recent war for "the preservation of the Union." New Bedford supplied 3,200 men for the army and navy in that conflict, he noted, among whom were "martyrs who died that our flag might still wave a symbol of freedom and the equal rights of all mankind." Their heroism, Crapo spoke for New Bedford's grateful citizens, "inspires us with faithfulness and determination to meet the needs and requirements of the coming age; it stimulates us to labor strenuously for the highest welfare of our country, believing that America holds in trust the destinies of the world." Numbered among that "noble ancestry," although unacknowledged by Crapo,[124] were helmsmen of the Hawaiian diaspora who had a hand in directing and renewing that precious birthright of liberty.

HAWAI'I CALLS

During his 1874 trip to Washington, D.C., Hawai'i's King Kalākaua visited San Francisco and New Bedford because of the historic ties linking the Islands with those portals to the continent. The king arrived on November 28 in San Francisco and on December 31 in New Bedford, where the town's finest entertained the royal entourage at Parker House and led them on an excursion to the cotton mills, and about a hundred ship captains greeted the king and his party. Mayor Richmond welcomed the king and hosted a public reception and banquet at city hall.[125] Among those who met the king was ninety-one-year-old Edmund Gardner, a crew member of one of the first whalers to stop in Hawai'i, in 1800, and who remembered that the Hawaiian queen, "a large woman, probably weighing 200 pounds," swam from the shore to the ship. Before leaving New Bedford the following day, Kalākaua thanked his hosts and offered his good wishes for the city's prosperity. After the farewell dinner, autograph hounds besieged the king, and throngs lined the streets to catch a last glimpse of the departing monarch. At the station, the king waved from the rear platform of his car "amid the cheer of the multitude."[126]

Some seven years later, King Kalākaua made a related visit to Sacramento, where he met Hawaiian Americans and their biracial children, including seventeen-year-old Mele Kainuha Ke'a'ala, daughter of Ioane Ke'a'ala o Ka'iana and his Maidu wife, Suwomine. Ke'a'ala recited for the king her genealogy, tracing her roots back on her paternal side to the famed Ka'iana. In recognition of her royal ancestry, Kalākaua designated Ke'a'ala his official *kahili* (standard) bearer and invited her to serve as a lady-in-waiting to Queen Kapi'olani. After six years in the kingdom, Ke'a'ala returned to California in 1887 in the entourage of the future and last queen of Hawai'i, Lili'uokalani. There she remained until King Kalākaua, on a vacation to California, died in San Francisco in January 1891. Ke'a'ala accompanied the king's body back to the Islands, and after a brief period as a lady-in-waiting to Queen Lili'uokalani, she returned to California and married John B. Azbill, a "Wailaki Indian man of the Maidu (people)."[127]

King Kalākaua's visits to New Bedford and Sacramento retraced the routes taken by Hawaiians in the diaspora. Some of those Hawaiians, like their king, moved between the Pacific islands and American continent and died while abroad. Many of them, like Mele Kainuha Ke'a'ala Azbill, received and created new varieties of Hawaiians and Americans in their bodies and cultures and left remarkable legacies in far-off places. Others of the Hawaiian diaspora favored by the ancestors found their way back to the Islands after oftentimes long and difficult sojourns over sea and land.

During the reign of King Kamehameha IV and Queen Emma (1854–1863), many Hawaiian laborers left the Islands for Micronesia, including Howland, Baker, and Kalama (Johnston) islands, to dig and load immense deposits of guano for Honolulu merchants and ship captains. Millions of fish-eating birds—pelicans, gannets, and cormorants—feed on the rich waters of the Pacific and nest on islands where rainfall is light. Washed away by rains, guano accumulates over the centuries only on dry, arid islands. In the glaring sun, heat, and stench, the dust rising from the nitrate-rich and hence valuable beds, which were used as fertilizer, could choke a man's breath and shorten his life.[128] A British observer described guano mining on islands off Peru's coast, worked by Chinese coolies about the same time that Hawaiians labored in Micronesia's guano beds: "No hell has ever been conceived . . . that can be equaled in the fierceness of its heat, the horror of its stink, and the damnation of those compelled to labor there, to a deposit of Peruvian guano when being shovelled into ships."[129]

Marooned about a thousand miles southwest of their home, one or several of those Hawaiian castaways, forsaken guano workers, composed a lei song, or love gift, for their queen, Emma, perhaps because she led the opposition to foreign domination and was the most visible symbol of Hawaiian sovereignty.[130] The chant, "Pua-ka-ʻilima," takes its name from the flat ʻilima blossom, which was the queen's favorite flower lei and the name given to the "pancake" Howland Island. The ʻilima was also called kanaka maikaʻi (good man) because the flower and its juice were precious and given to pregnant women and infants to maintain their health and vigor.[131]

There's beauty here on Pua-ka-ʻilima,
island-flower of the western sea
but the Kona wind blowing inland
strips every leaf and tree.
Along the ridge a sea eagle soars
calling, "Come, come back to Hawaiʻi and me."
Now let me walk with my love,
in quiet contentment, alone with my diamond ring.
I go to her soon.
Here's a song for my Queen.
Emalani is her name.[132]

Poetry in Motion

"Island music," a contemporary term that links Hawaiian, Latina/o, and African American music as that of tropical peoples, or "weak tropical races" in the words of Samuel Chapman Armstrong, has borne features of barbarism, stasis, and exoticism even as the "temperate races" and their "continental music" have conjured up notions of civilization, progress, and universalism. The uplift and liberation, then, of those inferior, mired, and subject races by those who shoulder the white man's burden included the elevation and improvement of their music and culture. Writing about the impact of white American missionaries on Hawai'i's music, a widely circulated essay claimed: "They found a heathen race musically addicted to rhythm and little else. They heard half-naked savages chant monotonous words, with little or no variation of pitch, accompanied by the beat of drums or the shaking of rattles. Of melody there was little and of harmony hardly a suggestion." Their work cut out for them, "the missionaries set to work to civilize the music as well as the manners and morals of their charges."[1]

Hawaiian music and culture, like those of Europe and the United States, were always susceptible to influence and change, and, as this chapter shows, they helped to shape some of the most "American" of music, especially during the first few decades of the twentieth century. Hawaiian music was rooted in indigenous structures and practices whose complexities contradict the myth of "savage monotony," but it also drew from alien instruments and traditions that Hawaiians absorbed and transformed into their own. And the flows, like the Hawaiian diaspora, moved in multiple directions and included the "uplift" and "regeneration" of the North American continent by Hawaiian island music.

MEXICAN COWBOY

Spanish Mexico engaged the Pacific long before the advent of British colonies in North America. Columbus's quest, to find a passage to India and its fabled riches, was fulfilled when Vasco de Balboa crossed Panama's isthmus in 1513 and gazed westward across El Mar del Sur (the "South Sea"), renamed by Ferdinand Magellan the Pacific. In an enactment of discovery, Balboa waited for hours for the tide to come in, waded out into the newly named Gulf of San Miguel, and made the absurdly grandiose claim of "real and corporeal and actual possession of these seas and lands and coasts and ports and islands of the south, and all their annexures and kingdoms and provinces to them pertaining . . . in the name of the Kings of Castile present or to come . . . both now and in all time, as long as the world endures until the final day of judgment of mortal man."[2]

Beginning in 1565, Acapulco became the American hub of Spain's Manila galleon trade that took the silver and gold mined in Spanish Mexico and Peru to the Philippines to pay for Asia's goods brought to Manila's entrepôt by East and Southeast Asian vessels.[3] In that marketplace, the Spaniards learned about the value of sea otter pelts to the Chinese and readily took to that trade commodity to reduce the outflow of specie from the Spanish realm. Accordingly, at missions strategically planted northward along California's *camino real* (royal road) Franciscan fathers encouraged their Indian communicants to hunt sea otter and fur-bearing seals. The 1783 Manila galleon would leave Acapulco with a cargo of more than seven hundred sea otter pelts collected by California's missions, and between 1786 and 1790 the missions assembled nearly ten thousand sea otter skins, an astonishing figure, valued at $3,120,000. So when Mexican businessmen formed the Philippine Company to corner the marketing of Asian products in Spanish America, they lobbied the officials of New Spain to establish trading posts in the northern reaches of the colony expressly to gather pelts, which they exchanged for Chinese quicksilver, essential for refining the gold ore being extracted from Mexican mines.[4] The natives of the Philippines, called "Indians" by their colonizers, crewed most of the galleons, and some of them settled in America and interacted and possibly mixed with its native peoples.[5] Within the Spanish colonial orbit, island "Indians" from Asia thus became continental "Indians" in America.

Besides fur-bearing mammals, another of Spanish America's exports was cattle, introduced to Hawai'i in 1793 from California by British captain George Vancouver. Soon thereafter, King Kamehameha I designated them as crown property to allow their increase and retain their economic value. For Hawai'i and California, meat from cattle and sheep, along with cattle hides and tallow, were valuable export commodities. Crews of whaling and trade ships consumed the meat, and they filled the ships' holds with hides and tallow for transportation from the Pacific to the Atlantic Northeast, where they more than doubled in value.[6] The kingdom's hides and tallow were also sold in Lima, Peru. William French, the Honolulu merchant who helped John Sutter gain entry into Spanish California, formed French and Company to cash in on the hides and tallow trade. In 1835, the first year of his company's operation, the Boston factor shipped from the Islands 587 hides and nineteen casks of tallow.[7]

Cattle herds thrived and grew so large, especially on the islands of Hawai'i and Maui, that they caused substantial damage to native gardens and fields.[8] Controlled hunting and an enclosure system of fenced cattle ranches helped to alleviate the wild cattle problem and allowed breeding to improve the quality of the stock. White ranchers, such as whale man John Palmer Parker from Newton, Massachusetts, obtained from the crown huge tracts of land on which to raise cattle. Parker arrived in the Islands in 1809, was the first to obtain permission to hunt wild cattle, and married Kipikāne, an offspring of Kamehameha I and a chief at Waimea on the island of Hawai'i.[9]

Because of the growing contact and trade between Hawai'i and Spanish America, Hawaiians gained an appreciation of cattle ranching in California, Mexico, and Chile. In 1828 a French ship introduced horses from San Diego to the Islands, and by the 1830s the kingdom had already secured highly regarded Mexican cowboys (*vaqueros*) from California, which after 1821 formed the northern reaches of an independent Mexico.[10] Liholiho, the son of Kamehameha I, and members of his court rode on horseback along the southwest slope of Mauna Kea in the summer of 1830. Both Liholiho and his mentor, perhaps a *vaquero,* chased and lassoed

172 ﹏ POETRY IN MOTION

wild cattle, and the next day other cowboys put on a display of horsemanship and cattle roping and subduing typical of Spanish America, much to the enjoyment of the youthful monarch and his party.[11]

The *vaqueros*, remembered as "Mexican Hispano-Indians" and "full-blooded Indians of Mexican origin," and called by Hawaiians Huanu (Juan), Hoke (José), and Hoakina (Joaquin), among other names, taught Hawaiians ranching skills and introduced specialized clothing, the saddle, spurs, and leather lariats.[12] One of those *vaqueros* was Joaquin Armas, born in San Diego in 1809 and a soldier and cowboy by trade.[13] He arrived in Hawai'i on board a British whaling ship in 1831, and despite his intention to sail with the ship to London, he stayed in the Islands, largely through the entreaties of the king, Kauikeaouli, Liholiho's successor, who wanted to use his skills as a cowboy. After a seven-month stay on O'ahu, Armas went to Waimea, Hawai'i, on direction from the king to trim the large herds of cattle and procure beef, hides, and tallow for visiting ships. There, for about nine years, he mainly worked alone, although there were other Mexican *vaqueros* in the vicinity, such as Federico Ramón Baesa and his Yaqui wife and brothers Federico and José Ramón, both of whom married Hawaiian women.[14] In 1843, Armas wrote about his life as an Island cowboy, noting that he stayed in the mountains four or five months at a time exposed to cold and hunger and, pressed by the king for more hides, was "frequently obliged to work at night running the risk of my life in capturing wild Bulls and receiving great injury in body from the falls." In return, the king provided Armas with a house and some land, but after about 1840, when cattle hunting ceased, he was, in his words, "turned adrift as a vagabond in poverty" and moved to Lahaina on the island of Maui. There he signed an agreement with the ubiquitous Bostonian William French to pen, slaughter, and sell his cattle to the whalers who visited Lahaina. Armas was briefly married to a Hawaiian woman, and he returned in September 1848 to his native California, which had earlier that year become a part of the United States. Two years later, Joaquin Armas was dead at the age of forty-one.[15]

Hawaiian cowboys, called *paniolos* after *Españoles*, replaced their Mexican tutors, who had apparently faded away by the 1850s, as was indicated by an 1859 report that observed that the *vaqueros* have "disappeared before the march of time. . . . In their place has sprung up a class of Hawaiian mountaineers, equally as skillful horsemen as their foreign predecessors, but leading a vagabond sort of life, alternating between hardships and privation on the mountain and plenty and lavish expenditure on their return to the settlements."[16] Some of the *paniolos* practiced their craft so well that they entered and won rodeo competitions both in the Islands and on the continent. In 1908, at a top venue—Cheyenne, Wyoming's, Frontier Day— Hawaiian cowboy Ikua Purdy was named the "world champion" steer roper, the featured category, and Archie Ka'au'a placed third.[17]

The counterparts of Mexican *vaqueros* in Hawai'i were Hawaiians in California involved in the coastal carrying trade, hauling stacks of stiff and smelly hides from the shore to waiting longboats, rowing them to transport ships anchored miles beyond the crashing surf, and ferrying the cargo to San Diego for cleaning and curing. At the processing works, as described by writer Richard Henry Dana Jr., Hawaiians, who lived in settlements around the harbor, soaked the hides in the ocean for two days, boiled them in huge, saturated brine vats for another two days, spread them on platforms, and stretched, staked, and scraped them. San Diego's Hawaiians, Dana wrote, were "quite a colony," who spoke a pidgin or trade language "amid the Babel of English, Spanish, French, Indian, and Kanaka," which shared "some words that we could understand in common." Gathering and hence likely generative places for that linguistic community, according to Dana, included the Kanaka Hotel and Oahu Coffee-House.[18]

Such was the importance of the hides and tallow trade that Mexican California depended almost entirely upon it to pay for its imports of clothing and manufactures and for civil and military expenditures up to the American period, when, during the 1850s, the trade declined.[19] In Hawai'i the value of the export trade in meat and hides was reported to exceed that of sugar production in 1855, and its livestock industry, unlike its counterpart in California, continued to thrive during the 1860s and reached its peak in the 1870s and '80s, despite being dwarfed by the rapid and enormous increase in the production of sugar and rice.[20] In the Northeast, shipowners realized profits from the hide and tallow trade that approached 300 percent, and the trade supplied the raw materials needed by the shoe and boot factories of Massachusetts and Connecticut while boosting the domestic production of such trade goods as tea, coffee, sugar, hardware, cutlery, clothing, shoes and boots, and jewelry. Accordingly, although Mexican California may have relied upon the Northeast for its imports during the first half of the nineteenth century, certain industries in New England benefited from and were similarly dependent upon the trade.[21]

Mexican *vaqueros,* it appears, introduced to Hawai'i not only ranching techniques and items of clothing but also the Spanish guitar. According to an 1888 account, "It seems that the guitar was brought to the Islands from Mexico at a time when there was considerable intercourse between the two countries, in the early part of the century."[22] Associations of the guitar with Spain, of course, commonly conjured romantic scenes of men serenading women, not unlike the later images of Hawaiian music's spell. One writer describing Hawaiian musicians summoned that magic and mood in 1906: "Then there are native serenaders with the same voices and same touches on the strings as the romantic troubadours that sung under the senoritas' lattices of old Spain's castles."[23]

The cowboy and his guitar have a long and storied association in the American West and, not surprisingly, among Mexican *vaqueros* and Hawaiian *paniolos* as well. "We can safely assume that the vaqueros played their guitars and sang their songs just as they had always done on the ranges in Mexico and that the paniolos were intrigued by what they heard," surmised educator and music historian George Kanahele. Still, he noted, it is puzzling that given that influence "there is almost no trace of either Spanish melodies or words in the Hawaiian songs" in the cattle regions of the island of Hawai'i, presumably to be explained by the fact that their presence was so brief that they contributed only the basics of guitar playing.[24]

Another and later impetus for the guitar, the steel guitar, in the Islands may have been Portuguese seamen from the Azores, many of whom knew Hawaiians as fellow whale men in the Atlantic and Pacific and who made landfall in Hawai'i as a result of the Confederate *Shenandoah*'s raids among the U.S. Pacific whaling fleet. Noted statesman Curtis P. 'Iaukea remembered as a youth the arrival of "dark complexioned . . . natives of the Azores" whose ships had been destroyed by the *Shenandoah* and who "brought their steel-stringed guitars with them, the first of the kind we had seen. At night-fall when the day's work was o'er, they would gather at one of their camps and entertain the crowd that had gathered to enjoy the music and see how these steeled guitars were played. Needless to say," he reported, "it took like wildfire."[25]

INDIGENIZING INSTRUMENTS

Whatever the origins of the guitar in the Islands, Hawaiians adapted and modified the instrument to suit their musics and tastes. A turning point in the guitar's career in Hawai'i, according to George Kanahele, was the 1883 coronation of King Kalākaua, at which guitar, *pahu* (wooden drum), and *ipu* (gourd drum) accompanied the hula and more specifically the *hula ku'i,* a style of dance and music developed in the 1870s and popularized in Kalākaua's court.[26] The guitar both added to and substituted for Hawaiian percussive instruments and became an essential element in what later became known as "modern" or "Westernized" hula performances.[27] Modernity, however, was not the sole engine for change; tradition too was evolving. The *pahu,* for instance, before the advent of the "West" in the Islands, underwent a conversion from its original association with sacred songs and use in temple service to its adaptation to the hula, and La'a, the bearer of the drum to Hawai'i, was also known as Laka, a patron of the hula.[28]

Perhaps the earliest Hawaiian guitar innovation was developed by the *paniolos,* like Ikua Purdy, who veered from their Mexican teachers in both ranching techniques and guitar playing. The style they developed was later known as *kī hō'alu,* or slack key, involving the loosening (slacking) of certain guitar strings to produce the right key for a particular Hawaiian song or vocal range. The Spanish tuning, they found, failed to meet their musical preferences. In addition, unlike solo Spanish guitarists, *paniolos* wanted a bass rhythm to accompany their melodies, and hence they developed the technique of plucking simultaneously the melody on the upper strings and the bass on the lower strings. "Slack key can be defined, therefore," summed up George Kanahele, "as the combination of loosening the strings, with the thumb playing the bass strings to produce tonic, dominant and sub-dominant harmonies, while the other fingers pluck the melody on the upper strings."[29]

Both the rhythms and the melody of slack key reflect hula rhythms and the vocal qualities of the chanter, making slack key a distinctively Hawaiian cultural expression that took hold within decades of the guitar's introduction to the Islands. Slack key's origins as Hawaiian music included its mimicking of chanting and vibrato, trills, and falsetto voicing. Like the guitar, falsetto singing probably came to the Islands from multiple directions. Its roots almost certainly reach back to pre-European Hawaiian chanting and the practices of ornamentation, including vibrato, falsetto, and glides between breaks, that distinguished one chanter from another. "Though there do not appear to be any requirements in chant practice for the use of falsetto," observed music scholar Elizabeth Tatar, "it does seem probable that some chanters would experiment with their voices, discover falsetto, and use it as their trademark. Innovation, at times radical, was a common practice of *hālau* (academy) chanters and dancers."[30] Another source may have been songs of dialogue between female and male characters that were chanted in different registers, including, sometimes and not a necessary correspondence, the female in falsetto. A new opportunity arose with the advent of missionaries and their introduction of choral singing, wherein boys and men may have easily moved into the female voice range. And Mexican *vaqueros* may have promoted their brand of singing, which included falsetto and yodeling.[31] Whatever its sources, falsetto singing was an established feature of Hawaiian music by the late nineteenth century, and its development paralleled and intersected the slack key style.[32]

Hawaiian music, at core, began as the unaccompanied chant, or *mele oli,* which was poetry and "chant that was not danced to." The later dance-accompanied chant was the *mele hula.* The *mele hula ku'i,* popularized by Kalākaua, involved the modification of the *mele hula* through adaptations of Western chant and dance styles. The *mele oli* varied by voice and style, was accompanied only occasionally by percussive instruments, displayed a minimum of gesture, and was appreciated on its own for its beauty and imagery. Men and women alike performed the *mele hula* with or without instruments in a standing or kneeling position, and like the *mele oli* it had its own distinctive styles that evolved and changed over time and place.[33]

An influence upon style and "tradition" was the class nature of the hula, involving patronage and prerogative, as recalled by Davida Malo, the esteemed nineteenth-century Hawaiian ethnographer. "The *hula* was a very popular amusement among the Hawaiian people," he reported. "It was used as a means of conferring distinction upon the *alii* [chiefs] and people of wealth. . . . The children of the wealthy were ardent devotees of the *hula*. . . . It was the custom of *hula* dancers to perform before the rich in order to obtain gifts from them."[34] By the late nineteenth century, that patronage system had evolved such that court favorites assumed "hereditary" status as chanters and dancers of certain chiefs and kings.

The union of chant with dance was described by David Samwell, a surgeon on board James Cook's *Discovery,* off the coast of Kona, Hawai'i, on January 10, 1779: "In the afternoon they [Hawaiian women] all assembled upon deck and formed a dance; they strike their Hands on the pit of their Stomack smartly & jump up all together, at the same time repeating the words of a song in responses." Samwell recorded songs that probably accompanied dances, which he saw as sexually charged when the women "wriggled their backsides and used many lascivious Gestures."[35] Those songs, as transliterated by Mary Kawena Pukui from Samwell's phonetic renderings, were perhaps composed in tribute to the visiting strangers, and they were performed, as Samwell explains, as songs, which "they repeat in responses when dancing":

> Where, oh where
> Is the hollow-stemmed stick, where is it,
> To make an arrow for the hawk?
> Come and shoot;
> Strike with the coconut-leaf midrib full on the head,
> Don't twist your way to your target
> Unsteady and turning; shoot straight to the bull's eye.
>
> An *ule* [penis], an *ule* to be enjoyed:
> Don't stand still, come gently,
> That way, all will be well here,
> Shoot off your arrow.[36]

The focus of the performance was the chant, not the dance movements, which were admired for their grace and not as enactments of the chant's meanings. John

Papa ʻĪʻī, historian, school superintendent, and official of the kingdom, described a performance around 1815, stressing the pairing of chant with dance while highlighting the former. "The dancers kept in unison and preserved the pleasing quality of chanting or reciting. Sometimes one would lead and others would join in; but while he was reciting, the others kept their silence and only gestured with their hands and swayed their drums."[37] Art forms that prized creativity and complexity, chants were divinely inspired and governed by an aesthetic; they recalled the past and praised rulers and genitals for their bounty, and they were sacred and powerful. In addition, crucial aspects of the art that enhanced the chant's musicality and potency were elocution, including an intricate range of sound patterns and vocal qualities, and body movements, the hula.[38]

The guitar, then, "went native" by learning to chant in slack key. The steel guitar, yet another immigrant to the Islands, underwent a similar transformation in Hawaiian hands. The story has several versions, but the most credible, sustainable account involves Joseph Kekuku, a student at the time, who claimed to have developed the slide technique in 1885. An intriguing and possible alternative is the Gabriel Davion story as told by well-known Hawaiian composer Charles E. King in the late 1930s. According to King, who was only ten years old at the time, "In 1884 I was living at Waiheʻe, Maui, and there appeared in the village a group of musicians from Honolulu, one of whom was Gabriel Davion—a young man who was born in India, kidnapped by a sea-captain and finally brought to Honolulu. . . . This Davion attracted a great deal of attention because he had a new way of playing the guitar. . . . All the playing was done on one string, and the strings were not elevated by a bar."[39] A South Asian, Davion may have learned the slide technique that defined the Hawaiian steel guitar from the *gōttuvādyam*, an Indian eight-stringed instrument played with a sliding bar of ebony or glass.

Kekuku developed the steel guitar sound when he was eleven years old. Walking along a railroad track strumming his guitar, Kekuku recalled, he picked up a bolt and ran it across the guitar strings. He liked the effect, and when he returned home he practiced with a metal knife and razor blade, trying to perfect the sound. "It took me seven years to master the guitar as I had no teacher to show me and no books to refer to for information," he later wrote. Simeon Nawaa, a fellow stu-

FIGURE 45. Joseph Kekuku playing the Hawaiian steel guitar. Jerry Byrd photograph. Courtesy of Centerstream Publishing.

dent at the Kamehameha School for Boys, where Kekuku enrolled in 1889, confirmed his claim. "To our astonishment," Nawaa testified, "Joe, besides playing the guitar the ordinary way, would shift to running a hair comb or tumbler on the strings producing a sweet sound." Kekuku's shop instructor noted that Kekuku spent many hours in the school's machine shop designing and producing a slim steel cylinder, about four inches long, to fit his hand comfortably. To enable the steel bar to slide over the strings without touching the frets, Kekuku raised the guitar strings and used wire instead of gut strings because they sustained the tones longer.[40]

The sound of the Hawaiian steel guitar, whoever its inventor, resembled chanting and its vibrato and glissando ornamentations, which were pleasing to the ear and signified individuality. In turn, Joseph Kekuku's slide Mexican guitar enabled the glissando sound that mimicked Hawaiian, and possibly Mexican *vaquero,* falsetto singing and became the staple of Hawaiian steel guitar playing.[41] Thus, the Spanish guitar was an import adapted to and for Hawaiian music's core. And in "going native" the Hawaiian steel guitar took off with its refinements, variations, and spread.[42] Island guitar innovations included the slide bar, usually made of steel because of its availability and sound-producing qualities, an adapter to raise the strings above the frets, and metal finger and thumb picks for a harder "bite" on the strings. Slack key tunings and playing style allowed for a plucked melody with an accompanying bass, but the steel, unlike slack key, played the entire melody from beginning to end as if sung by voice. On the continent, in the early 1920s, the resonator, or metal vibrating disc, amplified and sustained the guitar's sound, and jazz, blues, and ragtime required new tunings to accommodate their harmonic qualities.

BALMY AIRS

Joseph Kekuku and many other Hawaiian musicians and dancers left the Islands for the continent, both America and Europe, to forge and advance their careers and art. If the homeland was the site of the instruments and sensibilities for what became wildly popular as Hawaiian music and dance during the first few decades of the twentieth century, the diaspora was the place of engagement that enabled innovation as well as the invention of tradition.[43] After leaving Kamehameha School in 1904, Kekuku toured the United States and Europe and taught the slide guitar in several U.S. cities. As noted by his wife in 1932, the year of his death, Kekuku was "a great teacher of the Steel Guitar and is the possessor of one of the most beautiful guitars in the world. He taught either by notes or numbers."[44]

Commercial instruments like the National guitar with its resonator and the dobro with its cast aluminum spider and resonator, marketed in the early 1920s, gave Hawaiian musicians greater volume, vibrato, and glissando and a more sustained tone. The influences of ragtime, jazz, and the blues encouraged new tunings

FIGURE 46. In 1932 Joseph Kekuku was buried in Orchard Street Cemetery, Dover, New Jersey (top). It has been claimed that he was later returned to and buried in Laʻie, Oʻahu, where he was born (bottom). Note the different dates of Kekuku's death or burial at the two sites. Dover, New Jersey, 2005; Laʻie, Oʻahu, 2006. Gary Y. Okihiro photographs.

to accommodate the innovative sounds Hawaiian musicians created and played. And though artistic desires fueled those transformations, audiences and their tastes, no doubt, also directed the course of Hawaiian music. As Elizabeth Tatar points out, non-Hawaiians, including tourists and migrants, have influenced Hawaiian music since the 1780s.[45] "I think Hawaiian music is like the Negro spiritual," declared Alice Kamokila Campbell, respected performer, teacher, and supporter of Hawaiian culture. "And it includes a little bit of Japan, China, Spain, and just about everything else in the world. I think we've picked up this international atmosphere from our many tourists. I really do. Hawaiian music usually conveys a combination of the thoughts of tourists."[46]

The changes under way at home simply accompanied the inventions forged abroad by Hawaiians and non-Hawaiians alike. Hawaiian steel guitarists such as July Paka played to U.S. audiences in 1899, Frank Ferera did so in 1902, and Joseph Kekuku two years later. Some left the Islands never to return, playing in vaudeville, Chautauqua venues, clubs, theaters, and expositions throughout North America, Europe, and Asia. They opened music studios to teach the steel guitar—Kekuku in Boston, Chicago, and Detroit; Ben Hokea in Toronto and Ottawa; and Walter Kolomoku in New York City. They performed for the radio and movies and recorded for the phonograph, and they boosted the sales of guitars, sheet music, and records. Some of the biggest stars included Frank Ferera, Sol Ho'opi'i, Sam Ku West, Jim and Bob, and Ben (King Bennie) Nawahi.

Exemplary of that Hawaiian musical diaspora was Mike Keli'iahonui Hanapī, who left Hawai'i in 1912 when he was barely fourteen years old to perform at the Chicago World's Fair. In 1914 he moved to New York City, where he studied voice at the New York Conservatory of Music and joined Bill Kalama's Quartet during the Tin Pan Alley Hawaiian music craze. The quartet recorded with Edison and Okeh between 1926 and 1928, and as vocalist Hanapī was one of the first to popularize Hawaiian falsetto singing, called "yodeling" on record labels, on the U.S. continent. After eighteen years in New York City, Hanapī moved to Hartford, Connecticut, where he opened a music studio, formed his own band, and appeared on a weekly radio show under contract with the New England Mutual Insurance Company.[47]

FIGURE 47. Publicity photo of Sol Hoʻopiʻi by B. Dunn. Used with permission of Centerstream Publishing.

Solomon Hoʻopiʻi was born in Honolulu in 1902 and learned to play the guitar and ukulele as a child. At the age of seventeen, Hoʻopiʻi and two friends stowed away on a Matson liner bound for San Francisco, following the trail blazed by one of his idols, Joseph Kekuku. There, in California, he met other Hawaiian musicians, formed groups, played in Los Angeles nightclubs like the Hula Hutt, Singapore Spa, Seven Seas, Hawaiian Village, and Hawaiian Paradise, recorded for Columbia and Brunswick, and became one of the most prolific and influential steel guitarists of his time.[48] During the 1920s, Hoʻopiʻi played the acoustic guitar, and in recordings from this early period his voice was "marked by control in both vibrato and falsetto transitions" and his style of singing was "characteristically Hawaiian: a break in the voice, dynamic contrasts on prolonged sounds, rasping qualities in his articulation, slowly rising glides, and long-breath phrases." In the 1930s, when influenced by jazz and the blues, Hoʻopiʻi performed on the Rickenbacker electric, which allowed him to develop more continuous sound and his distinctive style: "improvised blueslike melodic ornaments, fast runs, syncopated rhythms, and various sound effects in chording and plucking."[49] As one of the first and most popular Hawaiian musicians to play American tunes and songs, black and white, Hoʻopiʻi helped to promote Hawaiian *hapa haole* (half white) music and the steel guitar.[50]

Perhaps the biggest single promoter of the Hawaiian music mania that swept the U.S. continent during the 1920s and '30s was the 1915 San Francisco PanamaPacific Exposition. The exposition, held to "commemorate the discovery of the Pacific Ocean and the construction of the Panama Canal," offered "a survey of the arts and a panorama of the achievements of Man," according to its official history.[51] A noted art critic and member of the exposition's international jury added: "While it is difficult to condense one's impressions of the Panama-Pacific Exposition into summary phrases, it nonetheless appears that its ultimate significance will prove social and psychological as well as aesthetic. The love of form and colour which you here saw displayed in such prodigal fashion suggested something pagan and Dionysian." The contrast, he offered, distinguished East from West Coast, with the former typified by "Puritan and Quaker constraint," the latter by freedom and spontaneity.[52] On a broader terrain, the exposition's memorialization of Balboa's 1513 gaze and claim and some 400 years of European occupation of the American continent and spread across the Pacific Ocean to Asia but also to the islands of the sea was indeed ironic in light of Hawaiʻi's indigenous peoples' reconquest of America through its music begun at that celebration of the achievements of (the European) "Man."

Hawaiʻi's building at the exposition, a small and undistinguished structure, was "a business proposition" designed "to gain more publicity for the islands, publicity which would attract the traveler, make the islands better known, and better understood, and cause them to become the tourist mecca of the travel world," according to the head of the territory's promotion committee.[53] The exhibit's creators chose music to lure the harried visitor into the Hawaiian pavilion, and color, including tropical flowers and plants and above all tropical fishes, to dazzle their senses and orchestrate unforgettable memories of paradise. In that scripting, they aspired to seed and propagate Mark Twain's dreamy ode to Hawai'i:

> No alien land in all the world has any deep, strong charm for me but that one; no other land could so longingly and beseechingly haunt me sleeping and waking, through half a life-time, as that one has done. Other things leave me, but it abides; other things change, but it remains the same. For me its balmy airs are always blowing, its summer seas flashing in the sun; the pulsing of its surf-beat is in my ear. I can see its garlanded crags, its leaping cascades, its plumy palms drowsing by the shore; its remote summits floating like islands above the cloud rack. I can feel the spirit of its woodland solitudes; I can hear the splash of its brooks; and in my nostrils still lives the breath of flowers that perished twenty years ago.[54]

Hawaiians, represented by tropical fishes from the aquarium in Waikīkī, were "transplanted bodily" to the exposition. Tanks lining three sides of the building's interior were filled "with the most beautiful fish ever seen, fish whose painted brilliance you could not vision in your wildest dreams; fish that were golden green, like a canary, fish that were striped black and orange, like some gaudy silk on a negress's head, fish that were mottled and dappled with flashing hues no less than gorgeous, as though a painter's palette had fallen into the sea and come to life." The fishes were the talk of the exposition, according to one account, and large crowds flocked to the exhibit, forming long lines, which guards had to keep moving. Like their human relatives, many of the Hawaiian fishes sickened and died in that strange and foreign place, and they had to be replaced with live infusions from the Islands.[55]

At the building's center, in a courtyard planted with palms and giant ferns from Kīlauea's volcanic forests, Hawaiian musicians played to as many as 34,000 visitors a day.[56] Although Hawaiian music was heard at several expositions and fairs on the U.S. continent before 1915 and as early as the 1893 Chicago World's Fair, where the Royal Hawaiian Band and hula dancers such as Kini Wilson performed, the Panama-Pacific Exposition made the largest impact on the American listening public. A

FIGURE 48. Tropical fishes and surf scenes entranced visitors to Hawai'i's pavilion at the 1915 Panama-Pacific Exposition. Courtesy of Hawai'i State Archives.

year after the 1915 exposition, *Paradise of the Pacific,* a magazine published in Hawai'i to promote tourism, featured in its November issue an article titled "Triumph of Hawaii's Music." "From Niihau to Nantucket, from Maine to Maui, from Weeka- wen to Waikiki Beach, from Hoboken to Hilo, from Washington, D.C., to Waiahole on Oahu Island, strains of Hawaiian music now win the hearts of music-loving hu- manity. . . . Everywhere you go, in music halls, vaudeville shows, hotels, cafes and cabarets, Hawaiian dance music is played and Hawaiian songs are sung." In New York City, the report continued, Rice & Webber had a "Hawaiian room" in one of their Broadway cafés, with paintings of Island scenes on the walls and ceiling, and a grass house, a Hawaiian orchestra, and hula dancing. "This room is so popular that to get a seat, reservations must be made several days ahead."[57]

The Royal Hawaiian Quartet, led by George E. K. Awa'i, was the "house band"

FIGURE 49. At the Panama-Pacific Exposition, the Hawaiʻiʻs pavilion's neoclassical façades were surely intended to impress upon the visitor Hawaiʻiʻs "civility." Set amid ferns from Kīlaueaʻs slopes were Hawaiian musicians. Courtesy of Hawaiʻi State Archives.

at the Panama-Pacific Exposition, but other noted guitarists performed at the Hawaiian pavilion, including Joseph Kekuku and Frank Ferera. The music created a sensation; *hapa haole* songs like "Waikiki Mermaid" and "Song of the Islands" became hits, and the greatest of them all was Henry Kaʻilimaʻiʻs "On the Beach at Waikiki," which was composed earlier but introduced at the exposition.[58] Capitalizing on the sound's popular appeal, the composers and publishers of Tin Pan Alley, who dominated much of the U.S. music scene during the first half of the century, produced dozens of Hawaiian songs in 1916, and major record companies such as Edison and Brunswick released "a torrent of Hawaiian records." Victor Records alone listing 146 Hawaiian records in its 1916 catalog. Hawaiian music outsold all other popular music in 1916, according to Victor, and "Good-bye Hono-lulu" was the number-one song in England and Europe.[59] Broadway contributed to the Hawaiian music craze with its 1912 hit show *Bird of Paradise,* which opened at Daly's Theater, and the many-faced minstrel Al Jolson went Hawaiian when he sang "Yaaka Hula Hickey Dula" in the 1916 musical comedy *Robinson Crusoe, Jr.*

Set in Puna on the Big Island of Hawai'i, *Bird of Paradise* tells a sorry tale of a young white man, a physician, who loses himself to the Islands' sensuous charms and "goes native" by becoming an alcoholic and marrying a Hawaiian of chiefly lin-eage. His counterpart, a newcomer, another white man and a beachcomber, searches for renewal by fleeing civilization. Luana, the protagonist's wife, with a "tempes-tuous childish love and anger," according to a January 10, 1912, *New York Dramatic Mirror* review, sacrifices herself in the "seething crater of Kilauea" and thereby res-cues her husband from his fallen state. Given a new lease on life, the physician and beachcomber return to the United States and civilization. The sets included the obligatory moonlight on the sea and a menacing volcano, establishing a tension be-tween a cool calm and a hot impetuousness, and the music of "simple melodies and harmonies" made it seem "credible that a man should fall prey to their sweet sad-ness." Hawaiian musicians, including Walter Kolomoku, used the guitar, steel gui-tar, ukulele, and *ipu* and introduced Broadway audiences to "the weirdly sensuous music of the island people," in the words of a *New York Times* review.[60]

The play's success led to a road tour of North American cities, and it played to packed houses in Boston and Toronto.[61] The *Pittsburgh Reader* described the "weird, cloyingly sweet" Hawaiian music that enhanced "the atmospheric effect," and it praised Lenore Ulrich, who played the Hawaiian princess, as expressing "all the passion, all the superstition of the savage, and at the same time all the exalted devotion of the soul of a woman. Physically she is a thing of tropical allure."[62] The *Detroit News* called the play an "exotic blossom" with a "cloying sweetness and tropic charm as sense-drugging as when it first appeared. . . ." The interracial romance, the review pointed out, would ordinarily elicit "frowns," but in this in-stance of regeneration and atmosphere—"the haunting strains of . . . Hawaiian melodies, the whisper of superstition and gods, the burning love that gives and in the giving brings death"—that "racial situation" instead "remains to fascinate and to bring forbearance."[63] Beginning in 1919, the Bird of Paradise Show toured Europe with Joseph Kekuku playing before audiences, including royalty, for eight years.[64] Even more influential were the 1932 RKO King Vidor movie version, *Bird of Paradise,* and its 1951 remake by Darryl F. Zanuck, starring Debra Paget and Jeff Chandler.[65]

Accompanying the phenomenal sale of records were the printing and distribution of sheet music with its cover, music, and lyrics, which promoted a vision of Hawai'i as a paradise of "balmy airs," eternal "summer seas flashing in the sun," tranquil shores lined with "plumy palms," and the sweet scent of flowers long faded, in the haunting words of Mark Twain. Covers designed to capture the consumer's eyes and release repressed sexual fantasies typically featured a "hula maiden" posed under palms with moonlight dancing on a glassy sea. Slippages that merged the unfamiliar with the familiar for white Americans included images of the erotic, exotic "Middle Eastern" belly dancer that scandalized sensibilities at the 1893 Chicago World's Fair and the American Indian maiden of Pocahontas fame.[66] The hula dancer as belly dancer appears on covers such as "My Hula Hula Love" (1911), "I Lost My Heart in Honolulu" (1916), and "My Hawaiian Sunshine" (1916), and Hawaiian as American Indian maiden on "Farewell My Love" (1914), "She Sang 'Aloha' to Me" (1915), and "Ola, My Sweet Hawaiian Love" (1916). Another convergence of Hawaiians with American Indians occurred at the 1893 World's Fair, where the band from the Carlisle Indian School, an offspring of the Islands' native education, played romanticized "Indian" songs composed by whites, such as "Hiawatha's Love Melody," "By the Waters of the Minnehaha," and "Indian Love Call."[67] In Philadelphia in the early 1900s, Anita Pineapple recalled, Hawaiians posed as American Indians. A Hawaiian musician with the stage name George Pinebird performed as an Indian in cowboy and Indian shows, and "I knew of other Hawaiians in Philadelphia who wore their hair long, wore cowboy hats and assumed Indian names," she testified.[68] Other couplings appeared in the lyrics, such as Hawai'i with the Philippine "jungle" and "a Bolo chieftain" from "savage Zinga Zulaland," a quick move to South Africa. These pairings allowed the sexually suggestive line "for you my bolo is swinging." The fine distinctions of culture and geography dissolved when it came to dark-eyed and dusky beauties who

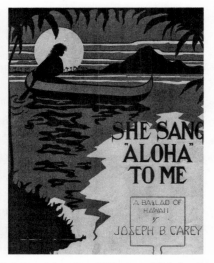

FIGURE 50. Sheet music covers of "My Hula-Hula Love" (1911) and "She Sang 'Aloha' to Me" (1915). Courtesy of Hawai'i Public Library.

"dressed like a Zulu," danced in "Oriental breezes" to oriental bands, and spoke an unintelligible and laughable "yacki, hacki, wicki, wacki, woo."[69]

By the 1920s the formula for success had been set, and the song lyrics followed a well-worn recipe. These were principally love songs of white men pining over Hawaiian women and longing for an escape to paradise, and they included tropic and coral isles, skies and ocean blue, gentle breezes and moonlit nights, silvery sands and swaying palms, tender sighs and kisses soft, pretty hula girls who wriggled and giggled, and love's story and wedding bells. Lovers yearned and sighed, shed tears and said long good-byes, and waited and called from across the sea, strumming ukuleles and guitars and singing sweet Hawaiian melodies.

Although Tin Pan Alley's version of Hawaiian music had a major impact upon the genre's popularity in the United States, it exercised little influence over the musical quality of Hawaiian songs. In fact, as noted by George Kanahele, pioneering Hawaiian composers such as Sonny Cunha and Henry Ka'ilima'i had a greater

FIGURE 51. Sheet music cover of "My Pearl of Honolulu (Hula Boola)" (1916). Hawai'i's voluptuous vegetation and available women promised an unbridled sensuality. Courtesy of Hawai'i Public Library.

FIGURE 52. Kini Wilson when she was a
dancer in the court of King Kalākaua.
Courtesy of Hawai'i State Archives.

FIGURE 53. At the 1893 Chicago World's Fair, the Hawaiian concession stood next to the Samoan pavilion on the midway. A description of this photograph, "Samoan Girls," reads: "So far from being forbidding in their looks and savage in their natures, the Samoans are among the mildest of people in disposition, and the most comely and symmetrical in form and feature." J. W. Buel, *The Magic City: A Massive Portfolio of Original Photographic Views of the Great World's Fair* (St. Louis: Historical Publishing, 1894). Courtesy of Avery Architectural and Fine Arts Library, Columbia University.

effect on Tin Pan Alley creations than the other way around. As an example, Kanahele observed that "Yaaka Hula Hickey Dula," performed by Al Jolson, resembles
Cunha's "Honolulu Hula-Hula Heigh!" (1906), with its incorporation of ragtime
and jazz, and Ka'ilima'i's "My Luau Girl" (1915).[70] Called a "Hawaiian love song"
on its cover, "Yaaka Hula Hickey Dula" (1916), written by E. Ray Goetz, Joe Young,
and Pete Wendling, declares, "Oh, I don't care if you've never loved before, / You'll
be captivated on that coral shore. / Yaaka hula hickey dula, / Yaaka hula hickey du."

Although Hawaiian musicians were almost always men, Hawaiian hula dancers
were invariably women, in contrast to hula's beginnings in Hawai'i, in which men
as well as women danced. The objects of men's longings as expressed in the lyrics
and specular bodies in performance, Hawaiian hula dancers on the continent
sought personal freedoms even as they reinforced social constraints.[71] Kini Wilson
acknowledged her problematic position as a dancer at the 1893 Chicago World's Fair.
Selected and trained by King Kalākaua as a court dancer, Kini (Jennie) Kapahukulaokamamalu was chosen and hired by a white theatrical agent for a tour of North
America after the king's death. Dance, she noted, was sacred, "very religious," and yet
at the Chicago World's Fair Wilson stood outside on a small box playing the ukulele,
rolling her eyes, wiggling seductively, and singing, "On the Midway, the Midway,
the Midway Plaisance, / Where the naughty girls from Honolulu do the naughty hula
dance, / At the naughty goings-on at the Midway Plaisance." Her beckoning hands
brought in the crowd, Wilson recalled, especially men, who winked at her and en-
joyed watching a jazzed-up version of the hula repeatedly.[72] At the same time, Wilson, who danced in the United States, Canada, Germany, Russia, Holland, Bel-
gium, France, and England, knew that her songs belonged to the *ali'i,* and she thus
consecrated the stage with a chant and hula and ended each performance with a
chant.[73]

Performances, recordings, and sheet music were just the leading edges of a
commercial sensation. Guitar manufacturers and schools for steel guitar playing
fed and satisfied the demand for Hawaiian music, and publishers such as Wm. J.
Smith released instructional books, for example *Famous Duets for Hawaiian Guitar, Hawaiian Guitar Duets,* and *Songs for Hawaiian Guitar,* in about 1928. Adver-
tisements assured, "You can play the Hawaiian guitar just like the Hawaiians!" and

they guaranteed proficiency "in five easy lessons."[74] The Honolulu Conservatory of Music of Cleveland, Ohio, was possibly the most successful of the guitar schools. Begun in Flint, Michigan, in 1926, the conservatory moved to Cleveland about four years later. An estimated 200,000 students took its guitar courses, and some of them became teachers who opened their own studios, as many as 1,200 of which were franchises across North America. The Oahu Publishing Company, an adjunct of the conservatory, sold books, guitars, and musical supplies until 1985. Although the founder of the conservatory and publishing company, Harry G. Stanley, capitalized on the Hawaiian image of palm trees, hula dancers, and tropical flowers, the conservatory's classes included Hawaiian music but also its cousins—folk, country, and gospel music.[75]

HULA BLUES

"Hula blues" embraces both a metaphorical and a literal coupling of Hawaiian and African American musics and musicians. In a way, like the hula, "hula blues" points to the resistances posed by Hawaiians and African Americans in popular culture to the vulgar cartoons of them as "weak tropical races"—idle, ignorant, but happy and given to dance and song.[76] Both African American and Hawaiian artists appropriated those representations to advance their interests and musical careers. At the same time, repossession might instead bespeak betrayal, and mimicry can buttress even as it can corrode the "original" and "real." Yet Hawaiian and African American musicians worked within the cramped quarters of race, gender, sexuality, and nation, and their labors should be multiply construed.

Exemplary is "Hula Blues" itself, composed by Johnny Noble in 1920 with lyrics by Sonny Cunha, which ends with the familiar refrain: "Hula girl, she will surely make you giggle, / Hula girl, with her naughty little wiggle." The popular hit was Noble's first and most enduring composition, and although he was heavily influenced by jazz and the blues, such that he was called the "Hawaiian King of Jazz," the *hapa haole* song's title was inspired, according to Noble, by tourists who loved the hula so much that when they left the Islands they must have felt blue. So he called the song "Hula Blues." Beneath those thin façades of title and lyrics, none-theless, Noble knew that both jazz and the blues were steeped in African Ameri-can folk music and the experiences of enslavement and racism and, in his words, "the urge of a whole people to express themselves in a language of their own." Compositions such as W. C. Handy's "St. Louis Blues" and "Beale Street Blues," Noble knew, were "melancholy—the cry of black men under oppression."[77] "Hula Blues," accordingly, was simultaneously for the tourist and for the Hawaiian ac-commodation and resistance, light and heavy.

Hawaiian and African American musics bore resemblances beyond the fact that some of the earliest "Hawaiian music" was marketed as "coon songs" and "oriental coon songs" in the late nineteenth and early twentieth centuries. Their covers also bore the racist stereotypical images of black men and women, and their lyrics were crude parodies—for example, "My Honolulu Lady" (1898), ad-vertised as "The Latest Coon Conquest," in which an Alabama narrator returns with "Honolulu Lou" to "show dem coons and wenches style and grace that is di-vine, when we both pass down de line. . . . We cut de pigeon wing, de coons did shout and sing."[78]

Both Hawaiian and African American musics drew heavily from Christian hymns and their harmonies, which lay a foundation for Hawaiian *hapa haole* music. Another source of this Hawaiian music was the *mele hula ku'i,* the hula chants and songs made popular by King Kalākaua's court.[79] The first hymnbook, *Na Himeni Hawaii,* was published in 1823, and it received wide and rapid distribution. In the first decade, 52,000 copies were printed, and several hundred singing schools en-rolled thousands of adults and children throughout the island chain.[80] By the turn of the century, remembered an enthralled Johnny Noble, "all over Honolulu, all over Hawaii, people gathered to listen to music or to sing, at concerts, at church, whenever and wherever they could. It was a land of music."[81] Hawaiians adapted the melody and harmony of hymns to the melodic and rhythmic patterns and con-tours and the voice qualities unique to Hawaiian musical expression and "created their own style of hymn singing."[82] They thereby indigenized New England hymns, like the imported instruments, to render them Hawaiian *himeni.*

Equally profound as hymns in shaping Hawaiian music were the influences of

FIGURE 54. Sheet music cover of "My Honolulu Lady" (1898). Courtesy of Sheldon Harris Blues, Jazz, and Black Music Culture Collections, Archives and Special Collections, University of Mississippi.

ragtime, jazz, and the blues. The century's end marked a transition from "coon music," performed by whites and blacks alike, to ragtime, which presented African American music relatively free of the odious linguistic and bodily caricatures associated with "coon music." Hawaiian musicians, racialized as black on the continent, found affinities between their condition and music and African Americans and their music. Besides providing an economic opportunity for Hawaiians, African American music conferred a measure of human dignity and was a point of intersection between divergent and yet analogous traditions and experiences.

Like the chant and hula, Johnny Noble pointed out, jazz was essentially dance music, and in the blues singers used their bodies and facial expressions to convey a song's message. Common to Hawaiian music and the blues, or "true jazz," Noble wrote, were "the use of the slur, (glissando or vibrato); the constant moving of the melodic line in and out of microtones; a tendency to mingle major and minor modes; and a regular beat, usually depending on drums, with stressed off-beat accents. Also, both jazz and early Hawaiian music were natural and spontaneous; both were personal and vocalized; and both effected the senses and feelings with a certain haunting quality."[83]

Eric Madis, a blues, jazz, and bottleneck guitar player,[84] saw connections between Hawaiian slack key and African American blues styles. "Like Hawaiians," he noted, "Afro-Americans developed a rich, syncopated, highly rhythmic approach to fingerpicking that developed into various styles and regional idioms within blues and ragtime guitar. Some of this playing was performed in open tunings and some was not. So, although we think Hawaiian slack key and blues styles both developed in isolation from each other, the parallels between them are quite astounding."[85] Bottleneck was also a precursor and relative of the Hawaiian steel guitar and its slide sound.

Hawaiian and African American musicians made crossover appearances, and each acquired the musical tongue of the other. Jazz's influence on Sol Hoʻopiʻi is clearly seen in his "I Like You," recorded in Los Angeles in 1934. Ben Nawahi was a key figure in introducing Hawaiian to African American music by playing the blues like his "California Blues" and "Black Boy Blues," forming the QRS Boys with the New Orleans singer and stride pianist Walter "Fats" Pichon and possibly

Robert Cloud, the saxophonist, in 1929, and playing with swing groups in the 1930s. He recorded in the 1920s and '30s with the QRS Boys, Red Devils (Harry Brooks, piano; Bruce Hinkson, violin; Ikey Robinson, banjo), and Georgia Jumpers (Socks Wilson, piano; Bruce Hinkson, violin; Robert Cloud, saxophone). Nawahi blended his Hawaiian guitar with jazz, pop, and hokum, and he and the Georgia Jumpers performed regularly at the Chinaland restaurant in New York City.[86]

The bottleneck blues tradition that appeared in the Mississippi Delta around the turn from the nineteenth to the twentieth century was probably unique to the region, although W. C. Handy heard "the mood for what we now call [the] blues" in 1903 at a Tutwiler, Mississippi, railroad station set by a guitar with a knife slide "in a manner popularized by Hawaiian guitarists who used steel bars." The guitarist, he wrote, was "a lean, loose-jointed Negro" whose clothes were "rags" and whose face displayed "the sadness of the ages."[87] It is more likely that the Hawaiian steel guitar influenced bottleneck blues north of the Delta from the 1910s through 1930s as touring musicians performed Hawaiian renditions at Chautauquas, at fairs, and in vaudeville. Such blues guitarists as Kokomo Arnold learned slide "lap style," and Robert Wilkins and Blind Willie Johnson played their slide guitar on their laps, Hawaiian style. As noted by Eric Madis, "Some of these early blues musicians acknowledged the influence of the Hawaiian steel guitar."[88] Oscar "Buddy" Woods is reported to have taken up the steel guitar after hearing a traveling Hawaiian troupe perform in his hometown of Shreveport, Louisiana, in the early 1920s and was among a handful of African American blues guitarists who played the steel on his lap. Woods taught the Texas-born bluesman B. K. Turner (better known as Black Ace) to play the Hawaiian guitar.[89]

Hawaiian musicians toured the United States and Europe as "colored artists," and their music and dance advanced and complemented the commerce-driven dreams of tropical paradise, gentle breezes, swaying palm trees, and moonlight on water. Evoking that exoticism, the all-girl band International Sweethearts of Rhythm, active from 1937 to 1949, played to white and black audiences. The band itself, like the Hawaiian tropical fishes at the Panama-Pacific Exposition, was a colorful mix of musicians. At different times it had different members, and sometimes it included whites. The *Chicago Defender* called the Sweethearts a "sensational mixed band which is composed of Race, Mexicans, Chinese, and Indian girls" who play "the savage rhythms of ancient African tom-toms, the weird beat of the Indian war dance, and the quaintness and charm of the Orient."[90] On the vaudeville stage, the Six Abdullah Girls and African American men's bands like the Ali Baba Trio, who sometimes wore turbans, suggested blends of black and brown and a hint of the Orient and Asia.[91] That "internationalism," of course, as "alien" and "foreign," functioned to exclude African, Asian, and Native Americans and Latina/os from the U.S. body, but it also had market appeal to black and white audiences alike and may have produced anxieties that destabilized dominant notions of race and miscegenation, gender and its separate spheres, and U.S. exceptionalism and its parochialism.[92]

Casey Bill Weldon personified the relative anonymity in which many bluesmen and African American musicians lived and labored. He may have been born in Pine Bluff, Arkansas, in 1909, and he worked the South as a singer and guitarist during the 1920s. He emerged more confidently during the 1930s in Kansas City and Chicago, hence his name, "Casey," from a phonetic rendering of "K. C." Kansas City Bill Weldon recorded during the 1930s under the byline "Hawaiian Guitar Wizard," to highlight the influence of the Hawaiian guitar, style, and technique in his playing. An encyclopedia entry described Weldon's playing: "Expressing himself in the classic Hawaiian-guitar style so fashionable in the early part of the century, he developed a profoundly personal approach to blues and ragtime. Most of his recordings display an exuberance, an intense rhythm, a joie de vivre and a lineage of Texan western-swing guitarists such as Leon McAuliffe and Strozer Quinn than that of black exponents of the bottleneck style."[93] If this description is true, Weldon, like several Hawaiian musicians, bridged Hawaiian and country music.

HAWAIIAN COUNTRY

Hawaiian troupes in vaudeville and Chautauqua performances and urban music clubs "took the country by storm, popularizing Hawaiian melodies and introducing the ukulele and steel guitar to American audiences," according to a widely read textbook on country music. "Fretted with a steel bar, the Hawaiian steel guitar emitted a melodious, but crying sound that has thrilled generations of country listeners."[94] The bottleneck sound of African American guitarists may have conditioned southern rural audiences to the Hawaiian steel guitar, pointing to a convergence of Hawaiian and African American music and their mutual influences on country. To designate this music, Al Hopkins and the Hill Billies was one of the first bands to use the term "hillbilly," which became a generic name for music of the rural South and commercial country music after 1925, and the band was one of the first to include a Hawaiian steel guitar.[95]

Perhaps typical of the way the Hawaiian steel guitar sound seeped into country music was the experience of noted guitarist Jerry Byrd. Growing up in Ohio during the 1920s, recalled Byrd, "I learned to play by listening to such greats as: Dick McIntire, Sol Hoopii, Andy Iona and others. Hawaiian music was my first love." But there were no Hawaiian bands in Lima, his small Ohio town, "so I fell into country music by default. But I played Hawaiian style on hundreds of records with some of the greatest country singers!" Hawaiian music was, then, pervasive, though unsung. Country, Byrd explained, is a "style" of playing, and that style of tone and expression is unique to each steel guitarist. Jimmie Rodgers, originator of the "blue yodel," was accompanied by the Hawaiian steel guitar played by Dick McIntire's brother, Lani, among others, in his first recordings of the late 1920s and early 1930s.[96] Hawaiian music became country through that incorporation, noted Byrd, and it moved into western swing, as performed by Bob Wills and his Texas Playboys, and country ballads, as exemplified by Eddy Arnold and Red Foley.[97]

A southerner, Jim Hand, described his first encounter with the Hawaiian steel guitar. In 1928, Hand's uncle was an evangelical preacher, and he had a Hawaiian steel guitarist play as part of his service. "They paid us a visit one day," recalled Hand, "and this fellow performed several numbers, church hymns and Hawaiian. Some numbers were *When the Roll is Called up Yonder, Sunshine in my Soul, In the Garden* and *Hilo March.* Well, Brother, that 'done it.' I dreamed of that sound for days."[98] Composed by Joseph Kapaeau Aeʻa in 1881, the "Hilo March" was popularized by steel guitarists Pale K. Lua and David Kaʻili, who recorded it during the 1920s.[99] It was not incongruous that the Hawaiian steel guitar accompanied singing

FIGURE 55. Jimmie Rodgers's Hawaiian Show and Carnival, which toured the Midwest in the spring and summer of 1925. Besides the lap guitar and leis, notice the women "hula" dancers, who could as well be "gypsies" or "belly dancers." Courtesy of House of Cash.

at an evangelical tent meeting in the South, or that the congregation raised their voices to the "Hilo March" along with "When the Roll Is Called up Yonder." After all, Christian missionaries from New England taught Hawaiians hymn singing, which Hawaiians adapted as *himeni,* and the Hilo Boarding School was an inspiration for a brand of education for African Americans, mainly in the South.

James "Jimmie" Charles Rodgers was born just north of Meridian, Mississippi, in 1897. As a teenager, Rodgers worked with his father on the railroad, and that association became his trademark, "the singing brakeman," made popular during the Great Depression. His influence on American country folk music was profound, broad, and long lasting. He set an example for countless others who would follow and seek to emulate him, and he made country music national rather than local in scope. Although he introduced innovations, his 111 recordings show the multiple strands that made up the South's musical culture. These included vaudeville and Tin Pan Alley, jazz and blues, hillbilly and folk. In 1928, on his second record, Rodgers sang to the sound of the Hawaiian steel guitar. He toured in the company of a Hawaiian band in 1930 and recorded with ukuleles and with Hawaiian steel guitarists Joe Kaipo and Charles Kama in 1929 and 1931. Moreover, according to an extravagant and intemperate claim, his famous yodeling "quite evidently stems from Hawaiian influences, as does the very structure of some of his work."[100] A more sober conclusion might cite the long history of yodeling in the South and its early appearance in blackface minstrel shows and in Mexican songs of the Southwest, all contexts in which Rodgers developed his music.[101] Still, it is clear that the "father of modern country music" absorbed and fused the Hawaiian sound, among other traditions, into a style that made him the country's first and most influential singing star.

A son of white South Carolina textile workers and folksingers, Jimmie (Johnny James Rimbert) Tarlton grew up listening to African American laborers sing the blues, which became a feature of his playing and singing. Tarlton hoboed as far north as New York and as far west as California, where he learned the steel technique from Hawaiian guitarists like Frank Ferera. In his travels around the country, Tarlton worked in the oil fields and cotton mills. His recordings from the late 1920s through the 1930s, with his distinctive instrumental and singing style, put him at the forefront of country singers of any period.[102] Like Jimmie Rodgers and other artists who stand at major crossings, Tarlton's style derived from several musical traditions, including the white and black working-class South, hillbilly, folk, and the blues, and the Hawaiian steel guitar.

In the Southwest, especially Louisiana, Oklahoma, and Texas, country music acquired the cowboy image of clothing and western themes. Cowboy, or western, music descended from southern music that accompanied the westward migrations of white and black southerners, and in the Southwest it merged with Mexican traditions. The romance of the West and cowboy lore, of course, were racialized as "white," as set in opposition to the "Indian" or "Mexican," and they engendered a rugged manliness and individualism. In fact, the *vaquero* set the standard for white cattlemen in techniques and implements. Besides musicians, novel writers and Hollywood film producers exploited the fictional version, which was as old as the nation, and catered to a public who knew virtually nothing about life on the range. As was noted by a music historian, "The farther Americans became removed from the cowboy past, the more intense became their interest in cowboy songs and lore. Hillbilly singers and musicians did much to implant the romantic cowboy image in the minds of their American audiences."[103]

Jimmie Rodgers, who toured and lived the last few years of his life in Texas, was an important figure in fusing country with western music. His deployment of a romantic cowboy image might well have inspired the idea of the "singing cowboy," and others copied his example, like Hank Snow, who dressed in cowboy outfits and called himself "the Yodeling Ranger," and Gene Autry, who early in his career sang as the "Oklahoma Yodeling Cowboy."[104] Although he began as a hillbilly and southern rural singer, Autry did Jimmie Rodgers imitations, and he moved in 1934 from Chicago to Hollywood and became the "Nation's Number One Singing Cowboy." Thus cast, Autry shifted from country to western themes, and his sound mellowed out to reach a broader U.S. audience, including the white, urban middle class.[105]

Like the bands and guitarists who alternated between country and Hawaiian styles during the first half of the twentieth century, the distinction between the two easily blurred and influences flowed in both directions. Those shifting boundaries have created classification problems in defining the limits of "Hawaiian" music and its reach. "It is, in retrospect, somewhat astonishing how popular Hawaiian music became on the American mainland in the early 1900s," a 1979 commentary observed. "What started out as a relatively pure Hawaiian musical style, with lyrics sung in Hawaiian, rapidly blended in with the mainstream of American pop music, the islanders contributing the steel guitar and ukulele and themes of island paradise, the mainlanders contributing the melodies and styles of contemporary jazz, urban blues, and middle-of-the-road pop music. Many early country musicians . . . affirmed their interest in Hawaiian music, and would as soon perform a concert of that as they would of hillbilly music."[106]

One of Gene Autry's rivals on the silver screen was Roy Rogers, who before his rise to movie and television stardom was a member of Bennie Nawahi's International Cowboys.[107] Nawahi, the noted Hawaiian steel guitarist, had moved, with vaudeville's decline, from the East to the West Coast to start anew and, like country music, took up western themes with his California band. Of course, unlike country music, which moved from hillbilly into a western or cowboy tradition, Nawahi could have claimed Hawaiian *paniolo* roots, which had origins in the Mexican North and U.S. Southwest among the *vaqueros*. Bob Dunn, one of the most influential steel guitarists in country and western music, became interested in the instrument after hearing a Hawaiian band in his hometown of Kusa, Oklahoma, in 1917, and after corresponding with Walter Kolomoku of Broadway's *Bird of Paradise* fame. Dunn joined the Panhandle Cowboys and Indians, played in vaudeville, and became one of the first electric steel guitarists in country and western music.[108] Although his sound differed from that of Hawaiian steel guitar greats like Sol Hoʻopiʻi and Dick McIntire, he played his converted Martin O-series acoustic guitar "with its strings raised high off the neck" and the instrument flat on his lap, Hawaiian style.[109]

Islands and Continents

"If cultures and civilizations are the tectonic plates of world history," a world historian once wrote, "frontiers are the places where they scrape against each other and cause convulsive change."[1] Accordingly, the historian's survey should contemplate the borders, because activity and movement are the stuff of history. Further, he noted, civilizations are commonly considered land-based formations, ignoring the fact that they "are grouped around waterways" from the China Sea to the Indian Ocean, the Mediterranean, and the Atlantic and Pacific.[2] Moreover, this historian neglected to point out that continents bed upon tectonic plates that exceed land's end, extending into ocean depths rarely penetrated by human comprehension. And along the plates' margins, where mass bumps up against mass, molten rock can ooze through the cracks and, given time, solidify and create seamounts, islands, and majestic mountain ranges packed with life's diversity.

In this rendering of Hawaiian and U.S. history, *Island World*, I center the islands of Oceania, widely held to be "tiny spaces" absent significance or moment and place on the periphery of the continent, which situates the United States. Commonly represented as feminine, islands remain passive, acted upon, stirred only by outside, manly manipulations.[3] Myths abound in the notions of islands and continents. An origin myth is the standard, gendered definition of islands as small bodies of land surrounded by water and of continents as large, unbroken landmasses. Boundedness appears to be an island's defining state, boundlessness a continent's. Yet, geologically, islands and continents are both anchored onto plates, which form the earth's mantle, beneath and above the oceans. From the perspective of the earth's surface at the ocean floor, the distinction between islands and continents disappears, and island chains are revealed as immense and high mountain ranges. Humans who act at different times upon political agendas, including the power to name and exert mastery over subject lands and peoples, are the ones responsible for the demarcations between islands and continents.

Geographical taxonomy at its most basic, a geographer and historian show, is the core problem. Whether segmenting the world into seven continents, or directions (east, west, north, and south), or political alignments (First, Second, and Third Worlds), they explain, "like areas are inevitably divided from like, while disparate places are jumbled together."[4] These authors make the obvious though often overlooked point that geographies, like the myths that surround continents and islands, are human inscriptions upon the earth and as such mirror ideologies specific to peoples, times, and places. Instead, those social constructions have carried the imprimatur of science, which claims to explain an objective reality transcendent of time and place, and, in that rendering, continents form the basic building blocks of landmass, biotic communities, and human groupings, all of which are conceived of as constituting a class apart because of alleged shared characteristics that differentiate it from other groups. Thus, the African continent's wildlife and peoples can be rendered as categories distinguishable from the European continent's flora, fauna, and peoples.

Continental divides were not always the rule, even within the European mind. The ancient Greeks conceived of their world as a "world island," consisting of the intersection of Europe, Asia, and Africa, lands circled by water. Despite being a cosmology that equated land with order and the familiar and that banished the oceans to land's fringes as chaotic and strange, unlike Hawaiians and Polynesians, the ancient Greeks' world was undivided.[5] After its discovery by Europeans, America shattered that world island idea and lent credence to the notion of separate landmasses that eventuated into solitary, continental communities estranged from one another. Still, as late as the nineteenth century, prominent geographers favored dividing the world into two parts, old (Europe, Asia, Africa) and new (America), and they saw them as islands or lands surrounded by water.[6] An exception that soon became the rule, however, was Carl Ritter, the most influential human geographer of the time, who viewed continents as the major organizing principle of metageography. "Each continent," he was positive, "is like itself alone. . . . Each one was so planned and formed as to have its own special function in the progress of human culture." Inevitably, bound to that notion of social evolution and design was Ritter's view that at the apex was Europe, the homeland of white people, followed by Asia, the homeland of yellow people, Africa, of black people, and America, of red.[7] Continents, accordingly, suggested a metageography and hierarchy of distinctive civilizations and racialized peoples.

By the twentieth century, continents were assumed not only to demarcate the earth's surface but also to be a "natural" and sometimes divinely ordained state. In the United States about mid-century, America was divided into North and South, Antarctica gained continental status, and Australia and New Zealand stood in for Oceania. The resulting seven-continent scheme gained rapid and widespread recognition, despite its glaring defects: zoogeography's demonstration that lifeforms move relatively freely across continental boundaries; geology's revelation that India is part of Australia, not Eurasia, and that North America connects seamlessly to Eurasia under the Bering Sea. Continents prove inadequate as a schema of physical geography and of human geography as well, insofar as they purport to map cultural and racial differences and ranks. Still, because they conform to "the basic patterns of land and sea that spring to the eye from a world map," the continental system appears natural and true.[8]

Likewise, visually, islands, with few exceptions, emerge as tiny specks of land, especially when seen from the perspective of the Pacific's immensity.[9] "Views of the Pacific from the level of macroeconomics and macropolitics often differ markedly from those from the level of ordinary people," explained Epeli Hau'ofa of his "sea of islands."[10] Most versions of world history envision "the Pacific" as its rim, where it washes against economic and political giants, continental Asia and America. And though seas may serve as fecund breeding grounds for exchanges of goods, peoples, and ideas, they are ordinarily conceived of not as places of generation and production but rather as mere watery routes, unlike landed roots, or even barren deserts, a land metaphor, to traverse and endure.[11]

Oceania's smallness is a state of mind, "mental reservations" imposed upon its peoples by European colonizers, Hau'ofa came to understand while driving from

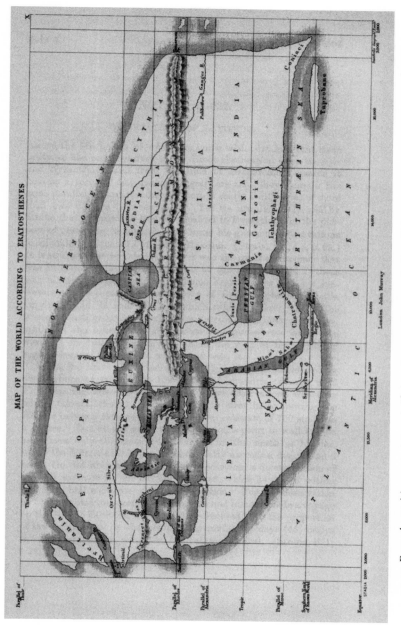

MAP 5. Eratosthenes (circa 276–196 B.C.), "father of systematic geography," used his position as head of Alexandria's massive library and its store of accumulated learning to produce this map of the world. Adapted from E. H. Bunbury, *A History of Ancient Geography* (New York: Dover Publications, 1959).

Kona to Hilo on the island of Hawai'i: "I saw such scenes of grandeur as I had not seen before: the eerie blackness of regions covered by recent volcanic eruptions; the remote majesty of Maunaloa, long and smooth, the world's largest volcano; the awesome craters of Kīlauea threatening to erupt at any moment; and the lava flow on the coast not far away. Under the aegis of Pele, and before my very eyes, the Big Island was growing, rising from the depths of a mighty sea. The world of Oceania is not small; it is huge and growing bigger every day."[12]

"Continental men," Hau'ofa continued, specifically Europeans and Americans, "drew imaginary lines across the sea, making the colonial boundaries that confined ocean peoples to tiny spaces for the first time." On the contrary, to Oceania's peoples, "their universe comprised not only land surfaces, but the surrounding ocean as far as they could traverse and exploit it, the underworld with its fire-controlling and earth-shaking denizens, and the heavens above with their hierarchies of powerful gods and named stars and constellations that people could count on to guide their ways across the seas. Their world was anything but tiny."[13]

Besides its physical expanse, added Albert Wendt, Oceania "nourishes my spirit, helps to define me, and feeds my imagination." Oceania is more than "mundane fact," he confessed, "my commitment won't allow me to confine myself to so narrow a vision. So vast, so fabulously varied a scatter of islands, nations, cultures, mythologies and myths, so dazzling a creature, Oceania deserves more." Like the diminution taught by colonialism and dependency, Wendt contended, cultural purity and visions of paradise contain half-truths and lies, and calls for a return to tradition and authenticity oftentimes result in stagnation, intolerance, and containment. Rather, he noted, Oceania's peoples traveled widely, interacted often, and changed frequently. Diversity abounds, and "there are no *true interpreters* or *sacred guardians* of any culture." "There was no Fall, no sun-tanned Noble Savages existing in South Seas paradises, no Golden Age, except in Hollywood films, in the insanely romantic literature and art by outsiders about the Pacific. . . . We, in Oceania, did not/and do not have a monopoly on God and the ideal life."[14]

By positioning Hawai'i as the core and the United States its periphery, accordingly, I have sought to untangle some of the myths of islands and continents by inverting their usual locations. A modern geographer mapped my challenge.

"Unlike the tropical forest or the continental seashore it [islands] cannot claim eco-logical abundance," he wrote, "nor—as an environment—has it mattered greatly in man's evolutionary past. Its importance lies in the imaginative realm."[15] More than a metaphor or a Pacific "crossroads" that receives the world, Hawai'i, in this version of the Islands' past, scrapes up against the continent by sending its peoples and their achievements abroad to its frontiers, causing convulsive change. Those agencies, I have tried to show, have influenced some of the most basic aspects of American society and culture. From that perspective, the island acts upon and moves the continent. Moreover, from that viewpoint of Island history, we come to understand that the mental separations of water from land and islands from con-tinents are inventions, like the fictions that embellish them, and that actual tres-passings routinely infringe upon the fences erected and patrolled by human imag-ination and wills.

Biotic communities with rich pasts and, one hopes, long futures exist and thrive within and beyond the radius of human concern. There is a notable void when history traces only the activities of humans and not their ancestry and connections with the land, water, and sky and their manifestations and lifeforms. In the Ku-mulipo, a Hawaiian creation song, life on earth appears through pairings, male and female, and all of its bodies, the celebrated child included, are related as shown by their interlocking genealogies. Motion—rotating, flowing, turning over—of sky against earth, male against female, causes the earth to heat and in its depths, its womb, from the ocean's muddy slime, first life is conceived. Begotten of salt water and soft earth, coupled by currents, are ocean invertebrates, sea and land plants, fishes, insects, birds, reptiles, and mammals. The infant chief, "a child of the gentle wrasse *[hilu]* that swims," traces his descent through those lineages back to the earth's beginnings.

The American sublime, by contrast, portrayed nature's creation as overwhelm-ing and threatening to humans. In its hands, the seas and mountains appear im-possibly large, whether as expanses, waves, or peaks, and the skies hang broodingly melancholic with extreme contrasts of light and dark.[16] The vast, uncharted terri-tories to the west of the Atlantic seaboard stirred the imagination of America's nonnative peoples, suggesting an immense, untamed wilderness of great promise

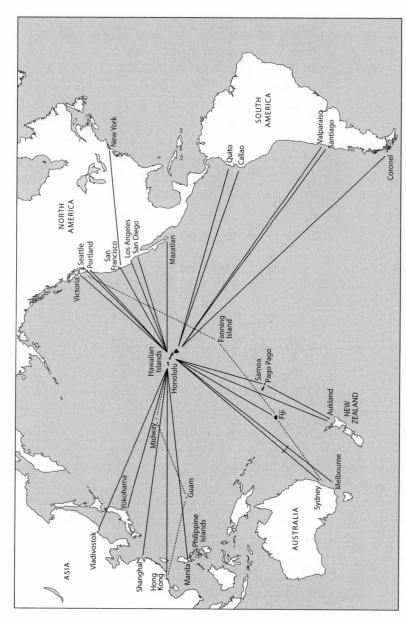

MAP 6. Copy of an early map of Hawai'i as the "Crossroads of the Pacific" by the Hawaii Promotion Committee in the journal "devoted to Hawaiian tourist interest." *Paradise of the Pacific* 15, no. 12 (1902).

FIGURE 56. Enoch Wood Perry Jr., *Manoa Valley from Waikiki* (1865). Born in Boston, Perry studied in Europe and painted the American West before visiting Hawai'i. The big skies and looming mountains, tranquil stream, and equestrians appear to be a Romantic composition of a pastoral paradise. Courtesy of Bishop Museum.

and extreme danger. The staggering enormity of the continent's natural wonders distinguished the United States from Europe, suggesting exceptionalism and nationalism, and stretched from the Atlantic to the Pacific by the late nineteenth century. The nation's westward march and search for new lands were aided and abetted by Romantic pens and brushes.

Pele's fires were both creative and consuming, as witnessed in volcanism's effects upon the earth's mantle, expanding its plates, which subduction then reduces. And while Hawaiians stressed Pele's life-giving qualities, Europeans and Americans saw her hellish, destructive powers.[17] Pele's presence in the dormant Lē'ahi (Diamond Head) and the exceedingly active Kīlauea were the most popular visual representations of Hawai'i's islands on the continental United States throughout the nineteenth and twentieth centuries. Those images appeared on postcards and sheet music, on canned goods and business cards, and in magazines, books, and motion pictures.[18] Diamond Head, a familiar backdrop for Waikīkī's fabled beach with its tranquil palm trees, mild surf, and hotel havens, assumed a quiet, passive pose, while the unpredictable and intractable Kīlauea inspired terror and invited bombing runs. Whether as art, religion, or science, Hawai'i's regions of fire left their imprint upon the U.S. imaginary and Romantic sublime, and as a symbol of creation and sin's final and everlasting end they affirmed central tenets of Christianity and stirred the emotions of enthusiastic religion of the Second Great Awakening.

Pele and Namaka, though they are unyielding and enduring antagonists, fire and water, are sisters—and fire's creation, islands, and the waters that surround them, along with their tenants, constitute pairs: liquid and solid, seaweeds and land plants, fishes and trees, as revealed by the Kumulipo. Many of Hawai'i's biotic communities, whether in the ocean or on land, were migrants from a region in Southeast Asia. Most floated upon liquid currents, water and air, whereas humans sailed against the prevailing patterns, especially those Polynesians who steered for the rising sun but then veered northward to the Hawaiian Islands. Because of the ocean's hospitality toward life and movement, the marine and human communities of Oceania are in regular contact despite the immense distances, and they inhabit a large world and number prodigious populations. In that sense, Polynesians constituted "by far the most extensive, nation upon earth," according to British captain James Cook.

Hawai'i's tropical fishes and wave sliding, natives both, are the Islands' unique endowments to the world. Often featured in exhibits, as at San Francisco's Panama-Pacific Exposition held to commemorate Balboa's extravagant 400-year-old claim of the Pacific for Spain, Hawai'i's colorful fishes suggested "something pagan and Dionysian," in the words of an art critic whose adjectives were aimed at the exposition's overall ambience, its "love of form and colour which you here saw displayed in such prodigal fashion," but were also appropriate for the fishes that dazzled the visitor to the Hawaiian pavilion. Those piscine relatives of Hawaiians, "whose painted brilliance you could not vision in your wildest dreams," attracted large crowds, as did the Hawaiians who swam in and later surfed California's waves at Santa Cruz and Redondo Beach. Olympian Duke Kahanamoku perhaps epitomized the "brown

Mercury" and "sea god" of Jack London's naughty tease to white American women and his recuperation of white masculinity and, allegedly, Hawaiian culture.

White tourists and settlers thrived in Hawai'i's gentle climate, unlike in other parts of the tropical "torrid zone," according to business and health experts, and Hollywood's South Seas cinema screened Gardens of Eden wherein feminine, lush abundance suggested sexual abandon and escape from modernity's conventions and constraints. Interracial romance between white men and brown women, the latter played by a range of whites, Latinas, Asians, and Pacific Islanders, was a prominent violation in this filmic genre, with the cautionary coda of the brown woman's sacrifice and atonement, typically in the volcano's cleansing fires, or recapture and courtroom justice and, sometimes, vindication for mutinous white men. Island paradises were pregnant with widely circulated caricatures of Hawaiian originals, including endless summers and eternal youth, surf culture of boards, cars, swim fashions and wetsuits, and beach parties and luaus, brightly colored sarongs, shirts, and dresses, leis, and food and drink. Promoted by dream weavers for profit, those pleasures of the flesh bruised the sensibilities of New England missionaries, who, from the start, tried to banish from the pristine garden the hideous serpent of Hawaiian culture.

Hawaiians like Hopu and 'Ōpūkaha'ia commuted to New England's alien shores on board American ships, serving as deckhands and crew members. They engaged a world bigger than their Oceania, which included Asia's trade cities and goods, Southeast Asia of their ancestral past, the Indian and Atlantic oceans, Africa's ports, Caribbean plantation societies, and America's Northeast. There, amid the mixed populations of bustling port cities, whites grouped Hawaiians as foreigners such as Chinese, Portuguese, and Jews but also as natives, as American Indians, and as blacks. Like American Indians, they became subjects for religious conversion and social uplift, Christianity and civilization, as was exemplified in Cornwall's Foreign Mission School. But unlike America's Indians, Hawaiians prompted the cause of foreign missions, away from the nation's expanding interior to its overseas, Pacific destiny. In that turn to trusteeships overseas, they were like African Americans, who suggested to some whites the imperative of taking the light of the gospel to the "dark continent."

Removing African Americans from the "reach of mixture," in Thomas Jefferson's words, appealed to abolitionists and slaveholders alike, and it was supported by the same doctrine of race held by the patrons of the Foreign Mission School, who pronounced the marriage of white women to American Indian men to be "criminal" and an "outrage upon public feeling." As lesser peoples, African Americans, American Indians, and Hawaiians merited separate and unequal treatment for their maladies administered by the "chosen people," who bore the remedies and the burden of Christianity and civilization to expand and conquer heathen lands and free their mired inhabitants. Coming at a time of spiritual awakening and the Romantic sublime, the rise of mercantile capitalism and westward expansion, and strivings for social reform, the Hawaiian foreign mission advanced and complemented those pivotal movements and opened the United States to the Pacific and the world.

An effect of New England's diaspora was the return of its children to its landings. Schooled in Hawai'i, Samuel Chapman Armstrong and other missionary sons transported to the continent baggage like paternalism when confronted with the spectacle of "weaker races" and their imperatives for charity and service. Christian education in the Islands involved the promotion of "mental and moral culture," and to enable and sustain those objects the schools' faculty and students engaged in manual labor for its discipline but mainly for its financial returns, upon which schools depended. Whether in Hawai'i or in the South, tending to "weak tropical races"—Hawaiians, African Americans, and American Indians—required a regime of constant care and thorough saturation. Armstrong's benevolence bequeathed "Negro and Indian education" to the nation in the Hampton Institute and its offspring, Booker T. Washington's Tuskegee Institute and Richard Henry Pratt's Carlisle Indian School. Those gifts, in return, influenced U.S. colonial education in Puerto Rico and the Philippines, and, having proved its success and value among African Americans and American Indians on the continent, the Hampton idea was carried back to the Islands to, in Armstrong's choice words, "make Kauai bloom with enlightened kanakas."

Polynesia's extensive spread, including its implantations in the Atlantic Northeast and Pacific Northwest, was accomplished through its peoples' seafaring skills and the Pacific's natural resources, not through the sole initiative of European peoples and their technologies and strategic interests. By the mid-nineteenth century, Hawaiians were in Tahiti and Peru to the south, in British Columbia and the Aleutian Islands to the north, and across the globe's girth from Mexico to China and along the Atlantic's western ports at Nantucket and New Bedford. They served, in bondage and freedom, as sailors on the open seas, steersmen and swimmers in the ocean's foam churning near land, soldiers and guards along contested frontiers, and shipbuilders, carpenters, farmers, and miners where the opportunities arose. The Hawaiian diaspora was significant in terms of numbers and effects on both Hawaiian society and the receiving places, whether on land or at sea.

Hawaiians were involved in the millions of dollars generated by investors in and builders and outfitters of expeditions in New England and by that region's factories that produced finished goods from whales in the Atlantic and Pacific and cattle hides from Mexico's territories and the Hawaiian kingdom. Lacking the gold and silver of Spain's colonies in America, the Atlantic Northeast relied upon the Pacific Northwest's sea otters and the Pacific's tropical trees, like sandalwood, to supply the currency demanded by the East Asian trade. Hawaiians helped harvest those products for American profiteers at the expense of their ocean's resources and their kingdom's development. And Hawaiian natives participated in U.S. wars against the continent's native peoples and settled among them and became counted as "Indians" out west and "blacks" in the east. A few fought against the British in the War of 1812, and more fought against the Confederacy in the U.S. Civil War. Given the chance to act as men and as "a long enslaved and oppressed people," in the words of Frederick Douglass, the Hawaiian soldier and sailor aided the cause of Union and freedom.

Hawaiʻi's contact with Spanish America—California, Mexico, Chile—brought to the Islands cattle, ranching, and the Mexican cowboy and his clothing, gear, and guitar. Hawaiians indigenized the instrument through tunings, producing *kī hōʻalu* (slack key), and through a refitting that enabled the steel slide sound. Those innovations germinated in the fertile ground of native chanting and falsetto singing as well as from hymns and their melodies introduced by New England missionaries, and they recirculated to the continent during the early twentieth century as "Hawaiian" music to become the most popular variety of music in the United

States. The blends, called *hapa haole,* complemented dreamy images of island paradises, pushed by Hollywood films, Tin Pan Alley lyrics, South Pacific literature, Broadway plays, and the colonizing economic and political objects of Hawaiian planters, shipping companies, the tourist industry, and the Hawaiian government.

Island music, as a tropical temptation, was sensuous and seductive, like the hula dancers who regularly accompanied Hawaiian musical troupes. And it harmonized with the musics of other "tropical races," including Caribbean island peoples, Latina/os, and African Americans.[19] Such influential Hawaiian musicians as Sol Hoʻopiʻi assimilated jazz and the blues in slide guitar renditions, African American blues musicians played the steel guitar on their laps, Hawaiian style, and Hawaiian sheet music was sold as "coon songs" and "oriental coon songs" at the turn of the century. The "all-girl" International Sweethearts of Rhythm capitalized on their exoticism inclusive of African, Asian, Latina, Native American, white, and biracial performers, like the Ali Baba Trio, an African American men's band suggestive of the "Orient."

Perhaps more surprising, because of racializations that attempt the segregation of "white" from "colored" music, is the footing of Hawaiian in country music, most notably in the steel guitar slide sound but also in its role in the professional careers of some of the most important country and cowboy or western music stars—Jimmie Rodgers and Bob Dunn among them. Upon reflection, such amalgamations and crossovers are unremarkable, because artists can be voracious consumers of cultures not their own, producing sounds that defy clear attribution and nomenclature. Musical forms evolve constantly, so boundaries shift and influences flow in multiple directions, like the ocean's currents. Those lessons underscore the permeability of cultural filters and classifications long before our present moment of "global cultures," and they finger the potentially liberating sight of history in worldview.

Whereas islands and continents offer a metageography of landmasses that rise above oceans, Samuel Chapman Armstrong's "weak tropical races" suggest another global metageography—of race, gender, and sexuality—which, like the idea of "world island," began with the ancient Greeks. Aristotle, it seems, conceived of the world as divided by climatic zones and speculated upon their effects on humans. In his schema, the band bordered by the "tropics" of Cancer, north, and Capricorn, south of the equator he called the "torrid zone" because, he claimed, its climate was unfit for human habitation. By contrast, the bands to the north and south of the tropics, which he named the "temperate zone," gave birth to Greek, and indeed human, civilization, allowing it to flourish. The extremities to the north and south of temperate climes, the "frigid zones," were perpetually frozen lands, making life there impossible. Accompanying Aristotle's hypothesis were speculations of monstrous creatures that roamed the tropics and, later, of primitive, uncivilized peoples whose ambitions rose no higher than their monotonous climate, which allegedly narcotized their natures and retarded their intellects. As put by Hippocrates, Greek physician and "father of medicine," "pleasure must be supreme" and "courage, endurance, industry and high spirit could not arise" in mild, uniform climates, "for uniformity engenders slackness, while variation fosters endurance in both body and soul."[20]

Island World offers an alternative to those archaic yet contemporary notions of places and peoples. The book's strategic and fleeting inversion of the representations of island and continent permits new perspectives on old ideas, but it ultimately fails to dismantle their binaries of space, race, gender, and sexuality because it leaves them intact. Instead and in the light of geology, zoogeography, and diaspora, much of the landed distinctions disappear, and although endemism produces differences, migration offers opportunities for mixtures that deny simpleminded discriminations and groupings. The ocean currents carry coral and fish larvae great distances, and migrating humans, with and against oceanic tides, populate the earth's seas and lands in all its climatic zones. Likely originating in the southwest Pacific, those biotic communities converged, in time, upon the Hawaiian chain of islands and seamounts and their waters, and from thence they spread to other oceans and lands.

In the course of those migrations separations occurred, as when Southeast Asians became Polynesians, who later became Hawaiians, and their encounters with Europeans, Asians, American Indians, Mexicans and other Latina/os, and African Americans resulted in hybrid peoples and cultures even as they promoted attempts at segregation. In the Pacific Northwest and West, Hawaiians, island natives, fought against and merged with American Indians, natives of the continent; in the Atlantic

Northeast, Hawaiians inspired a mission and education that homogenized them as colonial subjects with American Indians, Africans, Asians, and Latina/os and distinguished them from "whites." Hawaiian, or Island, music indigenized New England's Christian hymn singing and the Mexican guitar, and it influenced and was affected by musical, racialized traditions on the U.S. continent, notably jazz, the blues, and country.

Islands that move, islands of history, convey a Hawaiian and Polynesian erudition, uniting land with water, humans with other lifeforms, inanimate objects, and the totality of their environments. History's end, accordingly, languishes if limited to accounts of human activity or of landmasses absent the fullness of their pairs. And the violations of artificial borders, whether of geography, kingdom or nation, culture, or the imagination, testify lucidly to both the persistence and porosity of those divides. Although distinctions demand acknowledgment, unions oblige recognition. At those edges that mark meetings and separations, the fringes of earth's plates from whence liquid rock, and some believe life itself, emerges, coheres, and amplifies, creation works its wonders. Even as Kuai-he-lani, the Hawaiian homeland, floated on liquid currents, islands and continents, we now know, and the earth itself, our native home, are in constant motion. And the ceaseless movements and flows across space and time, in historical perspective, alert us to the verity and capaciousness of our island world.

NOTES

INTRODUCTION

1. As recounted in Ben R. Finney, *Hokule'a: The Way to Tahiti* (New York: Dodd, Mead, 1979), 119–25. On stellar navigation and orientation, see David Lewis, *We, the Navigators: The Ancient Art of Landfinding in the Pacific* (Honolulu: University of Hawai'i Press, 1972), 82–191; and Will Kyselka, *An Ocean in Mind* (Honolulu: University of Hawai'i Press, 1987), 36–67.

2. On "moving islands," see Lewis, *We, the Navigators,* 173–79.

3. Edward W. Said, *Culture and Imperialism* (New York: Vintage Books, 1993), 335, 336.

4. On "islands of the mind" as a Western way of bordered thinking, see John Gillis, *Islands of the Mind: How the Human Imagination Created the Atlantic World* (New York: Palgrave Macmillan, 2004).

5. Two exemplary recent books in this regard are Jonathan Kay Kamakawiwo'ole Osorio, *Dismembering Lāhui: A History of the Hawaiian Nation to 1887* (Honolulu: University of Hawai'i Press, 2002); and Noenoe K. Silva, *Aloha Betrayed: Native Hawaiian Resistance to American Colonialism* (Durham, N.C.: Duke University Press, 2004).

6. See, e.g., the Bush regime's *National Security Strategy of the United States of America,* September 2002, www.whitehouse.gov/nsc/nss.html.

7. Gary Y. Okihiro, "Islands of History: Hawai'i and Okinawa," *Okinawan Journal of American Studies* 3 (2006): 1–6.

8. See Gary Y. Okihiro, "Afterword: Toward a Black Pacific," in *AfroAsian Encounters: Culture, History, Politics,* ed. Heike Raphael-Hernandez and Shannon Steen (New York: New York University Press, 2006), 313–30.

9. As in Gary Y. Okihiro, "Toward a Pacific Civilization," in *Transcultural Localisms: Responding to Ethnicity in a Globalized World,* ed. Yiorgos Kalogeras, Eleftheria Ara-

poglou, and Linda Manney (Heidelberg, Germany: Universitätsverlag Winter GmbH Heidelberg, 2006), 15–25.

1. REGIONS OF FIRE

1. Gordon A. Macdonald and Agatin T. Abbott, *Volcanoes in the Sea: The Geology of Hawaii* (Honolulu: University Press of Hawai'i, 1970), 3, 5, 280. Some scientists believe the Hawaiian Ridge extends even farther as part of the Emperor Seamount Chain to the northwest. A much longer chain stretches from the Atlantic to the Pacific, some 40,300 miles. Alan C. Ziegler, *Hawaiian Natural History, Ecology, and Evolution* (Honolulu: University of Hawai'i Press, 2002), 7, 8, 19, 20.

2. Rubellite Kawena Johnson, *Kumulipo: The Hawaiian Hymn of Creation,* vol. 1 (Honolulu: Topgallant Publishing, 1981), 3. See the version by Martha Warren Beckwith, trans. and ed., *The Kumulipo: A Hawaiian Creation Chant* (Honolulu: University of Hawai'i Press, 1972), 58. Readers should note the inadequacy of translations to capture the beauty, nuances, and acuity of the original.

3. Johnson, *Kumulipo,* 18; and Beckwith, *Kumulipo,* 60.

4. Johnson, *Kumulipo,* 12, 13; and Beckwith, *Kumulipo,* 59.

5. Johnson, *Kumulipo,* 12, 13; and Beckwith, *Kumulipo,* 59, 60. On dualisms as oppositions, see Johnson, *Kumulipo,* 27–29.

6. Ziegler, *Hawaiian Natural History,* 135.

7. Ibid., 127, 128–30.

8. Ibid., 130–32.

9. Johnson, *Kumulipo,* 111; and Beckwith, *Kumulipo,* 64.

10. Beckwith, *Kumulipo,* 57, 61–62.

11. Johnson, *Kumulipo,* 109; and Beckwith, *Kumulipo,* 67.

12. Martha W. Beckwith, "Function and Meaning of the Kumulipo Birth Chant in Ancient Hawaii," *Journal of American Folklore* 62, no. 245 (1949): 290–93; and John Charlot, "A Pattern in Three Hawaiian Chants," *Journal of American Folklore* 96, no. 379 (1983): 64–68.

13. Johnson, *Kumulipo,* 26.

14. Ziegler, *Hawaiian Natural History,* 128, 145–46.

15. Ibid., 157–66.

16. H. W. Menard, *Islands* (New York: Scientific American Books, 1986), 1. On islands as scientific laboratories, see Menard, *Islands;* Robert H. MacArthur and Edward O. Wilson, *The Theory of Island Biogeography* (Princeton, N.J.: Princeton University Press, 1967); and Edward J. Larson, *Evolution's Workshop: God and Science in the Galapagos Islands* (New York: Basic Books, 2001).

17. Gordon A. Macdonald, *Volcanoes* (Englewood Cliffs, N.J.: Prentice-Hall, 1972), 351.

18. H. W. Menard, *Marine Geology of the Pacific* (New York: McGraw-Hill, 1964), 55, 57, 87–89, 95; and Macdonald, *Volcanoes,* 346.

19. Macdonald, *Volcanoes,* 344–45; and Alwyn Scarth, *Volcanoes: An Introduction* (College Station: Texas A&M University Press, 1994), 14–16.

20. Scarth, *Volcanoes,* 16–17. For an account by those who were instrumental in the development of the theory of plate tectonics, see Naomi Oreskes, ed., *Plate Tectonics: An Insider's History of the Modern Theory of the Earth* (Boulder, Colo.: Westview Press, 2003).

21. Scarth, *Volcanoes,* 17–19; and Thomas A. Jaggar, *My Experiments with Volcanoes* (Honolulu: Hawaiian Volcano Research Association, 1956), 116–17, 177.

22. Ziegler, *Hawaiian Natural History,* 11, 13, 14, 18–21.

23. Jaggar, *My Experiments,* 186. Some scientists have speculated that life on earth began in the dark and protective recesses of the deep seas around the "black smokers," plumes of hot, mineral-rich water pushing through vents along mid-ocean ridges. Peter Francis, *Volcanoes: A Planetary Perspective* (Oxford: Clarendon Press, 1993), 333–34.

24. Adrienne L. Kaeppler, "Music in Hawaii in the Nineteenth Century," in *Musikkulturen Asiens, Afrikas und Ozeaniens,* ed. Robert Günther (Germany: Gustav Bosse Verlag Regensburg, 1973), 311, 312.

25. Helen H. Roberts, *Ancient Hawaiian Music,* Bernice P. Bishop Museum Bulletin 29 (Honolulu: Bishop Museum Press, 1926), 57–69; Lorrin Andrews, "Remarks on Hawaiian Poetry," *Islander* 1, no. 7 (1875): 26–27; and Theodore Kelsey, "Unknown Poetry of Hawaii," *Paradise of the Pacific* 53, no. 6 (1941): 26–28, 31.

26. Kaeppler, "Music in Hawaii," 315.

27. Katherine Luomala, "Foreword" to Beckwith, *Kumulipo,* xi, xiii; and Johnson, *Kumulipo,* 26. See also Valerio Valeri, *Kingship and Sacrifice: Ritual and Society in Ancient Hawaii* (Chicago: University of Chicago Press, 1985), 4.

28. On January 6, 1895, a band of loyalists instigated an armed revolt to restore the de-

posed monarch, Lili'uokalani. The attempt failed dismally but the January uprising was celebrated in poetry collected and published that year in *Buke Mele Lahui,* which forms the basis of a provocative study by Amy K. Stillman, "History Reinterpreted in Song: The Case of the Hawaiian Counterrevolution," *Hawaiian Journal of History* 23 (1989): 1–30.

29. Beckwith, *Kumulipo,* 1–2, 35–36; Katherine Luomala, review of *The Kumulipo: A Hawaiian Creation Chant,* trans. and ed. Martha Warren Beckwith, *Journal of American Folklore* 64, no. 254 (1951): 429–30, 432; and Katherine Luomala, "Survey of Research on Polynesian Prose and Poetry," *Journal of American Folklore* 74, no. 294 (1961): 431, 435.

30. Samuel M. Kamakau, *Ruling Chiefs of Hawaii* (Honolulu: Kamehameha Schools Press, 1992), 241; and Beckwith, *Kumulipo,* 35–36.

31. I am indebted to Davianna Pomaka'i McGregor for this amazingly beautiful insight. See also Silva, *Aloha Betrayed,* 97–104, on the Kumulipo as resistance.

32. Kaeppler, "Music in Hawaii," 319–22; John R. Kaha'i Topolinski, "Musical Diggings: Na Mele Ohana (Family Songs)," *Ha'Ilono Mele* 2, no. 1 (1976): 3–6; "Musical Diggings: The Sumner Family: A Legacy of Family Mele and Chants," *Ha'Ilono Mele* 2, no. 2 (1976): 2–6; and "Musical Diggings: The Sumner Family," *Ha'Ilono Mele* 2, no. 3 (1976): 3–7.

33. The other patron of the hula was Laka, who, like Hi'iaka, was a forest deity and associated with the maile vine and lehua tree and blossom. Pualani Kanaka'ole Kanahele and Duke Kalani Wise, *Ka Honua Ola* [The Living Earth] (Honolulu: Center for Hawaiian Studies, University of Hawai'i, Mānoa, n.d.), 74; Shirley Garcia, "For the Life of the Land: Hula and Hawaii's Native Forests," in *Hawai'i: New Geographies,* ed. D. W. Woodcock (Honolulu: Department of Geography, University of Hawai'i, Mānoa, 1999), 2–3; and Nathaniel B. Emerson, *Unwritten Literature of Hawaii: The Sacred Songs of the Hula* (Honolulu: Mutual Publishing, 1998), 23–25.

34. On the complexities of the chant's language and imagery, see Kanahele and Wise, *Ka Honua Ola,* 65–73.

35. Ibid., 65–73; Pualani Kanaka'ole Kanahele and Davianna Pomaika'i McGregor, "Pele Beliefs, Customs, Practices," unpublished manuscript, Hawai'i Geothermal Project, August 1995, 8–9, 40–42; Nathaniel B. Emerson, *Pele and Hiiaka: A Myth from Hawaii* (Honolulu: Honolulu Star-Bulletin, 1915), 1–2, 162–63; and Martha Beckwith, *Hawaiian Mythology* (Honolulu: University Press of Hawai'i, 1970), 181.

36. Kanahele and Wise, *Ka Honua Ola,* 73.

37. For a review of the Pele literature, see H. Arlo Nimmo, *The Pele Literature: An Annotated Bibliography of the English-Language Literature on Pele, Volcano Goddess of Hawaiʻi,* Bishop Museum Bulletin in Anthropology 4 (Honolulu: Bishop Museum Press, 1992).

38. Kanahele and Wise, *Ka Honua Ola,* 6–8, 17–28; Beckwith, *Hawaiian Mythology,* 168–69, 179; and Nimmo, *Pele Literature,* 2.

39. Emerson, *Pele and Hiiaka,* ix; and K. R. Howe, *Where the Waves Fall: A New South Sea Islands History from First Settlement to Colonial Rule* (Honolulu: University of Hawaiʻi Press, 1984), 16–18.

40. Emerson, *Pele and Hiiaka,* xi. For variations on the migration story, see Beckwith, *Hawaiian Mythology,* 169–73.

41. Emerson, *Pele and Hiiaka,* xv–xvi, 25; and Kanahele and McGregor, "Pele Beliefs, Customs, Practices," 21–34.

42. Emerson, *Pele and Hiiaka,* xvi.

43. See, e.g., Samuel Manaiakalani Kamakau, *Ka Poʻe Kahiko: The People of Old,* trans. Mary Kawena Pukui and ed. Dorothy B. Barrère (Honolulu: Bishop Museum Press, 1964), 49–51.

44. Emerson, *Pele and Hiiaka,* v.

45. Ibid., 239, 240.

46. W. D. Westervelt, *Myths and Legends of Hawaii,* ed. A. Grove Day (Honolulu: Mutual Publishing, 1987), 37.

47. William Ellis, *Journal of William Ellis: Narrative of a Tour of Hawaii, or Owhyhee; with Remarks on the History, Traditions, Manners, Customs and Language of the Inhabitants of the Sandwich Islands* (1827; reprint, Honolulu: Advertiser Publishing, 1963), 64, 66.

48. Ibid., 76, 77.

49. Ibid., 117.

50. Mary K. Pukui and Alfons L. Korn, trans. and eds., *The Echo of Our Song: Chants & Poems of the Hawaiians* (Honolulu: University of Hawaiʻi Press, 1973), 52–56.

51. Ellis, *Journal,* 76–120. See also Mark Twain, *Roughing It* (Berkeley: University of California Press, 1993), 473.

52. See the story of Kapiʻolani's "defiance" of Pele in Pamela Frierson, *The Burning Island: A Journey through Myth and History in Volcano Country, Hawaiʻi* (San Francisco: Sierra Club Books, 1991), 117–31.

53. Ellis, *Journal,* 141, 148, 150, 152, 163, 164.

54. Ibid., 164, 165.

55. Ibid., 165–66. On Christianity, volcanoes, and the underworld, see Richard V. Fisher, Grant Heiken, and Jeffrey B. Hulen, *Volcanoes: Crucibles of Change* (Princeton, N.J.: Princeton University Press, 1997), 187, 191–94.

56. Ellis, *Journal,* 166–67.

57. Charles Wilkes, *Narrative of the U.S. Exploring Expedition during the Years 1838–1842,* vol. 4 (Philadelphia: Lee and Blanchard, 1845).

58. Julie Link Haifley, *Titian Ramsay Peale, 1799–1885* (Washington, D.C.: George Washington University, 1981), 13.

59. David C. Ward, *Charles Willson Peale: Art and Selfhood in the Early Republic* (Berkeley: University of California Press, 2004), xviii.

60. Frierson, *Burning Island,* 94.

61. Ibid., 85–92; and David W. Forbes, *Encounters with Paradise: Views of Hawaii and Its People, 1778–1941* (Honolulu: Honolulu Academy of Arts, 1992), 172–99. On anthropology's analogous genderings, see Frierson, *Burning Island,* 133–44.

62. Isabella L. Bird, *Six Months in the Sandwich Islands among Hawai'i's Palm Groves, Coral Reefs, and Volcanoes* (1881; reprint, Honolulu: Mutual Publishing, 1998), v.

63. Frierson, *Burning Island,* 97.

64. Bird, *Six Months,* 50–51.

65. Ibid., 54, 55.

66. Ibid., 57. For a description of the Volcano House Register and some of its contents, see Darcy Bevens, ed., *On the Rim of Kilauea: Excerpts from the Volcano House Register, 1865–1955* (Hawai'i National Park: Hawai'i Natural History Association, 1992).

67. On Twain's mixed estimation of missionaries, see David Zmijewski, "Mark Twain's Dual Visions of Hawai'i: Censoring the Creative Self," *Hawaiian Journal of History* 38 (2004): 112–17.

68. Bevens, *On the Rim,* 160–61. See also, Frierson, *Burning Island,* 98.

69. Bevens, *On the Rim,* 133, 134.

70. For a discussion of a "Volcano School" of painting, or "Little Hawaiian Renaissance," see Forbes, *Encounters with Paradise,* 174, 178.

71. On Dampier and his important Hawaiian portraits, see ibid., 78–83.

72. As cited in Peter C. Marzio, *The Democratic Art: Pictures for 19th-Century America* (Boston: David R. Godine, 1979), 48; and C. F. Gordon Cumming, *Fire Fountains: The Kingdom of Hawaii, Its Volcanoes, and the History of Its Missions* (Edinburgh: W. Blackwood, 1883). See also David W. Forbes and Thomas K. Kunichika, *Hilo, 1825–1925: A Century of Paintings and Drawings* (Hilo, Hawai'i: Lyman House Memorial Museum, 1983), 13.

73. Joseph Theroux, "Volcano Painter: Pioneer Artist Charles Furneaux Built on Success," *Hawaii Magazine* 9, no. 5 (1992): 71.

74. Forbes and Kunichika, *Hilo*, 13, 16; Theroux, "Volcano Painter," 72; Forbes, *Encounters with Paradise*, 174–77, 184–87; and William T. Brigham, *The Volcanoes of Kilauea and Mauna Loa on the Island of Hawaii*, Memoirs of the Bernice Pauahi Bishop Museum, vol. 2, no. 4 (Honolulu: Bishop Museum Press, 1909), 134.

75. Brigham, *Volcanoes*, 167, 178. For more on the limitations of photography to capture the sublime, see ibid., 134, 155.

76. Forbes and Kunichika, *Hilo*, 16; and Theroux, "Volcano Painter," 73.

77. Theroux, "Volcano Painter," 74. On the "Hawaiian" League, its origins, purposes, and membership, see Ralph S. Kuykendall, *The Hawaiian Kingdom*, vol. 3: *The Kalakaua Dynasty, 1874–1893* (Honolulu: University of Hawai'i Press, 1967), 347–50. Cf. Jonathan Kay Kamakawiwo'ole Osorio, *Dismembering Lāhui: A History of the Hawaiian Nation to 1887* (Honolulu: University of Hawai'i Press, 2002), 235–38.

78. Theroux, "Volcano Painter," 75.

79. Forbes and Kunichika, *Hilo*, 16–17; Forbes, *Encounters with Paradise*, 178–82, 190–98; and Frierson, *Burning Island*, 102.

80. *Pacific Commercial Advertiser*, January 31, 1885.

81. As quoted in Hitchcock's biography written by his daughter, Helen Hitchcock Maxon, *D. Howard Hitchcock: Islander* (Honolulu: Topgallant Publishing, 1987), 22. See also *Hawaiian Gazette*, October 2, 1888, on the early and close relationship between Tavernier and D. Howard Hitchcock.

82. Theodore E. Stebbins Jr., *American Master Drawings and Watercolors: A History of Works on Paper from Colonial Times to the Present* (New York: Harper and Row, 1976), 237; and Forbes, *Encounters with Paradise*, 201, 218–20. See also Henry Adams et al., *John La Farge* (New York: Abbeville Press, 1987); and Forbes and Kunichika, *Hilo*, 18–19.

83. John La Farge, *Reminiscences of the South Seas* (Garden City, N.Y.: Doubleday, Page, 1916), 49, 52.

84. *Report of the Hawaiian Volcano Observatory of the Massachusetts Institute of Technology and the Hawaiian Volcano Research Association, January–March 1912* (Boston: Society of Arts of the Massachusetts Institute of Technology, 1912), 6–16; Jaggar, *My Experiments,* 77–78, 86, 89; Macdonald, *Volcanoes,* 38–39; and T. A. Jaggar, *Volcanoes Declare War: Logistics and Strategy of Pacific Volcano Science* (Honolulu: Paradise of the Pacific, 1945), 16.

85. Jaggar, *Volcanoes Declare War,* i, ii. For an assessment of the textual war on Pele, see Houston Wood, *Displacing Natives: The Rhetorical Production of Hawai'i* (Lanham, Md.: Rowman and Littlefield, 1999), 63–84.

86. Jaggar, *Volcanoes Declare War,* 14–15, 16.

87. David Alapa'i, *Nani Wale nō'o Pele i ka Lua,* in *Nā Mele Welo: Songs of Our Heritage,* trans. Mary Kawena Pukui (Honolulu: Bishop Museum Press, 1995), 108, 109.

88. As quoted in Herb Kawainui Kane, *Pele: Goddess of Hawai'i's Volcanoes* (Captain Cook, Hawai'i: Kawainui Press, 1987), 7.

89. As quoted in Frierson, *Burning Island,* 216. On the Pele Defense Fund, see Davianna Pomaika'i McGregor, "Pele vs. Geothermal: A Clash of Cultures," in *Bearing Dreams, Shaping Visions: Asian Pacific American Perspectives,* ed. Linda A. Revilla et al. (Pullman: Washington State University Press, 1993), 45–60; Kanahele and McGregor, "Pele Beliefs, Customs, Practices," 11–12, 66–72; Frierson, *Burning Island,* 214–30; and Elizabeth Buck, *Paradise Remade: The Politics of Culture and History in Hawai'i* (Philadelphia: Temple University Press, 1993), 186–88. On the fund's legal challenges and its connections with Native Americans on the continental United States, see Frierson, *Burning Island,* 219–21.

90. As quoted in McGregor, "Pele vs. Geothermal," 48.

91. Ibid., 54, 55.

2. OCEANIA'S EXPANSE

1. Nathaniel B. Emerson, *Pele and Hiiaka: A Myth from Hawaii* (Honolulu: Honolulu Star-Bulletin, 1915), ix–x, xiv–xv; Martha Beckwith, *Hawaiian Mythology* (Honolulu: University Press of Hawai'i, 1970), 170; and Pualani Kanakaole Kanahele and Davianna Pomaika'i McGregor, "Pele Beliefs, Customs, Practices," unpublished manuscript, Hawai'i Geothermal Project, August 1995, 21–34.

2. Karl F. Lagler et al., *Ichthyology,* 2d ed. (New York: John Wiley and Sons, 1977), 2.

3. Beckwith, *Hawaiian Mythology,* 308, 309.

4. Alan C. Ziegler, *Hawaiian Natural History, Ecology, and Evolution* (Honolulu: University of Hawai'i Press, 2002), 308–9.

5. See the comprehensive, three-volume *Canoes of Oceania* by A. C. Haddon and James Hornell: *The Canoes of Polynesia, Fiji, and Micronesia,* vol. 1, Special Publication 27 (Honolulu: Bishop Museum, 1936); *The Canoes of Melanesia, Queensland, and New Guinea,* vol. 2, Special Publication 28 (Honolulu: Bishop Museum, 1937); and *Definition of Terms, General Survey, and Conclusions,* vol. 3, Special Publication 29 (Honolulu: Bishop Museum, 1938).

6. As quoted in Ben Finney, *Sailing in the Wake of the Ancestors: Reviving Polynesian Voyaging* (Honolulu: Bishop Museum Press, 2003), 137.

7. This was debated in Andrew Sharp, *Ancient Voyagers in Polynesia* (Sydney, Australia: Angus and Robertson, 1963); Jack Golson, ed., *Polynesian Navigation: A Symposium on Andrew Sharp's Theory of Accidental Voyages,* Polynesian Society Memoir, No. 34 (Wellington, New Zealand: Polynesian Society, 1963); and David Lewis, *We, the Navigators: The Ancient Art of Landfinding in the Pacific* (Honolulu: University of Hawai'i Press, 1972).

8. Myron "Pinky" Thompson, president of the Polynesian Voyaging Society, as quoted in Finney, *Sailing in the Wake,* 133. See also Ben R. Finney, "Voyagers into Ocean Space," in *Interstellar Migration and the Human Experience,* ed. Ben R. Finney and Eric M. Jones (Berkeley: University of California Press, 1985), 164–79.

9. For an account of Polynesian celestial navigation and the discovery voyage of the *Hōkūle'a,* see Ben R. Finney, *Hokule'a: The Way to Tahiti* (New York: Dodd, Mead, 1979); and Will Kyselka, *An Ocean in Mind* (Honolulu: University of Hawai'i Press, 1987).

10. Ben R. Finney, "New, Non-Armchair Research," in *Pacific Navigation and Voyaging,* comp. Ben R. Finney, Polynesian Society Memoir No. 39 (Wellington, New Zealand: Polynesian Society, 1976), 9.

11. Albert Wendt, "Towards a New Oceania," *Mana* 1, no. 1 (1976): 49–60; and Epeli Hau'ofa, "Our Sea of Islands," *Contemporary Pacific* 6, no. 1 (1994): 153–54.

12. Hau'ofa, "Our Sea," 160. See also O. H. K. Spate, *The Spanish Lake* (Minneapolis: University of Minnesota Press, 1979), 211.

13. Ben Finney and James D. Houston, *Surfing: A History of the Ancient Hawaiian Sport* (Rohnert Park, Calif.: Pomegranate Artbooks, 1996), 13. An earlier version of this book is Ben R. Finney and James D. Houston, *Surfing: The Sport of Hawaiian Kings* (Rutland, Vt.: Charles E. Tuttle, 1966). All references in this book are to the 1996 edition.

14. Mary K. Pukui and Alfons L. Korn, trans. and eds., *The Echo of Our Song: Chants & Poems of the Hawaiians* (Honolulu: University of Hawai'i Press, 1973), 36–41. See also Finney and Houston, *Surfing,* 40–41.

15. Charles Samuel Stewart, *A Residence in the Sandwich Islands* (Boston: Weeks, Jordan, 1839), 196.

16. Rubellite Kawena Johnson, *Kumulipo: The Hawaiian Hymn of Creation,* vol. 1 (Honolulu: Topgallant Publishing, 1981), 21.

17. Finney and Houston, *Surfing,* 47–49.

18. William Ellis, *Polynesian Researches during a Residence of Nearly Eight Years in the Society and Sandwich Islands,* vol. 4 (London: Fisher, Son and Jackson, 1853), 369.

19. Ibid., 371.

20. Ibid., 369, 370, 372.

21. Finney and Houston, *Surfing,* 27–40, 94–96; and Mary Kawena Pukui, Samuel H. Elbert, and Esther T. Mookini, *Place Names of Hawaii* (Honolulu: University of Hawai'i Press, 1974).

22. As cited in Finney and Houston, *Surfing,* 33.

23. On the possibility of earlier Spanish arrivals in Hawai'i, see Donald Cutter, "The Spanish in Hawaii: Gaytan to Marin," *Hawaiian Journal of History* 14 (1980): 16–17.

24. J. C. Beaglehole, ed., *The Voyage of the Resolution and the Discovery, 1776–1780,* part 1 (Cambridge: Cambridge University Press, 1967), 268.

25. A. Grove Day, "Foreword" to Mark Twain, *Roughing It in the Sandwich Islands* (Honolulu: Mutual Publishing, 1990), xx–xxi; Mark Twain, *Roughing It* (Berkeley: University of California Press, 1993), 501. See also Alex. Stevenson Twombly, *Kelea: The Surf-Rider, A Romance of Pagan Hawaii* (New York: Fords, Howard, and Hulbert, 1900), an early novel involving surfing, romance, war, and the volcano, or, in the author's words, "the Hawaiian savage at his best" (401).

26. Finney and Houston, *Surfing,* 81. On Kahanamoku, see Michael Nevin Willard, "Duke Kahanamoku's Body: Biography of Hawai'i," in *Sports Matters: Race, Recreation, and Culture,* ed. John Bloom and Michael Nevin Willard (New York: New York University Press, 2002), 13–38.

27. Jack London, "A Royal Sport: Surfing at Waikiki," *A Woman's Home Companion,* October 1907, republished in Jack London, *The Cruise of the Snark* (New York: Macmillan, 1911), 75–76.

28. London, *Cruise of the Snark,* 77.

29. On London and his redemption, through surfing, of his racialized and gendered self, see Willard, "Duke Kahanamoku's Body," 14–19; on surfing and interracial romance, see Jane C. Desmond, *Staging Tourism: Bodies on Display from Waikiki to Sea World* (Chicago: University of Chicago Press, 1999), 122–30.

30. Duke Paoa [Kahanamoku], "Riding the Surfboard," *Mid-Pacific Magazine* 1, no. 1 (1911): 3.

31. Kahanamoku, as a "world champion athlete," went on to endorse Pan Handle Scrap chewing tobacco, Wilbur chocolates, Sport Kings chewing gum, and Valspar varnish. Mark Blackburn, *Hula Girls & Surfer Boys* (Atglen, Pa.: Schiffer, 2000), 59, 76; and Nancy N. Schiffer, *Surfing* (Atglen, Pa.: Schiffer, 1998), 122.

32. Finney and Houston, *Surfing,* 82, 84; and Schiffer, *Surfing,* 53–109.

33. Finney and Houston, *Surfing,* 65.

34. Hi Sibley, "Better Ways to Build Surf Boards," *Popular Science Monthly,* August 1935, 56.

35. Finney and Houston, *Surfing,* 65–70; and Schiffer, *Surfing,* 55–79.

36. Finney and Houston, *Surfing,* 85–86, 89–90.

37. On population figures and the debate over numbers, see Gary Y. Okihiro, *The Columbia Guide to Asian American History* (New York: Columbia University Press, 2001), 45–55.

38. Chris Bongie, *Exotic Memories: Literature, Colonialism, and the Fin de Siècle* (Stanford, Calif.: Stanford University Press, 1991), 4–5, 10, calls these impulses "imperialist exoticism," which affirms the hegemony of modernity and civilization over savagery, and "exoticizing exoticism," in which colonies offer refuges from a dehumanizing modernity.

39. William Samuel W. Ruschenberger, *Narrative of a Voyage Round the World,* vol. 2 (London: Richard Bentley, 1838), 373.

40. Hiram Bingham, *A Residence of Twenty-one Years in the Sandwich Islands* (New York: Converse, 1847), 136–37.

41. Finney and Houston, *Surfing,* 50–57.

42. Ibid., 51–57.

43. For an interpretation on how representations shaped Hawai'i's tourist industry, see Desmond, *Staging Tourism.*

44. Van Norden, "Hawaii for the White Man," *Mid-Pacific Magazine* 1, no. 6 (1911): 629, 634.

45. Frederic J. Haskin, "The White Man in the Tropics," *Mid-Pacific Magazine* 20, no. 1 (1920): 17–19. For more on this subject of white acclimatization in the tropics, see the forthcoming second volume of this trilogy.

46. "The Lure of Hawaii," *Mid-Pacific Magazine* 22, no. 5 (1921): 409, 411, 415.

47. *Paradise of the Pacific* 1, no. 1 (1888): 1.

48. *Paradise of the Pacific* 1, no. 2 (1888): 6.

49. Isabella L. Bird, *Six Months in the Sandwich Islands among Hawai'i's Palm Groves, Coral Reefs, and Volcanoes* (1881; reprint, Honolulu: Mutual Publishing, 1998), v.

50. Jonathan Kay Kamakawiwoʻole Osorio, *Dismembering Lāhui: A History of the Hawaiian Nation to 1887* (Honolulu: University of Hawaiʻi Press, 2002), 235–37, 240.

51. *Paradise of the Pacific* 3, no. 10 (1890): 1.

52. As quoted in A. Grove Day, *Mad about Islands: Novelists of a Vanished Pacific* (Honolulu: Mutual Publishing, 1987), 107.

53. Charles Warren Stoddard, "Halcyon Hawaii," *Paradise of the Pacific* 2, no. 12 (1889): 2, 3.

54. Robert C. Schmitt, *Hawaiʻi in the Movies, 1898–1959* (Honolulu: Hawaiian Historical Society, 1988), vi, 1, 4, 14, 17, 19. See also Robert C. Schmitt, "South Seas Movies, 1913–1943," *Hawaii Historical Review* 2, no. 11 (1968): 433–52.

55. See, e.g., the Edison Company's 1906 documentary, filmed by Robert K. Bonine, that includes scenes of Honolulu, Waikīkī, sugar plantations, and railroads and streetcars; Schmitt, *Hawaii in the Movies*, 19; James Baldwin, *Our New Possessions: Cuba, Puerto Rico, Hawaii, Philippines* (New York: American Book Company, 1899); and Murat Halstead, *Our New Possessions: Natural Riches, Industrial Resources of Cuba, Porto Rico, Hawaii, the Ladrones, and the Philippine Islands* (Chicago: Dominion, 1898).

56. Luis I. Reyes, *Made in Paradise: Hollywood's Films of Hawaiʻi and the South Seas* (Honolulu: Mutual Publishing, 1995), xxv–xxvi.

57. For a theoretical consideration of women as islands, see Judith Williamson, "Woman Is an Island: Femininity and Colonization," in *Studies in Entertainment: Critical Approaches to Mass Culture,* ed. Tania Modleski (Bloomington: Indiana University Press, 1986), 99–118.

58. For a distinction of brown and black women in white representations, see Desmond, *Staging Tourism,* 60–97.

59. Schmitt, *Hawai'i in the Movies,* 12, 13, 19–21, 36–37; and Reyes, *Made in Paradise,* 40–41, 44–45. *Bird of Paradise* would fly again in the 1951 remake by producer Darryl F. Zanuck, starring Debra Paget in the role originally played by Dolores del Rio.

60. Gary D. Keller, *A Biographical Handbook of Hispanics and United States Film* (Tempe, Ariz.: Bilingual Press, 1997), 43–44.

61. Schmitt, *Hawai'i in the Movies,* 13; and Keller, *Biographical Handbook,* 122–23, 200.

62. Schmitt, *Hawai'i in the Movies,* 33, 50; Keller, *Biographical Handbook,* 209; and Reyes, *Made in Paradise,* 56.

63. As quoted in Reyes, *Made in Paradise,* xxvii, 57.

64. Ibid., xxiv, 47–48.

65. Ibid., 38, 39.

66. *Rudyard Kipling's Verse* (New York: Doubleday, Doran, 1940), 233–36, 321–23.

67. Schmitt, *Hawai'i in the Movies,* 41; and Reyes, *Made in Paradise,* 49–50. Latino actor Anthony Quinn played a Hawaiian named Kimo in *Waikiki Wedding.*

3. PAGAN PRIEST

1. *Boston Recorder,* October 23 and 30, 1819, 175, 179.

2. "Memoirs of Thomas Hopoo," *Hawaiian Journal of History* 2 (1968): 42–54.

3. E. W. Dwight, *Memoir of Henry Obookiah, a Native of the Sandwich Islands, Who Died at Cornwall, Connecticut, February 17, 1818, Aged 26* (New York: American Tract Society, 1818), 16.

4. "Memoirs of Thomas Hopoo," 42–44.

5. Ibid., 44. Cf. *A Narrative of Five Youth from the Sandwich Islands, Now Receiving an Education in This Country* (New York: J. Seymour, 1816), 18, which claims that Hopu fell overboard "near the Cape of Good Hope."

6. Dwight, *Memoir,* 17–18.

7. "Memoirs of Thomas Hopoo," 45.

8. Ibid., 46.

9. Ibid., 47.

10. Susan N. Bell, "Owhyhee's Prodigal," *Hawaiian Journal of History* 10 (1976): 28; and *Narrative of Five Youth,* 25.

11. Dwight, *Memoir,* 7, 9–10, 11.

12. Gardiner Spring, *Memoirs of the Rev. Samuel J. Mills* (New York: New York Evangelical Missionary Society, 1820), 48.

13. *Narrative of Five Youth,* 19.

14. Ibid., 12.

15. Dwight, *Memoir,* 92. For an assessment of ʻŌpūkahaʻia and his memoirs, see Jeffrey K. Lyons, "Memoirs of Henry Obookiah: A Rhetorical History," *Hawaiian Journal of History* 38 (2004): 35–57.

16. On the "whitening" of Hawaiians generally, or creation of the "ideal" native, see Jane C. Desmond, *Staging Tourism: Bodies on Display from Waikiki to Sea World* (Chicago: University of Chicago Press, 1999), 34–59.

17. Dwight, *Memoir,* 98–99.

18. Ibid., 115, 119.

19. Otto G. Reuman, "The Influence of One Man—Henry Obookiah" (Cornwall: First Church of Christ, 1968), in folder "Material on Obookiah Ceremony," Archives, Cornwall Historical Society, Cornwall, Connecticut.

20. This sermon by Lyman Beecher delivered at the funeral of ʻŌpūkahaʻia on February 18, 1818, is appended to *Memoirs of Henry Obookiah, a Native of Owhyhee, and a Member of the Foreign Mission School; Who Died at Cornwall, Conn., Feb. 17, 1818, Aged 26 Years* (Elizabeth-Town, N.J.: Edson Hart, 1819), 27, 28, 32. For an example of the use of ʻŌpūkahaʻiaʻs death to raise contributions for the mission work in Hawaiʻi, see American Board of Commissioners for Foreign Missions, *Mission to the Sandwich Islands* (Boston: U. Crocker, 1819), a pamphlet published by the American Board's Prudential Committee.

21. Samuel Eliot Morison, "Boston Traders in the Hawaiian Islands, 1789–1823," *Proceedings of the Massachusetts Historical Society* 54 (October 1920): 11.

22. *Memoirs of Henry Obookiah* (1819), 10–14.

23. *Narrative of Five Youth,* 30, 31, 33, 34, 37.

24. Kaumualiʻi, George's father, was a king of the island of Kauaʻi when the boy left Hawaiʻi but was a tributary chief to Kamehameha II, who ruled all the Islands when George returned in 1820.

25. As quoted in Catherine Stauder, "George, Prince of Hawaii," *Hawaiian Journal of History* 6 (1972): 31. For skepticism over this claim to service in the War of 1812, see ibid., 28–44.

26. Letter from Kaumualiʻi to his father dated October 19, 1816, published in the *Recorder,* November 26, 1816, in which he claims, "I was neglected very much by the man you sent me with." As quoted in Stauder, "George, Prince of Hawaii," 33.

27. Quoted in ibid., 36.

28. Ibid., 38.

29. *Narrative of Five Youth,* 41, 42, 43, 44. The relations between civilization and Christianity were debated and negotiated both among missionaries and between missionaries and their objects of conversion. See Paul William Harris, *Nothing but Christ: Rufus Anderson and the Ideology of Protestant Foreign Missions* (New York: Oxford University Press, 1999).

30. *Memoirs of Henry Obookiah* (1819), 9.

31. *Foreign Mission School* 19 (June 1825), Archives, Cornwall Historical Society. See also the student lists in folder "Foreign Mission School," Archives, Cornwall Historical Society. For a detailed consideration of Chinese at the Foreign Mission School, see Karen Sánchez-Eppler, "Copying and Conversion: An 1824 Friendship Album 'from a Chinese Youth,'" *American Quarterly* 59, no. 2 (2007): 301–39.

32. Commonplace book belonging to Cherry Stone, August 25, 1824–September 6, 1826, in folder "Foreign Mission School," Archives, Cornwall Historical Society.

33. Ibid.

34. *The Missionary Spelling Book, and Reader. Prepared at the Foreign Mission School, Cornwall, Conn. and Designed Especially for Its Use* (Hartford: George Goodwin and Sons, 1822).

35. Ibid., 13, 18.

36. Paul H. Chamberlain Jr., *The Foreign Mission School* (Cornwall, Conn.: Cornwall Historical Society, 1968), 1.

37. As quoted in Ralph Henry Gabriel, *Elias Boudinot: Cherokee & His America* (Norman: University of Oklahoma Press, 1941), 61.

38. Quoted in Chamberlain, *Foreign Mission School,* 15. See also Gabriel, *Elias Boudinot,* 62–64.

39. For more information on the Ridge and Boudinot families, see Edward Everett Dale and Gaston Little, *Cherokee Cavaliers: Forty Years of Cherokee History as Told in the Correspondence of the Ridge-Watie-Boudinot Family* (Norman: University of Oklahoma Press, 1939).

40. Mary Brinsmade Church, "Elias Boudinot: An Account of His Life Written by His

Granddaughter," unpublished paper of the Woman's Club, Washington, Connecticut, October 1, 1913, 6–7.

41. On the Gold-Boudinot marriage, see Chamberlain, *Foreign Mission School,* 7, 9, 15–19; and Gabriel, *Elias Boudinot,* 66–92.

42. Letter published in *Foreign Mission School* 19 (June 1825).

43. Chamberlain, *Foreign Mission School,* 20. See Clifton Jackson Phillips, *Protestant America and the Pagan World: The First Half Century of the American Board of Commissioners for Foreign Missions, 1810–1860* (Cambridge, Mass.: Harvard University East Asian Research Center, 1968), 67–68, for disagreement in the board over the question of miscegenation.

44. On Rufus Anderson, see Harris, *Nothing but Christ;* on the Brethren, see Phillips, *Protestant America,* 23–28. It is noteworthy that Asa Thurston and Hiram Bingham of the first mission to Hawai'i were both graduates of Andover and members of the Brethren. Phillips, *Protestant America,* 93.

45. Harris, *Nothing but Christ,* 25–26. See also Phillips, *Protestant America,* 20–22.

46. Spring, *Memoirs,* 50.

47. "On Educating Heathen Youth in Our Own Country," *Panoplist and Missionary Magazine,* July 1816, 297–302, and August 1816, 356–62. See also October 1816, 453; February 1817, 77–80; April 1818, 190–92; and November 1819, 526–28.

48. John Jay and Alexander Hamilton organized in 1785 in New York City the African Free Schools, run by the New York Manumission Society, for free blacks. Lamin Sanneh, *Abolitionists Abroad: American Blacks and the Making of Modern West Africa* (Cambridge, Mass.: Harvard University Press, 1999), 190.

49. Spring, *Memoirs,* 129.

50. P. J. Staudenraus, *The African Colonization Movement, 1816–1865* (New York: Columbia University Press, 1961), 18.

51. Spring, *Memoirs,* 139.

52. Phillips, *Protestant America,* 3.

53. For the connections between the "two Englands," see Phillips, *Protestant America,* 12–17; and Joan Jacobs Brumberg, *Mission for Life: The Story of the Family of Adoniram Judson . . .* (New York: Free Press, 1980), 25–26.

54. As quoted in Phillips, *Protestant America,* 16.

55. Ibid., 18; and Staudenraus, *African Colonization Movement,* 4–5.

56. Phillips, *Protestant America,* 22.

57. Patricia Grimshaw, *Paths of Duty: American Missionary Wives in Nineteenth-Century Hawaii* (Honolulu: University of Hawai'i Press, 1989), xi–xvi, 1–23.

58. See, e.g., the popular tract by James D. Knowles, *Memoir of Mrs. Ann H. Judson* (London: Littlewood and Co., 1829).

59. Brumberg, *Mission for Life,* 28, 79–106.

60. Thomas Jefferson, *Notes on the State of Virginia,* ed. William Peden (Chapel Hill: University of North Carolina Press, 1954), 143. On the pre-1816 roots of the colonization movement, see Staudenraus, *African Colonization Movement,* 1–11.

61. Sanneh, *Abolitionists Abroad,* 190–92; and Staudenraus, *African Colonization Movement,* 15–22.

62. Kay Brundage Takara, "Who Is the Black Woman in Hawaii?" in *Montage: An Ethnic History of Women in Hawaii,* ed. Nancy Foon Young and Judy R. Parrish (Honolulu: General Assistance Center for the Pacific, University of Hawaii, 1977), 86; and Miles M. Jackson, *And They Came: A Brief History and Annotated Bibliography of Blacks in Hawaii* (Durham, N.C.: Four-G Publishers, 2001), 6. For biographies of two other prominent African Americans in Hawai'i, see Marc Scruggs, "Anthony D. Allen: A Prosperous American of African Descent in Early 19th Century Hawai'i," *Hawaiian Journal of History* 26 (1992): 55–93; and Albert S. Broussard, "Carlotta Stewart Lai, a Black Teacher in the Territory of Hawai'i," *Hawaiian Journal of History* 24 (1990): 129–54.

63. Manumission was not the issue for many key supporters of colonization but was a means to relieve the United States of the "troublesome" free black presence, not the useful slave. For others, colonization was a step toward abolition. On the diverse motivations for colonization, see Sanneh, *Abolitionists Abroad,* 182–237.

64. Martin E. Marty, *Righteous Empire: The Protestant Experience in America* (New York: Dial Press, 1970), Foreword, 48.

65. Jared Sparks, *The Life of John Ledyard, the American Traveller* (Cambridge, Mass.: Hilliard and Brown, 1829), 6.

66. Ledyard kept a journal, but this was confiscated by the Admiralty upon the expedition's return to Britain because of the desire for a single, official account of the voyage. His journal, accordingly, was based upon his recollections years later, written in Hartford, rather than upon his notes at sea. See James Kenneth Munford, ed., *John Ledyard's Journal of Captain Cook's Last Voyage* (Corvallis: Oregon State University

Press, 1963); and Lynne Withey, *Voyages of Discovery: Captain Cook and the Exploration of the Pacific* (Berkeley: University of California Press, 1987), 402–5.

67. Munford, *John Ledyard's Journal,* 70.

68. See Philip Chadwick Foster Smith, *The Empress of China* (Philadelphia: Philadelphia Maritime Museum, 1984); and John Kuo Wei Tchen, *New York before Chinatown: Orientalism and the Shaping of American Culture, 1776–1882* (Baltimore: Johns Hopkins University Press, 1999), 26–40.

69. Munford, *John Ledyard's Journal,* xxxii.

70. Andrew A. Lipscomb et al., eds., *The Writings of Thomas Jefferson,* 20 vols. (Washington, D.C.: Thomas Jefferson Memorial Association, 1903), vol. 18, 143–44, 148–49, 154. On the relations between Jefferson and Ledyard, see Lipscomb, *Writings,* vol. 6, 130; vol. 7, 78, 360, 363–64; and vol. 19, viii–ix.

71. Munford, *John Ledyard's Journal,* 122, 123; and Sparks, *Life of John Ledyard,* 96–101.

72. Samuel Eliot Morison, *The Maritime History of Massachusetts, 1783–1860* (Boston: Houghton Mifflin, 1921), 43–44.

73. Ibid., 44.

4. SCHOOLING FOR SUBSERVIENCE

1. *Missionary Album: Portraits and Biographical Sketches of the American Protestant Missionaries to the Hawaiian Islands* (Honolulu: Hawaiian Mission Children's Society, 1969), 30–31, 33.

2. Clarissa Armstrong, letter addressed to her children and grandchildren, dated May 15, 1885, in Clarissa Armstrong, *C. C. A.: May 15, 1885, 80 Years* (Hampton, Va.: Normal School Steam Press, 1885), 29, 30.

3. Samuel Chapman Armstrong, letter addressed to his mother, dated May 5, 1885, in Armstrong, *C. C. A.,* 21.

4. Edith Armstrong Talbot, *Samuel Chapman Armstrong: A Biographical Study* (New York: Doubleday, Page, 1904), 3.

5. S. C. A. [Samuel Chapman Armstrong], "Reminiscences," in *Richard Armstrong: America, Hawaii* (Hampton, Va.: Normal School Steam Press, 1887), 103.

6. Samuel Chapman Armstrong to "Dear Cousins," February 5, 1881, and May 11, 1881, Hampton, Virginia, in "Children of the Mission, 1830–1900," Hawaiian Mission Children's Society, Honolulu. For more of Armstrong's views of the Chinese, see

S. C. Armstrong, "Lessons from the Hawaiian Islands," *Journal of Christian Philosophy*, January 1884, 226–28; and "Address by General S. C. Armstrong," *Hawaiian Gazette*, August 30, 1880.

7. Quoted in Helen W. Ludlow, *Clarissa Chapman Armstrong* (n.p., n.d.), Hawaiian Mission Children's Society, Honolulu; and Patricia Grimshaw, *Paths of Duty: American Missionary Wives in Nineteenth-Century Hawaii* (Honolulu: University of Hawaiʻi Press, 1989), 57–58.

8. Folder "Richard Armstrong," 1805–1860, M5, B, Ar5, Hawaiian Mission Children's Society, Honolulu.

9. As quoted in Talbot, *Samuel Chapman Armstrong*, 27.

10. SCA [Samuel Chapman Armstrong], "Memoranda," December 31, 1890, Hampton, Virginia, Samuel Chapman Armstrong Collection, 1826–1947, Box 3, Folder 28, Archives and Special Collections, Williams College, Williamstown, Mass. [henceforth, Armstrong Collection, Williams College].

11. Letter, Samuel Chapman Armstrong to Clarissa Chapman Armstrong, May 5, 1885, Hampton, Virginia, in Armstrong, *C. C. A.*, 21.

12. Ibid., 22.

13. Talbot, *Samuel Chapman Armstrong*, 35–36.

14. Armstrong, "Lessons from the Hawaiian Islands," 213.

15. *Missionary Album*, 33. To contextualize Clarissa Chapman Armstrong's account within the wider world of missionary wives in Hawaiʻi, see Grimshaw, *Paths of Duty*.

16. Excerpts from a letter written by Clarissa C. Armstrong, September 25, 1831, Bridgeport, Connecticut, in Journal of Clarissa C. Armstrong, 1831–1838, vol. 1, 1–2, Journal Collection, 1819–1900, MsJ, Ar52, v. 1, Hawaiian Mission Children's Society, Honolulu [henceforth, Journal of Clarissa C. Armstrong].

17. Journal entry for November 26, 1831, in Journal of Clarissa C. Armstrong, vol. 1, 3. Armstrong was, in addition to seasick, pregnant throughout the voyage.

18. Journal entry for February 12, 1832, in Journal of Clarissa C. Armstrong, vol. 1, 10.

19. Journal entries for May 21, 1832, May 28, 1832, and October 31, 1832, in Journal of Clarissa C. Armstrong, vol. 1, 20, 23, 56.

20. Letter by Clarissa C. Armstrong, January 24, 1865, Stone House, Honolulu, in Journal of Clarissa C. Armstrong, vol. 1.

21. As quoted in Grimshaw, *Paths of Duty*, 71.

22. Journal entries for May 4, 1835, May 9, 1835, and June 28, 1835, in Journal of Clarissa C. Armstrong, 1831–1838, vol. 2, 4, 5, 11, MsJ, Ar52, v.2, Journal Collection, 1819–1900, Hawaiian Mission Children's Society, Honolulu; and Grimshaw, *Paths of Duty*, 92.

23. *Richard Armstrong*, 10.

24. *Missionary Album*, 30–31.

25. *Richard Armstrong*, 30. For the influence of missionaries on Hawai'i's school system, see Merze Tate, "The Sandwich Island Missionaries Lay the Foundation for a System of Public Instruction in Hawaii," *Journal of Negro Education* 30, no. 4 (1961): 396–405.

26. Grimshaw, *Paths of Duty*, 180.

27. Benjamin O. Wist, *A Century of Public Education in Hawaii, 1840–1940* (Honolulu: Hawaii Education Review, 1940), 59.

28. Ibid., 59, 60. On the distinction between manual labor and manual training systems of education, see Carl Kalani Beyer, "Manual and Industrial Education during Hawaiian Sovereignty: Curriculum in the Transculturation of Hawai'i" (Ph.D. dissertation, University of Illinois, Chicago, 2003), 3–5 [henceforth, Beyer, "Manual and Industrial Education"]; and Carl Kalani Beyer, "Manual and Industrial Education for Hawaiians during the 19th Century," *Hawaiian Journal of History* 38 (2004): 2–6 [henceforth, Beyer, "Manual and Industrial Education for Hawaiians"]. See also Robert Frances Engs, *Educating the Disfranchised and Disinherited: Samuel Chapman Armstrong and Hampton Institute, 1839–1893* (Knoxville: University of Tennessee Press, 1999), 79–80.

29. Beyer, "Manual and Industrial Education," 48–50; and Beyer, "Manual and Industrial Education for Hawaiians," 27.

30. Richard Armstrong in *Answers to Questions Proposed by His Excellency, R. C. Wyllie, His Hawaiian Majesty's Minister of Foreign Relations, and Addressed to all the Missionaries in the Hawaiian Islands, May, 1846* (Honolulu, March 27, 1848), 12, 32, 33.

31. Richard Armstrong to R. Anderson, December 21, 1839, Wailuku, Maui, folder "Richard Armstrong," October 1832–October 1835, ABCFM-Hawaii Papers, Houghton Library (Harvard), 1820–1900, Hawaiian Mission Children's Society, Honolulu.

32. Samuel Chapman Armstrong, two-page autobiography, Folder 28, Series 1, Box 3, Armstrong Collection, Williams College. See also, Engs, *Educating the Disfranchised*, 9, 11, 13, 20.

33. "Address of Gen'l S. C. Armstrong," *Pacific Commercial Advertiser,* June 26, 1891.

34. Samuel Chapman Armstrong to "Dear Cousins," May 11, 1881, Hampton, folder "Samuel Chapman Armstrong," Letters to Cousin's Society, 1860–1890, Children of the Mission, 1830–1900, Hawaiian Mission Children's Society, Honolulu; and Samuel Chapman Armstrong, "Notes on my Vacation," 1855, Folder 7, Series 1, Box 1, Armstrong Collection, Williams College.

35. Samuel Chapman Armstrong to "Dear Cousins," December 22, 1860, Williamstown, folder "Samuel Chapman Armstrong," Letters to Cousin's Society, 1860–1890, Children of the Mission, 1830–1900, Hawaiian Mission Children's Society, Honolulu.

36. Armstrong credits abolitionist missionary Jonathan Green with his introduction to slavery and abolitionism. See S. C. A., "Reminiscences," 79.

37. Talbot, *Samuel Chapman Armstrong,* 86, 101.

38. Ibid., 139, 148, 152. For more on Armstrong's work in the Freedmen's Bureau, see Engs, *Educating the Disfranchised,* 57–69.

39. Talbot, *Samuel Chapman Armstrong,* 155.

40. Mary F. Armstrong and Helen W. Ludlow, *Hampton and Its Students* (New York: G. P. Putnam's Sons, 1874), 22–23.

41. As quoted in Edwin A. Start, "General Armstrong and the Hampton Institute," *New England Magazine,* n.s., 6 (1892): 444. I am grateful to Greg Robinson for bringing this article to my attention. Also quoted in Ludlow, *Clarissa Chapman Armstrong.*

42. S. C. A., "Reminiscences," 74–75.

43. Talbot, *Samuel Chapman Armstrong,* 157. Also quoted in Start, "General Armstrong," 446–47.

44. James D. Anderson, "The Hampton Model of Normal School Industrial Education, 1868–1900," in *New Perspectives on Black Educational History,* ed. Vincent P. Franklin and James D. Anderson (Boston: G. K. Hall, 1978), 61. See also Donald Spivey, *Schooling for the New Slavery: Black Industrial Education, 1868–1915* (Westport, Conn.: Greenwood Press, 1978), 16–44.

45. Anderson, "Hampton Model," 62, 63–71; and Spivey, *Schooling for the New Slavery,* 24–26, 32. For a more positive view of Armstrong and Hampton, see Engs, *Educating the Disfranchised,* especially chapters 7 and 11.

46. Beyer, "Manual and Industrial Education," 71–72; and Beyer, "Manual and Industrial Education for Hawaiians," 7.

47. For an account of Lahainaluna High School, see Beyer, "Manual and Industrial

242 🐟 NOTES TO PAGES 108–112

Education," 97–108; and Beyer, "Manual and Industrial Education for Hawaiians," 8–12.

48. Wist, *Century of Public Education,* 87–89.

49. Beyer, "Manual and Industrial Education," 78–79, 93.

50. Ibid., 119–20.

51. As quoted in ibid., 122.

52. Henry T. Cheever, *Life in the Sandwich Islands: Or, The Heart of the Pacific, as It Was and Is* (New York: A. S. Barnes and Company, 1851), 105.

53. Grimshaw, *Paths of Duty,* 161.

54. As quoted in Cheever, *Life in the Sandwich Islands,* 106.

55. Wist, *Century of Public Education,* 96; and Beyer, "Manual and Industrial Education for Hawaiians," 12–16, 20–21.

56. Beyer, "Manual and Industrial Education," 93. See also Harris, *Nothing but Christ,* 20–21, for the exemplar of the Cornwall Foreign Mission School, where the most promising Indian students were sent "for complete immersion in New England culture."

57. Wist, *Century of Public Education,* 98.

58. *Hilo Boarding School: A Glance at the Oldest School on the Island of Hawaii* (n.p., n.d.), Hawaiian Mission Children's Society, Honolulu.

59. *Hilo Boarding School for Boys: Seventy Five Years of Progress, 1836–1917* (n.p., n.d.), Hawaiian Mission Children's Society, Honolulu.

60. For a general, popular account of the Lyman family, see MacKinnon Simpson, *The Lymans of Hawai'i Island: A Pioneering Family* (Hilo, Hawai'i: Orlando H. Lyman Trust, 1993).

61. Beyer, "Manual and Industrial Education," 157–58.

62. On the centrality of finances in the early years of the school, see Lyman's summary history as recalled in his letter to R. Anderson of the American Board, November 12, 1840, Folder 20, Letters Pertaining to Hilo Boarding School, 1834–1889, Board of Trustees Records, Box 2, Lyman House Memorial Museum, Hilo, Hawai'i, 12–15.

63. David Belden Lyman Journal, 1831–37, 42, 42–43, McJ, L982, Journal Collection, 1819–1900, Hawaiian Mission Children's Society, Honolulu.

64. All of the annual reports cited in this section are from folder "Schools—Hilo Boarding School, Reports, 1837–63," Sandwich Islands Mission Collection, 1820–1853, Hawaiian Mission Children's Society, Honolulu.

65. Titus Coan, *Life in Hawaii: An Autobiographic Sketch of Mission Life and Labors (1835–1882)* (New York: Anson D. F. Randolph, 1882), 28.

66. Ibid., 61, 62. For a daily record of Sarah Lyman's educational labors from her letters and journals, see Margaret Greer Martin, ed., *The Lymans of Hilo,* rev. ed. (Hilo, Hawai'i: Lyman House Memorial Museum, 1992), 39–40, 47, 53, 58, 60, 61, 71, 73, 74, 81, 195–201.

67. D. B. Lyman to R. Anderson, Hilo, June 29, 1848, Folder 20, Letters Pertaining to Hilo Boarding School, 1834–1889, Board of Trustees Records, Box 2, Lyman House Memorial Museum, Hilo.

68. For a distinction between Hampton and mission society ideas of industrial education, see Anderson, "Hampton Model," 84–90.

69. Armstrong, "Lessons from the Hawaiian Islands," 213. See also Anderson, "Hampton Model," 64–65.

70. Spivey, *Schooling for the New Slavery,* 20.

71. M. F. Armstrong, *Hampton Institute: Its Work for Two Races, 1868 to 1885* (Hampton, Va.: Normal School Press Print, 1885), 8, 9. Hampton consisted of three levels, the preparatory, night, and normal schools. This curriculum reflects the work of the night school. For a more sympathetic account of this curriculum, see Engs, *Educating the Disfranchised,* 103–6.

72. Quote from Booker T. Washington in Talbot, *Samuel Chapman Armstrong,* 208.

73. Armstrong and Ludlow, *Hampton and Its Students,* 56; see also 40–47.

74. Samuel Chapman Armstrong, *Education for Life* (Hampton, Va.: Press of the Hampton Normal and Agricultural Institute, 1913), 40; and Anderson, "Hampton Model," 77–78.

75. *Hilo Boarding School for Boys;* and Anderson, "Hampton Model," 71.

76. Armstrong, *Education for Life,* 21, 29.

77. "Address by General S. C. Armstrong," *Hawaiian Gazette,* August 30, 1880.

78. Two-page autobiography by SCA, no date, Folder 28, Series 1, Box 3, Armstrong Papers, Williams College.

79. Anderson, "Hampton Model," 69.

80. Quoted in Anderson, "Hampton Model," 78, 80, 82.

81. *Dedication of the General Samuel Chapman Armstrong Memorial,* January 30, 1913, Pauahi Hall, Oahu College, B, Ar683d, P, Hawaiian Mission Children's Society, Honolulu.

82. Quoted in Talbot, *Samuel Chapman Armstrong*, 206, 207. Armstrong called his white supporters "the best class of Southern people"; two-page autobiography by SCA, no date, Folder 28, Series 1, Box 3, Armstrong Collection, Williams College.

83. Booker T. Washington to J. F. B. Marshall, July 18, 1881, Tuskegee, Alabama, Folder 3, Series 1, Box 2, Armstrong Collection, Williams College. For more on Washington's dependence on Armstrong, see Engs, *Educating the Disfranchised*, 139–42.

84. Booker T. Washington to Samuel Chapman Armstrong, June 29, 1881, Tuskegee, Alabama, Folder 3, Series 1, Box 2, Armstrong Collection, Williams College.

85. J. F. B. Marshall to Booker T. Washington, April 5, 1883, Hampton, Virginia, Folder 3, Box 2, Armstrong Collection, Williams College. See also Folder 6.

86. Booker T. Washington, *Some Results of the Armstrong Idea* (Hampton, Va.: Institute Press, 1909), 3.

87. Ibid., 3–4, 5–6, 8, 9.

88. Booker T. Washington, *Up from Slavery* (Oxford: Oxford University Press, 1995), 56–57.

89. *Southern Workman,* February 1885, 20. On Washington's contradictions in his views of American Indians, see David Wallace Adams, "Education in Hues: Red and Black at Hampton Institute, 1878–1893," *South Atlantic Quarterly* 67, no. 2 (1977): 172–76.

90. Washington, *Up from Slavery,* 57, 58. See also Helen W. Ludlow, ed., *Ten Years' Work for Indians at the Hampton Normal and Agricultural Institute, at Hampton, Virginia, 1878–1888* (Hampton, Va.: Hampton Institute, 1888), 12–17. For contrasting white racializations of Indians and African Americans, see Washington, *Up from Slavery,* 59–60, and for African American prejudices toward Indians, see Engs, *Educating the Disfranchised,* 118.

91. Adams, "Education in Hues," 169–72.

92. Ludlow, *Ten Years' Work for Indians,* 14.

93. Two of Pratt's prisoners, captives of the "Red River War" of 1874, attempted suicide en route to Florida. David Wallace Adams, *Education for Extinction: American Indians and the Boarding School Experience, 1875–1928* (Lawrence: University of Kansas Press, 1995), 37–39.

94. Richard Henry Pratt, *Battlefield and Classroom: Four Decades with the American Indian, 1867–1904,* ed. Robert M. Utley (New Haven, Conn.: Yale University Press, 1964), 118, 119, 120, 121; see also chapter 12, "Prison Industries"; chapter 13, "Anthropological Interest in the Prisoners"; and chapter 15, "Prison Educational Programs."

For a study of Pratt and his brand of education, see Joel Pfister, *Individuality Incorporated: Indians and the Multicultural Modern* (Durham, N.C.: Duke University Press, 2004).

95. Pratt, *Battlefield and Classroom,* 122, 123.

96. Engs, *Educating the Disfranchised,* 117.

97. As quoted in Mary Lou Hultgren and Paulette Fairbanks Molin, *To Lead and to Serve: American Indian Education at Hampton Institute, 1878–1923* (Virginia Beach: Virginia Foundation for the Humanities, 1989), 18. See also Pfister, *Individuality Incorporated,* 38.

98. Talbot, *Samuel Chapman Armstrong,* 214, 278. See also S. C. Armstrong, *The Indian Question* (Hampton, Va.: Normal School Steam Press, 1883), 4, 6–8, 15; and Start, "General Armstrong," 452.

99. Armstrong, *Hampton Institute,* 8. For more on Indian education at Hampton, see Ludlow, *Ten Years' Work for Indians;* Start, "General Armstrong," 451–53; William H. Robinson, "Indian Education at Hampton Institute," in *Stony the Road: Chapters in the History of Hampton Institute,* ed. Keith L. Schall (Charlottesville: University of Virginia Press, 1977), 1–33; Adams, "Education in Hues," 159–76; Paulette Fairbanks Molin, "'Training the Hand, the Head, and the Heart': Indian Education at Hampton Institute," *Minnesota History* 51, no. 3 (1988): 82–98; Hultgren and Molin, *To Lead and to Serve;* and Engs, *Educating the Disfranchised,* 115–29.

100. Ludlow, *Ten Years' Work for Indians,* 12; and Engs, *Educating the Disfranchised,* 118.

101. Pratt, *Battlefield and Classroom,* 192–95; and Richard H. Pratt, "A Way Out," in *Americanizing the American Indians: Writings by the "Friends of the Indians,"* ed. Francis Paul Prucha (Cambridge, Mass.: Harvard University Press, 1973), 272–76. Pratt, according to one account, devised the "outing system" for Indian prisoners in Florida as a way of integrating them into white St. Augustine. Adams, *Education for Extinction,* 54. For critical views of the "outing" program, see Robert A. Trennert, "Educating Indian Girls at Nonreservation Boarding Schools, 1878–1920," *Western Historical Quarterly* 13, no. 3 (1982): 276–77, 280, 283; and Margaret L. Archuleta, Brenda J. Child, and K. Tsianina Lomawaima, eds., *Away from Home: American Indian Boarding School Experiences, 1879–2000* (Phoenix, Ariz.: Heard Museum, 2000), 35–37.

102. Richard H. Pratt, "The Advantages of Mingling Indians with Whites," in Prucha, *Americanizing the American Indians,* 260–61. On this metaphor of redemptive death, see Pfister, *Individualism Incorporated,* 41–49.

103. Armstrong, *Indian Question*, 21. For an extended discussion of assimilation and the before and after photographs (figure 35) at Hampton, see Laura Wexler, *Tender Violence: Domestic Visions in an Age of U.S. Imperialism* (Chapel Hill: University of North Carolina Press, 2000), 52–53, 106–14.

104. Pratt, "Advantages," 262, 263, 268, 270–71.

105. Pratt, *Battlefield and Classroom,* 196; see also 222–24.

106. Molin, "Training the Hand," 86.

107. Pratt, *Battlefield and Classroom,* 202, 220, 227. For an accounting of Pratt's 1878 recruitment trip for Hampton, see 204, n. 11.

108. Adams, *Education for Extinction,* 47–48.

109. Ibid., 215–17.

110. Ibid., 220, 227; and Henry E. Fritz, *The Movement for Indian Assimilation, 1860–1890* (Philadelphia: University of Pennsylvania Press, 1963), 165–66.

111. Pratt, *Battlefield and Classroom,* 220–25. See also Molin, "Training the Hand," 85, in which the author quotes Pratt as having stated, "the Sioux were selected on the principle of taking the most pains with those who give the most trouble."

112. Ludlow, *Ten Years' Work for Indians,* 11, 18, 19–20.

113. Hultgren and Molin, *To Lead and to Serve,* 28. For autobiographical stories first published between 1900 and 1902, see Zitkala-Sa, *American Indian Stories* (Lincoln: University of Nebraska Press, 1985); and for a perceptive reading of those, see Wexler, *Tender Violence,* 115–24.

114. K. Tsianina Lomawaima, "Estelle Reel, Superintendent of Indian Schools, 1898–1910: Politics, Curriculum, and Land," *Journal of American Indian Education* 35, no. 3 (1996): 12, 14.

115. Ibid., 13, 14.

116. Jenichiro Oyabe, *A Japanese Robinson Crusoe* (Boston: Pilgrim Press, 1898), 134–42. I am grateful to Greg Robinson for providing me with a copy of this book.

117. José-Manuel Navarro, *Creating Tropical Yankees: Social Science Textbooks and U.S. Ideological Control in Puerto Rico, 1898–1908* (New York: Routledge, 2002), 124–25; and see the evidence provided at http://www.epix.net/~landis/portorican.html.

118. Carter Godwin Woodson, *The Mis-education of the Negro* (1933; reprint, New York: AMS Press, 1972), xiii.

119. Anderson, "Hampton Model," 84–90, 91.

120. Engs, *Educating the Disfranchised,* 166.

121. Adams, "Education in Hues," 160. See also Archuleta, Child, and Lomawaima, *Away from Home.*

122. Trennert, "Educating Indian Girls," 271–90; and W. Roger Buffalohead and Paulette Fairbanks Molin, "'A Nucleus of Civilization': American Indian Families at Hampton Institute in the Late Nineteenth Century," *Journal of American Indian Education* 35, no. 3 (1996): 59–94. On the complexities of the boarding school experience, see Sally J. McBeth, *Ethnic Identity and the Boarding School Experience of West-Central Oklahoma American Indians* (Lanham, Md.: University Press of America, 1983).

123. Historical marker at Carlisle, Pennsylvania, adjacent to the cemetery where 186 of Carlisle's Indian students lie buried. On the mixed results of the Carlisle idea for American Indian students, see Pfister, *Individualism Incorporated,* 97–132; on the Hampton notion for African American students, see Engs, *Educating the Disfranchised,* 130–43.

124. Items in folder "Schools—Kaua'i Industrial School (Koloa), 1890–1900," Hawaiian Evangelical Association Archives, 1853–1947, Hawaiian Mission Children's Society, Honolulu. See also Beyer, "Manual and Industrial Education," 224–29.

125. Items and letters in folders "Schools—Kauai Industrial School, Building Plans, Prospectus, 1889–1891," and "Schools—Kauai Industrial School, Accounts & Correspondence, 1888–1890," Smith Papers, Koloa, Kauai, 1865–1900, Hawaiian Mission Children's Society, Honolulu.

126. Lloyd L. Lee, "A Brief Analysis of the Role and Status of the Negro in the Hawaiian Community," *American Sociological Review* 13, no. 4 (1948): 423; and Jackson, *And They Came,* 11. See also Merze Tate, "Decadence of the Hawaiian Nation and Proposals to Import a Negro Labor Force," *Journal of Negro History* 47, no. 4 (1962): 248–63.

5. HAWAIIAN DIASPORA

1. This account of Peter Kakua is taken from W. J. Illerbrun, "Kanaka Pete," *Hawaiian Journal of History* 6 (1972): 156–66.

2. Illerbrun, "Kanaka Pete," 158, 164.

3. Ibid., 162–64.

4. David G. Miller, "Ka'iana, the Once Famous 'Prince of Kaua'i,'" *Hawaiian Journal of History* 22 (1988): 1–19.

5. David Kalakaua, *The Legends and Myths of Hawaii: The Fables and Folk-Lore of a Strange People* (Honolulu: Mutual Publishing, 1990), 383. See also Ralph S. Kuykendall, *The Hawaiian Kingdom*, vol. 1: *Foundation and Transformation, 1778–1854* (Honolulu: University Press of Hawaiʻi, 1938), 35.

6. John Meares, *Voyages Made in the Years 1788 and 1789, from China to the North West Coast of America* (London: Logographic Press, 1790), 7–8; Nathaniel Portlock, *A Voyage Round the World; But More Particularly to the North-West Coast of America* . . . (London: John Stockdale, 1789), 359–63; and George Mortimer, *Observations and Remarks Made during a Voyage to the Islands of Teneriffe* . . . (London: T. Cadell, 1791), 51.

7. Meares, *Voyages*, 10, 28–29, 36; Janice K. Duncan, *Minority without a Champion: Kanakas on the Pacific Coast, 1788–1850* (Portland: Oregon Historical Society, 1972), 1–3; Janice K. Duncan, "Kanaka World Travelers and Fur Company Employees, 1785–1860," *Hawaiian Journal of History* 7 (1973): 93–94; and Miller, "Kaʻiana," 5, 6. In 1792, two Hawaiian women sailed from Hawaiʻi to Nootka Sound, and they returned in 1794. "Menzies' California Journal," *California Historical Society Quarterly* 2 (January 1924): 265.

8. The *North West America*'s maiden voyage in 1788 was to Hawaiʻi, and the location and circumstances of its construction sparked Kamehameha I's interest in building his own ship in the Islands. Meares, *Voyages*, 2–3, 221, 334, 338.

9. On the British, Russian, and Spanish rivalries in the Pacific Northwest, see Warren L. Cook, *Flood Tide of Empire: Spain and the Pacific Northwest, 1543–1819* (New Haven, Conn.: Yale University Press, 1973); and Arrell Morgan Gibson, *Yankees in Paradise: The Pacific Basin Frontier* (Albuquerque: University of New Mexico Press, 1993), 69–72.

10. Edmond S. Meany, *History of the State of Washington* (New York: Macmillan, 1909), 29. British merchant ship captain James Colnett led that ill-fated expedition against which the Chinese lodged complaints about having been deceived into thinking they were headed for Bengal and not the Pacific Northwest. Cook, *Flood Tide*, 144; and Gibson, *Yankees in Paradise*, 68.

11. For a measured discussion of Kaʻiana's role in the Hawaiian arms race, see Miller, "Kaʻiana," 8–12.

12. See ibid., 12–14, for a consideration of the allegation of an affair between Kaʻiana and Kaʻahumanu as a cause for Kaʻiana's turn against Kamehameha. Also, Kalakaua, *Legends and Myths*, 384, 403–8.

13. Kuykendall, *Hawaiian Kingdom*, vol. 1, 312–13. See *The Friend* 2, no. 9 (1844): 79, for statistics for the period January 1, 1843, to June 1, 1844.

14. Robert C. Schmitt, *Demographic Statistics of Hawaii: 1778–1965* (Honolulu: University of Hawai'i Press, 1968), 39. See also Robert C. Schmitt, "Migration Statistics of Hawaii, 1823–1962," *Hawaii Historical Review* 1, no. 4 (1963): 59–68; and Robert C. Schmitt, "Population Characteristics of Hawaii, 1778–1850," *Hawaii Historical Review* 1, no. 11 (1965): 199–211.

15. George Simpson, *Narrative of a Journey Round the World, during the Years 1841 and 1842*, vol. 2 (London: Henry Colburn, 1847), 78. See Robert Wyllie's "Notes," in *The Friend* 2, no. 9 (1844): 79, which states that ship captains had to sign a $200 bond against the safe return of their Hawaiian crews within three years; and Richard A. Greer, "Wandering Kamaainas: Notes on Hawaiian Emigration before 1848," *Journal of the West* 6, no. 2 (1967): 222. Cf. George Verne Blue, "A Hudson's Bay Company Contract for Hawaiian Labor," *Oregon Historical Quarterly* 25 (March 1924): 72–75; and E. Momilani Naughton, "Hawaiians in the Fur Trade: Cultural Influence on the Northwest Coast, 1811–1875" (M.A. thesis, Western Washington University, 1983), 21. For receipts to the Hawaiian government from those taxes, see Janice K. Duncan, "Minority without a Champion: The Kanaka Contribution to the Western United States, 1750–1900" (M.A. thesis, Portland State University, 1972), 83, 84.

16. Greer, "Wandering Kamaainas," 223.

17. As quoted in ibid., 224.

18. Ibid., 223.

19. "Letters of A. Rotchev, Last Commandant of Fort Ross and the Resumé of the Report of the Russian-American Company for the Year 1850–51," trans. and ed. Frederick C. Cordes, *California Historical Society Quarterly* 39, no. 2 (1960): 109. See also Duncan, "Minority without a Champion," 92–96, on Hawaiians and the Russian-American Company.

20. British Canadians accused American fur traders of special cruelty toward American Indians. Gibson, *Yankees in Paradise*, 111–13.

21. As reproduced in Samuel Eliot Morison, "Boston Traders in the Hawaiian Islands, 1789–1823," *Proceedings of the Massachusetts Historical Society* 54 (October 1920): 27.

22. Marion O'Neil, "The Maritime Activities of the North West Company, 1813 to 1821," *Washington Historical Quarterly* 21, no. 4 (1930): 253, 258–59.

23. Morison, "Boston Traders," 14.

24. E. E. Rich, *The History of Hudson's Bay Company, 1763–1820*, vol. 2 (London: Hudson's Bay Record Society, 1959), 615; "Edward Vischer's First Visit to California," trans. and ed. Erwin Gustave Gudde, *California Historical Society Quarterly* 19, no. 3

(1940): 194; Richard Henry Dana Jr., *Two Years before the Mast: A Personal Narrative of Life at Sea* (reprint; New York: Penguin Books, 1981), 204; and David A. Chappell, *Double Ghosts: Oceanian Voyagers on Euroamerican Ships* (Armonk, N.Y.: M. E. Sharpe, 1997), 56.

25. David Kittelson, "Hawaiians and Fur Traders," *Hawaii Historical Review* 1, no. 2 (1963): 17; and Naughton, "Hawaiians," 27.

26. As reproduced in Morison, "Boston Traders," 27.

27. Gabriel Franchère, *Narrative of a Voyage to the Northwest Coast of America, 1811–1814,* trans. J. V. Huntington (New York: Bedfield, 1854), 229.

28. Ross Cox, *Adventures on the Columbia River . . . ,* vol. 1 (London: Henry Colburn and Richard Bentley, 1831), 26–27. For more on contract terms and wages, see Naughton, "Hawaiians," 21–26; and Chappell, *Double Ghosts,* 56–59, 158–59.

29. See David Kittelson, "John Coxe: Hawaii's First Soldier of Fortune," *Hawaii Historical Review* 1, no. 10 (1965): 194, 197, n. 2, on the possibility that Naukane was John Coxe.

30. On Astor and his continental ambitions, see Gibson, *Yankees in Paradise,* 117–21, 128; Kenneth W. Porter, *John Jacob Astor: Business Man,* 2 vols. (Cambridge, Mass.: Harvard University Press, 1931); and James P. Ronda, *Astoria and Empire* (Lincoln: University of Nebraska Press, 1990).

31. On the North West Company's activities, see O'Neil, "Maritime Activities," 243–67. The War of 1812 was also fought in the Pacific between British and U.S. war and whale ships. Gibson, *Yankees in Paradise,* 137.

32. Cox, *Adventures,* 104–5; Franchère, *Narrative,* 294–98; and O'Neil, "Maritime Activities," 243–44, 248–54.

33. Duncan, "Kanaka World Travelers," 96.

34. Most of this account comes from Kittelson, "John Coxe," 194–98.

35. O'Neil, "Maritime Activities," 261.

36. Alexander Ross, *The Fur Hunters of the Far West,* ed. Kenneth A. Spaulding (Norman: Oklahoma University Press, 1956), 61, 70, 83, 91, 110, 121, 173, 175–76, 193, 194; and Franchère, *Narrative,* 229.

37. Duncan, "Kanaka World Travelers," 99–100; Guy Vernon Bennett, "Early Relations of the Sandwich Islands to the Old Oregon Territory," *Washington Historical Quarterly* 4, no. 2 (1913): 122–23, 125; M. Melia Lane, "The Migration of Hawaiians to Coastal British Columbia, 1810 to 1869" (M.A. thesis, University of Hawai'i, 1985),

32; Alexander Spoehr, "Fur Traders in Hawai'i: The Hudson's Bay Company in Honolulu, 1829–1861," *Hawaiian Journal of History* 20 (1986): 27–66; and Alexander Spoehr, "A 19th Century Chapter in Hawai'i's Maritime History: Hudson's Bay Company Merchant Shipping, 1829–1859," *Hawaiian Journal of History* 22 (1988): 71, 72–73, 93.

38. Gibson, *Yankees in Paradise*, 115, 125, 160–62; Kuykendall, *Hawaiian Kingdom*, vol. 1, 85–92; and Noel J. Kent, *Hawaii: Islands under the Influence* (New York: Monthly Review Press, 1983), 17–21.

39. Gibson, *Yankees in Paradise*, 111.

40. Ibid., 103–30; Kent, *Hawaii*. For a detailed account of a U.S. ship's involvement in this trade network, from its construction in Boston in 1821 to its travels to Hawai'i and North America's west coast, its trans-Pacific crossing to China, and its return to Martha's Vineyard in 1828, see F. W. Howay, "Brig Owhyhee in the Columbia, 1827," *Oregon Historical Quarterly* 34, no. 4 (1933): 324–29.

41. For a social history of Hawaiians in British Columbia, see Jean Barman, "New Land, New Lives: Hawaiian Settlement in British Columbia," *Hawaiian Journal of History* 29 (1995): 1–32; for an engaging account of a remarkable daughter of a Hawaiian man and Indian woman, see Jean Barman, *Maria Mahoi of the Islands* (Vancouver: New Star Books, 2004); and for a history of Hawaiians in the Pacific Northwest that includes useful biographies, see Jean Barman and Bruce McIntyre Watson, *Leaving Paradise: Indigenous Hawaiians in the Pacific Northwest, 1787–1898* (Honolulu: University of Hawai'i Press, 2006).

42. Duncan, "Kanaka World Travelers," 102, 106.

43. Duncan, "Minority without a Champion," 44, 45; and Lane, "Migration," 47, 48, 50. For a discussion of the patterns of Hawaiian migration in British Columbia, see Lane, "Migration," 38–61.

44. *The Friend* 2, no. 9 (1844): 79. Cf. Spoehr, "Fur Traders," 33.

45. Samuel C. Damon, *A Journey to Lower Oregon & Upper California, 1848–49* (San Francisco: John J. Newbegin, 1927), 21; Duncan, *Minority without a Champion*, 12; and Lane, "Migration," 45.

46. Duncan, *Minority without a Champion*, 11–12; and Bennett, "Early Relations," 124–25.

47. For a more optimistic appraisal of Hawaiian experiences in British Columbia, especially as contrasted with their counterpart in the United States, see Barman, "New Land, New Lives," 1, 3–6.

48. Duncan, "Kanaka World Travelers," 101–2, 107; and Spoehr, "19th Century Chapter," 72, 94.

49. Sutter claimed to have employed ten Hawaiians, eight men and two women, but William Heath Davis counted eight Hawaiians, four men and four women. Charles W. Kenn, "Sutter's Canacas," Conference of California Historical Societies, *Newsletter* 2, no. 2 (1955): 3; and Charles W. Kenn, "Descendants of Captain Sutter's Kanakas," *Proceedings of the Second Annual Meeting of the Conference of California Historical Societies,* ed. Richard Coke Wood (Stockton, Calif.: College of the Pacific, 1956), 87–88.

50. Kenn, "Sutter's Canacas," 3; and William J. Breault, *John A. Sutter in Hawaii and California, 1838–1839* (Rancho Cordova, Calif.: Landmark Enterprises, 1998), 3–8, 27–36.

51. Breault, *John A. Sutter,* 26; and Kenn, "Sutter's Canacas," 3–4.

52. Breault, *John A. Sutter,* 43–44, 61, 72; Kenn, "Descendants," 90–101; and Kenn, "Sutter's Canacas," 3–6.

53. Schmitt, "Population Characteristics of Hawaii," 207.

54. Richard H. Dillon, "Kanaka Colonies in California," *Pacific Historical Review* 24, no. 1 (1955): 19; and Kenn, "Descendants," 99. See also C. W. Haskins, *The Argonauts of California* (New York: Fords, Howard and Hulbert, 1890), 77–78; and Richard A. Greer, "California Gold—Some Reports to Hawaii," *Hawaiian Journal of History* 4 (1970): 157–73, for contemporary accounts in Hawai'i of the gold rush; and Duncan, "Minority without a Champion," 98–109.

55. From an assembly committee report, as cited in Charles J. McClain, *In Search of Equality: The Chinese Struggle against Discrimination in Nineteenth-Century America* (Berkeley: University of California Press, 1994), 10.

56. Duncan, *Minority without a Champion,* 15.

57. On the 1852 Foreign Miners' Tax, see McClain, *In Search of Equality,* 10, 12–13, 18–20, 24–25, 40–41. Californios were Mexican landowners who long predated the gold-rushing, American immigrants.

58. Dillon, "Kanaka Colonies," 18.

59. *The Friend* 12, no. 2 (1863): 10. On intermarriage between Hawaiian men and Indian women in British Columbia, see Lane, "Migration," 88–95; and Naughton, "Hawaiians," 29–41.

60. Dillon, "Kanaka Colonies," 19–20; *The Friend* 11, no. 7 (1862): 49; *The Friend* 18, no. 8 (1868): 69; and Kenn, "Descendants," 88, 97.

61. *The Friend* 11, no. 7 (1862): 49; and *The Friend* 18, no. 8 (1868): 69.

62. Samuel Manaiakalani Kamakau, *Ka Po'e Kahiko: The People of Old,* trans. Mary Kawena Pukui (Honolulu: Bishop Museum Press, 1964), 96; David Malo, *Hawaiian Antiquities,* trans. Nathaniel B. Emerson (Honolulu: Bishop Museum Press, 1951), 29, 87–88, 151–52; and Caroline Ralston, "Changes in the Lives of Ordinary Women in Early Post-Contact Hawaii," in *Family and Gender in the Pacific: Domestic Contradictions and the Colonial Impact,* ed. Margaret Jolly and Martha Macintyre (Cambridge: Cambridge University Press, 1989), 52, 53.

63. Apparently during the 1880s and '90s in Utah and the 1930s and '40s in New York City, Hawaiians could not get taro so they used wheat flour instead to make their poi. Duncan, "Minority without a Champion," 72; and Adria L. Imada, "Hawaiians on Tour: Hula Circuits through the American Empire," *American Quarterly* 56, no. 1 (2004): 139.

64. From a translated letter dated October 30, 1865, in Naughton, "Hawaiians," 49–50.

65. Spoehr, "Fur Traders," 57.

66. Robert Carlton Clark, "Hawaiians in Early Oregon," *Oregon Historical Quarterly* 35, no. 1 (1934): 31. See also Duncan, "Minority without a Champion," 107–8.

67. Kenn, "Descendants," 92.

68. Duncan, "Minority without a Champion," 120–23; and Damon, *Journey to Lower Oregon,* 19–20.

69. Quoted in Duncan, *Minority without a Champion,* 17–18. See also Duncan, "Minority without a Champion," 124–28.

70. *Oregon Spectator,* June 27, 1850, as quoted in Duncan, "Minority without a Champion," 115.

71. Chappell, *Double Ghosts,* xiii, 41–42, 186, n. 5; Gibson, *Yankees in Paradise,* 146–48; and J. Ross Browne, *Etchings of a Whaling Cruise,* ed. John Seelye (Cambridge, Mass.: Harvard University Press, 1968), 504.

72. MacKinnon Simpson and Robert B. Goodman, *Whale Song: A Pictorial History of Whaling and Hawai'i* (Honolulu: Beyond Words Publishing, 1986), 98.

73. As reproduced in Simpson and Goodman, *Whale Song,* 96–97; and New Bedford Whaling Museum, Kendall Institute, Mss 55, S-g 2, Ser O, S-s 1, Folder 4.

74. Chappell, *Double Ghosts,* 57, 58, 158–59; and New Bedford Whaling Museum, Kendall Institute, Mss 78, S-g 3, Ser E, S-s 4, Folder 2.

75. New Bedford Whaling Museum, Kendall Institute, Mss 55, S-g 2, Ser L, S-s 3, Folder 3.

76. New Bedford Whaling Museum, Kendall Institute, Swift & Allen Collection, Labor Records, Mss 5, Box 17, S-g 3, Ser C, Volume 16.

77. Zephaniah W. Pease, ed., *History of New Bedford,* vol. 1 (New York: Lewis Historical Publishing, 1918), 37, 38; and Leonard Bolles Ellis, *History of New Bedford and Its Vicinity, 1602–1892* (Syracuse, N.Y.: D. Mason and Co., 1892), 418, 421–22.

78. Gibson, *Yankees in Paradise,* 149.

79. Herman Melville, *Moby-Dick,* ed. Charles Child Walcutt (Toronto: Bantam Books, 1967), 40.

80. Kuykendall, *Hawaiian Kingdom,* vol. 1, 309.

81. Unlike the fur traders who operated mainly in the Pacific Northwest and traversed the Pacific in an east-west traffic, whalers, in tracking their quarry, ranged across the Pacific east and west and north and south, although there were distinctive hunting grounds for particular species of whales during certain seasons.

82. Kuykendall, *Hawaiian Kingdom,* vol. 1, 307; and Kent, *Hawaii,* 21–22.

83. As quoted in Kuykendall, *Hawaiian Kingdom,* vol. 1, 94.

84. As quoted in Chappell, *Double Ghosts,* 163. See Kuykendall, *Hawaiian Kingdom,* vol. 1, 304–5, 308–11, and Kent, *Hawaii,* 22–25, for estimates of the value of this trade.

85. *The Friend* 2, no. 7 (1844): 61.

86. As quoted in Foster R. Dulles, *Lowered Boats: A Chronicle of American Whaling* (New York: Harcourt, Brace, 1933), 242.

87. Francis Allyn Olmsted, *Incidents of a Whaling Voyage* (New York: D. Appleton, 1841), 238–39.

88. Kuykendall, *Hawaiian Kingdom,* vol. 1, 311–12; Gibson, *Yankees in Paradise,* 144–46; Kent, *Hawaii,* 22, 23; and Simpson and Goodman, *Whale Song,* 94–95, 99.

89. Ellis, *History of New Bedford,* 307–11.

90. Ibid., 266, 276, 304; and Melville, *Moby-Dick,* 17–18, 39.

91. *Nantucket Inquirer,* May 9, 1822, as quoted in Frances Karttunen, "Far-Away Neighbor Islands: Pacific Islanders on Nantucket during the Whaling Era," unpublished paper, 4. Karttunen's paper forms the second of a three-part social history of Nantucket, "The Other Islanders."

92. Chappell, *Double Ghosts,* 132.

93. Especially helpful are Mary Malloy, *African Americans in the Maritime Trades: A Guide to Resources in New England,* Kendall Whaling Museum Monograph Series, No. 6 (Sharon, Mass.: Kendall Whaling Museum, 1990); and Marilyn Halter, *Between Race and Ethnicity: Cape Verdean American Immigrants, 1860–1965* (Chicago: University of Illinois Press, 1993).

94. Randolph L. Chambliss, "The Blacks," *Social Process in Hawaii* 29 (1982): 113; Eleanor C. Nordyke, "Blacks in Hawai'i: A Demographic and Historical Perspective," *Hawaiian Journal of History* 22 (1988): 243; and Jackson, *And They Came,* 7, 8–9.

95. From the New Bedford Whaling Museum's website, http://www.whalingmuseum.org.

96. New Bedford Whaling Museum, Kendall Institute, Mss 55, S-g 2, Ser I, S-s 3, Folder 5.

97. Crews from the whaling voyages crewlist of the New Bedford Free Public Library, www.ci.new-bedford.ma.us/SERVICES/LIBRARY/signin.htm.

98. 1860 U.S. Census, U.S. and Massachusetts Census Tracts, Bristol County, New Bedford, and Fairhaven, Microfilm Department, New Bedford Free Public Library. *The 1860 New Bedford Census: Index to Persons 20 Years Old and Older* (New Bedford, Mass.: New Bedford Free Public Library, 1992) offers a quick way to identify those born in Hawai'i and China. Without their birthplace, it is virtually impossible to locate Hawaiians in the 1840 and 1850 census tracts, especially because they were commonly given non-Hawaiian names.

99. 1870 U.S. Census, Massachusetts, Bristol County, New Bedford; and Paul Albert Cyr, compiler, *Index to the 1870 U.S. Census of New Bedford, Massachusetts* (New Bedford, Mass.: New Bedford Free Public Library, 1992).

100. On Chinese men and Irish women in New York City, see Tchen, *New York before Chinatown,* 71–86, 225–59.

101. 1880 U.S. Census, Massachusetts, Bristol County, New Bedford; and Paul Albert Cyr, compiler, *Index to the 1880 U.S. Census of New Bedford, Massachusetts by Streets & House Numbers,* 2 vols. (New Bedford, Mass.: New Bedford Free Public Library, 1994).

102. Information on Pacific Islanders on Nantucket is from Karttunen, "Far-Away Neighbor Islands" (see note 91).

103. I am grateful to Frances Karttunen, who shared the fruits of her research on Nantucket with me. Personal correspondence, Karttunen to Gary Y. Okihiro, August 20, 2003.

104. Ellis, *History of New Bedford*, 276, 277. The Emancipation Act of 1833 abolished slavery in the British West Indies, but its formal end came on August 1, 1834.

105. Frederick Douglass, *My Bondage and My Freedom* (New York: Miller, Orton and Mulligan, 1855), 340–54.

106. Ellis, *History of New Bedford*, 306, 307.

107. As quoted in ibid., 317.

108. Ibid., 346, 349–50. On the reticence to deploy African American troops and the varying responses by African Americans to military service, see Hondon B. Hargrove, *Black Union Soldiers in the Civil War* (Jefferson, N.C.: McFarland, 1988), 1–113; Ira Berlin, Joseph P. Reidy, and Leslie S. Rowland, eds., *Freedom's Soldiers: The Black Military Experience in the Civil War* (Cambridge: Cambridge University Press, 1998), 1–23; and John David Smith, "Let Us All Be Grateful That We Have Colored Troops That Will Fight," in *Black Soldiers in Blue: African American Troops in the Civil War Era,* ed. John David Smith (Chapel Hill: University of North Carolina Press, 2002), 1–77.

109. Ellis, *History of New Bedford*, 347.

110. S. C. A. [Samuel Chapman Armstrong], "Reminiscences," in *Richard Armstrong: America, Hawaii* (Hampton, Va.: Normal School Steam Press, 1887), 84.

111. Civil War Sailors Database, posted at http://www.itd.nps.gov/cwss/sailors.htm.

112. Berlin, Reidy, and Rowland, *Freedom's Soldiers,* 20–21.

113. See, e.g., Record Group 94, Records of the Adjutant General's Office, Book Records of Volunteer Union Organizations, 31st USCT Infantry, Regimental Descriptive Book, vol. 1, National Archives, Washington, D.C. Among the Asian Americans were Chinese Ab Dold and Juan Lodigo, both of whom deserted, and South Asian John Bank, who was wounded in battle and rose to the rank of sergeant.

114. Record Group 94, Records of the Adjutant General's Office, Book Records of Volunteer Union Organizations, 20th Regiment, Company A, USCT Infantry, Regimental Descriptive Book, vol. 2; and 29th Regiment, Connecticut Colored Infantry, Company F, Descriptive Book, Companies A–K, vol. 2, National Archives, Washington, D.C.

115. For recent studies of African American soldiers in battle and in the routine of camp life, see Noah Andre Trudeau, *Like Men of War: Black Troops in the Civil War, 1862–1865* (Boston: Little, Brown, 1998); and Keith P. Wilson, *Campfires of Freedom: The*

Camp Life of Black Soldiers during the Civil War (Kent, Ohio: Kent State University Press, 2002).

116. Smith, "Let Us All Be Grateful," 54. On casualties in African American regiments, see Hargrove, *Black Union Soldiers,* 212–13.

117. As reproduced in Berlin, Reidy, and Rowland, *Freedom's Soldiers,* 115–16.

118. Military service may have widened the gender gap between African American men and women. Ibid., 43–44.

119. As quoted in Smith, "Let Us All Be Grateful," 28.

120. Ellis, *History of New Bedford,* 350–51.

121. Ralph S. Kuykendall, *The Hawaiian Kingdom,* vol. 2: *Twenty Critical Years, 1854–1874* (Honolulu: University of Hawai'i Press, 1953), 65–66.

122. Gavan Daws, *Shoal of Time: A History of the Hawaiian Islands* (Honolulu: University Press of Hawai'i, 1968), 172.

123. Gibson, *Yankees in Paradise,* 340–41; James D. Horan, ed., *C.S.S. Shenandoah: The Memoirs of Lieutenant Commanding James I. Waddell* (New York: Crown Publishers, 1960), 1, 34, 47; R. Gerard Ward, ed., *American Activities in the Central Pacific, 1790–1870,* vol. 6 (Ridgewood, N.J.: Gregg Press, 1967), 193–200; and Murray Morgan, *Dixie Raider: The Saga of the C.S.S. Shenandoah* (New York: E. P. Dutton, 1948).

124. As quoted in Ellis, *History of New Bedford,* 380–81.

125. Ibid., 378.

126. *Evening Standard* (New Bedford), December 31, 1874, and January 1, 1875; and *Daily Mercury* (New Bedford), December 31, 1874, and January 1, 1875.

127. Breault, *John A. Sutter,* 82–94.

128. On U.S. involvement in the Pacific guano trade, see Gibson, *Yankees in Paradise,* 165–67.

129. As quoted in Watt Stewart, *Chinese Bondage in Peru: A History of the Chinese Coolie in Peru, 1849–1874* (Westport, Conn.: Greenwood Press, 1970), 96.

130. Jonathan Kay Kamakawiwo'ole Osorio, *Dismembering Lāhui: A History of the Hawaiian Nation to 1887* (Honolulu: University of Hawai'i Press, 2002), 145–92; and George S. Kanahele, *Emma: Hawai'i's Remarkable Queen* (Honolulu: Queen Emma Foundation, 1999), esp. 245–354.

131. E. S. Craighill Handy and Elizabeth Green Handy, *Native Planters in Old Hawaii:*

Their Life, Lore, and Environment, Bernice P. Bishop Museum Bulletin 233 (Honolulu: Bishop Museum Press, 1972), 227–28.

132. "Song of the Workers on Howland Island," in *The Echo of Our Song: Chants & Poems of the Hawaiians,* trans. and ed. Mary K. Pukui and Alfons L. Korn (Honolulu: University of Hawai'i Press, 1973), 80–82.

6. POETRY IN MOTION

1. Sigmund Spaeth, "Hawaii Likes Music," *Harper's Monthly Magazine,* March 1938, 423.

2. O. H. K. Spate, *The Spanish Lake* (Minneapolis: University of Minnesota Press, 1979), 1, 32, 33.

3. On the impact of the galleon trade on the Philippines and Spanish America, see William Lytle Schurz, *The Manila Galleon* (Manila: Historical Conservation Society, 1985).

4. Warren L. Cook, *Flood Tide of Empire: Spain and the Pacific Northwest, 1543–1819* (New Haven, Conn.: Yale University Press, 1973), 107; and Arrell Morgan Gibson, *Yankees in Paradise: The Pacific Basin Frontier* (Albuquerque: University of New Mexico Press, 1993), 70, 106–7.

5. Schurz, *Manila Galleon,* 174. Similarly, Europeans and European Americans routinely called Hawaiians "Indians," which was an equivalent of "natives." See, e.g., James Kenneth Munford, ed., *John Ledyard's Journal of Captain Cook's Last Voyage* (Corvallis: Oregon State University Press, 1963), 121, 123.

6. Samuel Eliot Morison, *The Maritime History of Massachusetts, 1783–1860* (Boston: Houghton Mifflin, 1921), 267.

7. Bernard Brian Wellmon, "The Parker Ranch: A History" (Ph.D. dissertation, Texas Christian University, 1970), 54, 55.

8. Ralph S. Kuykendall, *The Hawaiian Kingdom,* vol. 1: *Foundation and Transformation, 1778–1854* (Honolulu: University Press of Hawai'i, 1938), 318.

9. Joseph Brennan, *The Parker Ranch of Hawaii: The Saga of a Ranch and a Dynasty* (New York: John Day Company, 1974), 32, 34, 40, 41; Billy Bergin, *Loyal to the Land: The Legendary Parker Ranch, 750–1950* (Honolulu: University of Hawai'i Press, 2004), 25–29; and Larry Kimura, "Old-Time Parker Ranch Cowboys," *Hawaii Historical Review* 1, no. 9 (1964): 161.

10. Kuykendall, *Hawaiian Kingdom,* vol. 1, 318; Wellmon, "Parker Ranch," 42, 43; and George Kanahele, *Kī hōʻalu: The Story of Slack Key* (Honolulu: Hawaiian Music Foundation, 1973).

11. Wellmon, "Parker Ranch," 42–43.

12. Curtis J. Lyons, "Traces of Spanish Influence in the Hawaiian Islands," *Papers of the Hawaiian Historical Society,* no. 2 (April 27, 1892): 26. See also W. D. Alexander, "The Relations between the Hawaiian Islands and Spanish America in Early Times," *Papers of the Hawaiian Historical Society,* no. 1 (January 28, 1892): 10–11; Wellmon, "Parker Ranch," 43, 44; Bergin, *Loyal to the Land,* 32–36; John Rogers and Tim Knott, "The Paniolos," *Ko Kākou* 1, no. 2 (1975): 14, 15; and Kimura, "Old-Time Parker Ranch," 162–63, 166–67.

13. Information on Joaquin Armas is from Rossie and Locky Frost, "The King's Bullock Catcher," *Hawaiian Journal of History* 11 (1977): 175–87.

14. Kyle Ko Francisco Shinseki, "El pueblo mexicano de Hawaiʻi: Comunidades en formación" (M.A. thesis, University of California, Los Angeles, 1997), 11.

15. For brief mention of other Mexicans in Hawaiʻi during this period and their influence, see ibid., 13–14.

16. *Pacific Commercial Advertiser,* August 11, 1859. See also *Pacific Commercial Advertiser,* December 9, 1907.

17. Rogers and Knott, "Paniolos," 14; and Joseph Brennan, *Paniolo* (Honolulu: Ku Paʻa Publishing, 1978), 77–78, 106–7. Cf. Philip Sampaio, Joy Kalawaia, and Debra Arii, "Sol Bright: 'Hawaiian Cowboy,'" *Ko Kākou* 1, no. 2 (1975): 11–12, which claims that racism denied Purdy the "gold plaque," which he received after the rodeo in San Francisco.

18. Richard Henry Dana Jr., *Two Years before the Mast: A Personal Narrative of Life at Sea* (1840; New York: Penguin Books, 1981), 211–13.

19. Gibson, *Yankees in Paradise,* 163–65; Robert Glass Cleland, *A History of California: The American Period* (New York: Macmillan, 1927), 43; and Morison, *Maritime History,* 267.

20. Ralph S. Kuykendall, *The Hawaiian Kingdom,* vol. 2: *Twenty Critical Years, 1854–1874* (Honolulu: University of Hawaiʻi Press, 1953), 153; and Brennan, *Parker Ranch,* 56.

21. Morison, *Maritime History,* 266–69; and Cleland, *History of California,* 3, 44–45.

22. "Native Music in Honolulu," *Paradise of the Pacific,* July 1888, 3. For a brief discus-

sion of the various possibilities of the guitar's introduction to Hawai'i, see George Kanahele, ed., *Hawaiian Music and Musicians: An Illustrated History* (Honolulu: University Press of Hawai'i, 1979), 351–53.

23. *Paradise of the Pacific,* February 1906, 11.

24. Kanahele, *Kī hōʻalu.* Cf. Shinseki, "El pueblo mexicano de Hawai'i," 14, who cites Mexican influences in Spanish words spoken around Waimea, the song "Adiós Ke Aloha" (1870), and Lili'uokalani's songs written in Spanish. Cf. Kanahele, *Hawaiian Music,* 1–2; and *Nā Mele Paniolo: Songs of Hawaiian Cowboys,* CD collection by the Hawaii State Foundation on Culture and the Arts, 1990 and 2004. In *Hawaiian Buckaroo* (1938), Hollywood's *paniolos* fight, hula dancers shake, and steel guitars sing. Luis I. Reyes, *Made in Paradise: Hollywood's Films of Hawai'i and the South Seas* (Honolulu: Mutual Publishing, 1995), 52; and Robert C. Schmitt, *Hawai'i in the Movies, 1898–1959* (Honolulu: Hawaiian Historical Society, 1988), 43.

25. *Honolulu Advertiser,* May 7, 1939. See James Clifford, *Routes: Travel and Translation in the Late Twentieth Century* (Cambridge, Mass.: Harvard University Press, 1997), 26, which cites a claim by noted guitarist Bob Brosman that the steel guitar was invented by a Czech immigrant living in California.

26. Kanahele, *Hawaiian Music,* 201, 353; and Adrienne L. Kaeppler, "Music in Hawaii in the Nineteenth Century," in *Musikkulturen Asiens, Afrikas und Ozeaniens,* ed. Robert Günther (Germany: Bustav Bosse Verlag Regensburg, 1973), 327, 328.

27. Amy Ku'uleialoha Stillman, *Sacred Hula: The Historical Hula 'Āla'apapa,* Bishop Museum Bulletin in Anthropology 8 (Honolulu: Bishop Museum Press, 1998), 2–3.

28. Kanahele, *Hawaiian Music,* 288.

29. Kanahele, *Kī hōʻalu.*

30. Elizabeth Tatar, "Falsetto," in Kanahele, *Hawaiian Music,* 86.

31. Thanks to Brenda M. Romero and Ted Solis for confirming this about Mexican singing, which included yodeling, especially in Huastecan music of the Mexican gulf coast and falsetto in Vera Cruz. See also Ricardo D. Trimillos, *"He Mo'olelo:* Historical and Artistic Notes," in *Nā Mele Paniolo,* 6.

32. Tatar, "Falsetto," 86–92.

33. Kaeppler, "Music in Hawaii," 313; and Dorothy B. Barrère, Mary Kawena Pukui, and Marion Kelly, *Hula: Historical Perspectives,* Pacific Anthropological Records, No. 30 (Honolulu: Bishop Museum, 1980), 12, 13. For a helpful description of writings on the hula before Europeans, see Mazeppa King Costa, "Dance in the Society and Hawaiian

Islands as Presented by the Early Writings, 1767–1842" (M.A. thesis, University of Hawaii, 1951).

34. David Malo, *Hawaiian Antiquities,* trans. Nathaniel B. Emerson (Honolulu: Bishop Museum Press, 1951), 231.

35. J. C. Beaglehole, ed., *The Voyage of the Resolution and Discovery, 1776–1780,* part 2 (Cambridge: Cambridge University Press, 1967), 1157, 1222.

36. As translated in ibid., 1234.

37. John Papa ʻĪʻī, *Fragments of Hawaiian History,* trans. Mary Kawena Pukui (Honolulu: Bishop Museum Press, 1959), 137.

38. Elizabeth Tatar, "Chant," in Kanahele, *Hawaiian Music,* 53–68; Mary Kawena Pukui, "Songs *(Meles)* of Old Kaʻu, Hawaii," *Journal of American Folklore* 62, no. 245 (1949): 247–58; Elizabeth Buck, *Paradise Remade: The Politics of Culture and History in Hawaiʻi* (Philadelphia: Temple University Press, 1993), 43–46, 101–13; and Mantle Hood, "Musical Ornamentation as History: The Hawaiian Steel Guitar," in *The Hawaiian Steel Guitar and Its Great Hawaiian Musicians,* ed. Lorene Ruymar (Anaheim Hills, Calif.: Centerstream Publishing, 1996), 12–13.

39. As quoted from radio transcripts, Donald D. Kilolani Mitchell and George S. Kanahele, "Steel Guitar," in Kanahele, *Hawaiian Music,* 366–67. See also Ruymar, *Hawaiian Steel Guitar,* 8–9, 14, 16–20.

40. Mitchell and Kanahele, "Steel Guitar," 367–68. See also Ruymar, *Hawaiian Steel Guitar,* 2–8, 11, 16–26; and Helen H. Roberts, *Ancient Hawaiian Music,* Bulletin 29 (Honolulu: Bishop Museum, 1926), 10–11.

41. Hood, "Musical Ornamentation," 12–15; and *Vintage Hawaiian Music: The Great Singers, 1928–1934,* Rounder Records, 1989.

42. Besides the guitar, another imported musical instrument that became indigenized and was exported with great success to the continental United States was the ukulele. For a succinct and well-researched account, see John King and Jim Tranquada, "A New History of the Origins and Development of the ʻUkulele, 1838–1915," *Hawaiian Journal of History* 37 (2003): 1–32.

43. On Hawaiian musical adaptations, see Buck, *Paradise Remade,* 114–20, 173–91. For a broader discussion on the "whitening" of Hawaiian cultural forms, especially dance and music, see Jane C. Desmond, *Staging Tourism: Bodies on Display from Waikiki to Sea World* (Chicago: University of Chicago Press, 1999), 60–78.

44. As quoted in Mitchell and Kanahele, "Steel Guitar," 368. Joseph Kekuku died on Jan-

uary 16, 1932, and was buried in Orchard Street Cemetery, Dover, New Jersey. His ashes, it has been claimed, were returned to and buried in Laʻie, Oʻahu, where he was born; see Lorene Ruymar, ed., *The Hawaiian Steel Guitar and Its Great Hawaiian Musicians* (Anaheim Hills, Calif.: Centerstream Publishing, 1996), 24. James Little, director of the board of trustees of the Orchard Street Cemetery, told me in 2006 that neither the cemetery records, which date back to 1880, nor his twenty-plus years overseeing the cemetery offer any evidence that Kekuku's body or ashes were exhumed. I am grateful to James Little for this information, and to Kekela Kuhia Miller, who directed me to the gravesite in Laʻie.

45. Elizabeth Tatar, *Strains of Change: The Impact of Tourism on Hawaiian Music,* Bishop Museum Special Publication 78 (Honolulu: Bishop Museum Press, 1987).

46. *Honolulu Star Bulletin,* May 12, 1967.

47. Emperor Hanapi, "Mike Keliiahonui Hanapi," *Haʻllono Mele* 3, no. 10 (1977): 6–7; and "Mike Keliiahonui Hanapi," in Kanahele, *Hawaiian Music,* 104–6. For Hawaiian musicians who toured Asia, see "The Tau Moe Story," *Hawaiian Steel Guitar Association Newsletter* 5, no. 19 (1990): 3–6; 5, no. 20 (1990): 8–10; 6, no. 21 (1991): 16–17; 6, no. 22 (1991): 16–18; 6, no. 23 (1991): 22–23; and George S. Kanahele, "Ernest Kaai, a Giant in Hawaiian Music," *Haʻllono Mele* 3, no. 11 (1977): 3–4.

48. *Sol Hoopii: Master of the Hawaiian Guitar,* vol. 1, original recordings from 1926–1930, Rounder Records 1024, Cambridge, Massachusetts, 1991; and "Solomon Hoopii Influenced the World," *Haʻllono Mele* 3, no. 7 (1977): 1–2, 6.

49. "Solomon Kaaiai Hoopii," in Kanahele, *Hawaiian Music,* 145.

50. Kanahele, *Hawaiian Music,* 106–7, provides a working definition of *hapa haole* music. A prominent Hawaiian musician, Charles E. King, bemoaned the mixtures of jazz with Hawaiian music and urged a strict definition of "Hawaiian music." See George S. Kanahele, "Charles E. King, Consensus Dean of Hawaiian Music," *Haʻllono Mele* 3, no. 8 (1977): 5–6; and 3, no. 9 (1977): 6–7.

51. Frank Morton Todd, *The Story of the Exposition: Being the Official History of the International Celebration Held in San Francisco in 1915 to Commemorate the Discovery of the Pacific Ocean and the Construction of the Panama Canal* (New York: G. P. Putnam's Sons, 1921), xiii.

52. Christian Brinton, *Impressions of the Art at the Panama-Pacific Exposition* (New York: John Lane Company, 1916), 49.

53. Albert P. Taylor, "Hawaii: The Best-Known Building at the Panama-Pacific Exposi-

tion, 1915," *Hawaiian Almanac and Annual for 1916* (Honolulu: Thos. G. Thrum, 1915): 149.

54. As quoted in Todd, *Story of the Exposition,* 321–22.

55. Ibid., 322, 323.

56. Ward Warren Thayer, *Report to Hon. Lucius E. Pinkham, Governor of Hawaii . . . Concerning Hawaii's Exhibit at the Panama-Pacific International Exposition* (Honolulu: Hawaiian Gazette, 1917), 15, 16.

57. *Paradise of the Pacific* 29, no. 11 (1916): 10–11. On the Hotel Lexington's "Hawaiian Room," which operated from the 1930s to 1966, see Adria L. Imada, "Hawaiians on Tour: Hula Circuits through the American Empire," *American Quarterly* 56, no. 1 (2004): 126–34.

58. "George E. K. Awai Fueled the Hawaiian Music Craze in 1915," *Ha'Ilono Mele* 3, no. 9 (1977): 5–6.

59. Kanahele, *Hawaiian Music,* 290–92; and *Paradise of the Pacific* 29, no. 11 (1916): 11.

60. *New York Times,* January 9, 1912.

61. "Bird of Paradise," in Kanahele, *Hawaiian Music,* 45–46.

62. *Pittsburgh Reader,* February 16, 1915.

63. *Detroit News,* September 4, 1917. For these reviews of *Bird of Paradise,* I am indebted to Michelle S. Liu, who researched and recovered them for me.

64. Kanahele, *Hawaiian Music,* 46.

65. Reyes, *Made in Paradise,* 44–45, 64–67.

66. See, e.g., Aeko Sereno, "Images of the Hula Dancer and 'Hula Girl': 1778–1960" (Ph.D. dissertation, University of Hawai'i, 1990), 168–69, 173, 179–80; and Gary Y. Okihiro, *Common Ground: Reimagining American History* (Princeton, N.J.: Princeton University Press, 2001), 31–34, 87–94.

67. Margaret L. Archuleta, Brenda J. Child, and K. Tsianina Lomawaima, eds., *Away from Home: American Indian Boarding School Experiences, 1879–2000* (Phoenix: Heard Museum, 2000), 67–69.

68. "Mrs. Johnny Pineapple Recalls Some of Hawaiian Musicians on the U.S. Mainland in Early 1900s," *Ha'Ilono Mele* 3, no. 3 (1977): 4.

69. "My Hula Hula Love" (1911), words by Edward Madden; "Oh! How She Could Yacki Hacki Wicki Wacki Woo" (That's Love in Honolulu) (1916), words by Stanley Murphy and Chas. McCarron; "On the South Sea Isle" (1916), words by Harry Von Tilzer;

and "Since Maggie Dooley Learned the Hooley Hooley" (1916), words by Edgar
Leslie and Bert Kalmar.

70. Kanahele, *Hawaiian Music,* 387.

71. Live performances, especially hula dancing, promoted an "imagined intimacy" between
the United States and Hawai'i, according to Imada, "Hawaiians on Tour," 134–36.

72. Interview with Aunt Jennie Wilson, February 4, 1961, Charlot Tape 008, Special Collections, Hamilton Library, University of Hawai'i. See also Interview with Jennie Kapahukulaokamamalu Wilson, January 1, 1962, Archives, HAW 59.3.1, Bishop Museum, Honolulu; "Last Living Court Dancer," *Honolulu Star-Bulletin,* May 29, 1960
("Hawaiian Life"); Sereno, "Images of the Hula Dancer," 154–74; and "Kini (Jennie)
Kapahu Wilson," in *Notable Women of Hawaii,* ed. Barbara Bennett Peterson (Honolulu: University of Hawai'i Press, 1984), 406–8.

73. Interview with Jennie Kapahukulaokamamalu Wilson, July 1962, Archives, HAW
59.8.2, Bishop Museum, Honolulu.

74. Ruymar, *Hawaiian Steel Guitar,* 66, 68, 69.

75. Ibid., 70–72.

76. For a contrary interpretation of Hawaiian representations of race, gender, and sexuality as distinctive from those of African Americans, see Desmond, *Staging Tourism.*

77. Gurre Ploner Noble, *Hula Blues: The Story of Johnny Noble, Hawaii, Its Music and
Musicians* (Honolulu: Tongg Publishing, 1948), 45–46, 53. Kanahele, *Hawaiian
Music,* 154–55.

78. See, e.g., "Ma Honolulu Queen" (1896), words and music by Dorothy K. Crapser;
"My Honolulu Lady" (1898) and "The Belle of Honolulu" (1898), words and music
by Lee Johnson; "My Gal from Honolulu" (1899), words by Maggie D. Branard,
music by George E. Ebert; "Ma Honolulu Man" (1899), words and music by Lee
Johnson; "My Bamboo Queen" (1903), words and music by Harry Von Tilzer; and
"When Old Bill Bailey Plays the Ukalele" (1915), words and music by Charles Mc-
Carron and Nat Vincent.

79. Tatar, *Strains of Change,* 5, 11.

80. Kanahele, *Hawaiian Music,* 131, 132.

81. Noble, *Hula Blues,* 9. See also interview with Auntie Genoa Keawe in *Da Kine
Sound: Conversations with the People Who Create Hawaiian Music,* by Burl
Burlingame and Robert Kamohalu Kasher, vol. 1 (Kailua, Hawai'i: Press Pacifica,
1978), 27–28.

82. Kanahele, *Hawaiian Music,* 136.

83. Noble, *Hula Blues,* 46–47.

84. The bottleneck style of guitar playing imitated the sliding of a broken bottle's neck over the steel guitar strings to produce a melancholy, blues sound.

85. As quoted in Ruymar, *Hawaiian Steel Guitar,* 51.

86. *King Bennie Nawahi: Hawaiian String Virtuoso,* Yazoo Records, 2000; *Hawaiian Music: Honolulu, Hollywood, Nashville, 1927–1944,* 2 CDs, Frémeaux & Associés, 1995; and for recordings of the QRS Boys and Georgia Jumpers, *Florida Rhythm,* BDW 8011, Jazz Oracle Phonograph Record Co.

87. W. C. Handy, *Father of the Blues: An Autobiography,* ed. Arna Bontemps (New York: Macmillan, 1941), 78.

88. Ruymar, *Hawaiian Steel Guitar,* 51–52.

89. Al Handa, "The National Steel Guitar, Part Four," July 1998, www.nationalguitars .com/part4.html. For Black Ace sound clips, http://www.arhoolie.com/titles/374 .shtml. See Joe Goldmark, *The International Steel Guitar and Dobro Discography* (San Francisco, 1994), 3, for a distinction between the blues slide and Hawaiian slide guitar technique and sound.

90. As quoted in Sherrie Tucker, *Swing Shift: "All-Girl" Bands of the 1940s* (Durham, N.C.: Duke University Press, 2000), 183–84.

91. Ibid., 185.

92. For an extended discussion of the band's "internationalism," see ibid., 163–94.

93. *Casey Bill: The Hawaiian Guitar Wizard, 1935–1938,* APM, 1994.

94. Bill C. Malone, *Country Music, U.S.A.* (Austin: University of Texas Press, 2002), 26.

95. Ibid., 39–40.

96. McIntire was born in Honolulu in 1904 and was a steel guitarist, composer, singer, and band leader; his Hawaiians were the resident band of New York City's Hotel Lexington from 1947 to 1951. "Lani McIntire," in Ruymar, *Hawaiian Steel Guitar,* 100.

97. Jerry Byrd, "Musical Diggings," *Ha'Ilono Mele* 1, no. 2 (1975): 4, 6; "Jerry Byrd," in Ruymar, *Hawaiian Steel Guitar,* 84; and Malone, *Country Music,* 128. For a history, annotated discography, and bibliography of the steel guitar, see Daniel Kahn's three-part "Steel Guitar Development," *Ha'Ilono Mele* 2, no. 3 (1976): 4–6; no. 4 (1976): 4–6; and no. 5 (1976): 1–5. On Bob Wills and the Texas Playboys, including steel

guitarist Leon McAuliffe, a member of the Playboys, see Malone, *Country Music,* 170–74; and Rich Kienzle, "Steel Guitar: The Western Swing Era," *Guitar Player* 13 (December 1979): 48, 50–52.

98. Jim Hand, "From the Beginning," *Pedal Steel Newsletter* 18, no. 5 (1991): 8–10.

99. "Hilo March," in Kanahele, *Hawaiian Music,* 129. On David Kaʻili, see "David Kaʻili: Senior Steel Guitarist of the World," *Hawaiian Steel Guitar Association Newsletter* 8, no. 29 (1993): 3–5.

100. *Hawaiian Music: Honolulu, Hollywood, Nashville, 1927–1944* (see note 86).

101. Malone, *Country Music,* 82, 85, 86, 87; and Nolan Porterfield, *Jimmie Rodgers: The Life and Times of America's 'Blue Yodeler'* (Urbana: University of Illinois Press, 1992), 10, 11.

102. Malone, *Country Music,* 104, 127; and *Slidin' on the Frets: The Hawaiian Steel Guitar Phenomenon,* Yazoo Records, 2000.

103. Malone, *Country Music,* 138.

104. Ibid., 141, 142.

105. Ibid., 142–44.

106. *JEMF* [John Edwards Memorial Foundation] *Quarterly* 15, no. 54 (1979): 127.

107. *King Bennie Nawahi* (see note 86).

108. See a claim for Sol Hoʻopiʻi as the first to perform on the electric steel guitar before an audience. Hoʻopiʻi, because of his extensive involvement in film, was known as the "Hollywood Hawaiian." Ruymar, *Hawaiian Steel Guitar,* 90; and Kanahele, *Hawaiian Music,* 145.

109. Malone, *Country Music,* 157–58; and Kienzle, "Steel Guitar," 48.

7. ISLANDS AND CONTINENTS

1. Felipe Fernández-Armesto, *Millennium: A History of the Last Thousand Years* (New York: Charles Scribner's Sons, 1995), 20.

2. Ibid., 720.

3. See, e.g., Judith Williamson, "Woman Is an Island: Femininity and Colonization," in *Studies in Entertainment: Critical Approaches to Mass Culture,* ed. Tania Modleski (Bloomington: Indiana University Press, 1986), 99–118; and Patty O'Brien, *The Pacific Muse: Exotic Femininity and the Colonial Pacific* (Seattle: University of Washington Press, 2006).

4. Martin W. Lewis and Kären E. Wigen, *The Myth of Continents: A Critique of Metageography* (Berkeley: University of California Press, 1997), 1.

5. For a summary of ancient Greek views of the ocean, see John Gillis, *Islands of the Mind: How the Human Imagination Created the Atlantic World* (New York: Palgrave Macmillan, 2004), 5–10.

6. Lewis and Wigen, *Myth of Continents*, 26, 29. American exceptionalism and its claim of distinction from "old" Europe abetted that continental metageography.

7. Ibid., 30.

8. Ibid., 31–35.

9. For evolving European views of islands, see especially Gillis, *Islands of the Mind;* Rod Edmond and Vanessa Smith, eds., *Islands in History and Representation* (London: Routledge, 2003); and John Fowles, *Islands* (Boston: Little, Brown, 1978). On Pacific islands, see Bernard Smith, *European Vision and the South Pacific* (New Haven, Conn.: Yale University Press, 1960); Greg Dening, *Islands and Beaches: Discourse on a Silent Land, Marquesas 1774–1880* (Honolulu: University Press of Hawai'i, 1980); Rod Edmond, *Representing the South Pacific: Colonial Discourse from Cook to Gauguin* (Cambridge: Cambridge University Press, 1997); Nicholas Thomas, *In Oceania: Visions, Artifacts, Histories* (Durham, N.C.: Duke University Press, 1997); K. R. Howe, *Nature, Culture, and History: The "Knowing" of Oceania* (Honolulu: University of Hawai'i Press, 2000); and O'Brien, *Pacific Muse.*

10. Epeli Hau'ofa, "Our Sea of Islands," *Contemporary Pacific* 6, no. 1 (1994): 49–60, or see an earlier version and responses in Eric Waddell, Vijay Naidu, and Epeli Hau'ofa, eds., *A New Oceania: Rediscovering Our Sea of Islands* (Suva, Fiji: University of the South Pacific, 1993).

11. For a study of the social construction of oceanic space, its uses, regulations, and representations, see Philip E. Steinberg, *The Social Construction of the Ocean* (Cambridge: Cambridge University Press, 2001).

12. Hau'ofa, "Our Sea," 151, 152.

13. Ibid., 152, 153. See also Steinberg, *Social Construction*, 39–67, for a comparative view, including a Micronesian perspective, of the ocean.

14. Albert Wendt, "Towards a New Oceania," *Seaweeds and Constructions* 7 (1983): 71, 76, 77. This essay was originally published in *Mana* 1, no. 1 (1976).

15. Yi-Fu Tuan, *Topophilia: A Study of Environmental Perception, Attitudes, and Values* (Englewood Cliffs, N.J.: Prentice-Hall, 1974), 118.

16. See, e.g., Thomas Weiskel, *The Romantic Sublime* (Baltimore: Johns Hopkins University Press, 1976); and Mary Arensberg, ed., *The American Sublime* (Albany: State University of New York Press, 1986).

17. For a coupling of geology with the Pele account, see Jelle Zeilinga de Boer and Donald Theodore Sanders, *Volcanoes in Human History: The Far-Reaching Effects of Major Eruptions* (Princeton, N.J.: Princeton University Press, 2002), 22–46.

18. Jane C. Desmond, *Staging Tourism: Bodies on Display from Waikiki to Sea World* (Chicago: University of Chicago Press, 1999), 34–59.

19. Beginning in the 1970s, reggae, with its message of freedom from oppression, appealed to Hawaiian cultural and sovereignty movement activists, who produced "Jawaiian" (Jamaican and Hawaiian) music. A similar development occurred with rap and hip hop during the 1990s. See Amy Kuʻuleialoha Stillman, "Hula Hits, Local Music and Local Charts: Some Dynamics of Popular Hawaiian Music"; and Andrew N. Weintraub, "Jawaiian Music and Local Cultural Identity in Hawaiʻi," in *Sound Alliances: Indigenous Peoples, Cultural Politics and Popular Music in the Pacific,* ed. Philip Hayward (London: Cassell, 1998), 78–88, 88–103; Fay Yokomizo Akindes, "Sudden Rush: *Na Mele Paleoleo* (Hawaiian Rap) as Liberatory Discourse," *Discourse* 23, no. 1 (2001): 82–98; and Kuʻualoha Hoʻomanawanui, "Yo Brah, Itʻs Hip Hop Jawaiian Style: The Influence of Reggae and Rap on Contemporary Hawaiian Music," *Hawaiʻi Review* 56 (Summer 2001): 136–75. I am indebted and grateful to Amy Kuʻuleialoha Stillman for advice and assistance on Hawaiian music.

20. W. H. S. Jones, trans., *Hippocrates,* vol. 1 (Cambridge, Mass.: Harvard University Press, 1923), 105–33. For versions of that hypothesis contemporary with this bookʻs time period, see Charles H. Pearson, *National Life and Character* (London, 1893); and Lothrop Stoddard, *The Rising Tide of Color against White World-Supremacy* (New York: Charles Scribnerʻs Sons, 1920).

BIBLIOGRAPHY

ARCHIVES AND COLLECTIONS

Archives and Special Collections, Williams College, Williamstown, Mass.

Bernice Pauahi Bishop Museum, Honolulu, Hawai'i

Black Sailors Research Project, Howard University, http://www.itd.nps.gov/cwss/sailors.htm

Cemeteries: Carlisle, Pa.; Cornwall, Conn.; Dover, N.J.; Hampton, Va.; La'ie, Hawai'i; Honolulu, Hawai'i

Cornwall Historical Society, Cornwall, Conn.

Hawaiian Evangelical Association Archives, Hawaiian Mission Children's Society, Honolulu, Hawai'i

Hawaiian Mission Children's Society, Honolulu, Hawai'i

Hawai'i State Archives, Honolulu, Hawai'i

Hawai'i State Library, Honolulu, Hawai'i

Lyman House Memorial Museum, Hilo, Hawai'i

National Archives, Washington, D.C.

New Bedford Free Public Library, New Bedford, Mass.

New Bedford Whaling Museum, Kendall Institute, New Bedford, Mass.

Special Collections, Hamilton Library, University of Hawai'i, Mānoa, Honolulu, Hawai'i

U.S. Census, 1840, 1850, 1860, 1870, 1880

NEWSPAPERS AND MAGAZINES

Boston Daily Journal

Boston Evening Courier

Boston Recorder

Daily Mercury (New Bedford, Mass.)

Detroit News

Evening Standard (New Bedford, Mass)

The Friend
HaʻIlono Mele
Hawaiian Gazette
Hawaiian Steel Guitar Association
   Newsletter
Honolulu Advertiser
Honolulu Star-Bulletin
Nantucket Inquirer

New York Times
Oregon Spectator
Pacific Commercial Advertiser
   (Honolulu)
Panoplist and Missionary Magazine
Paradise of the Pacific
Pittsburgh Reader
Southern Workman

SECONDARY SOURCES

Adams, David Wallace. 1977. "Education in Hues: Red and Black at Hampton Institute, 1878–1893." *South Atlantic Quarterly* 67, no. 2 (Spring): 159–76.

———. 1995. *Education for Extinction: American Indians and the Boarding School Experience, 1875–1928*. Lawrence: University of Kansas Press.

Adams, Henry, et al. 1987. *John La Farge*. New York: Abbeville Press.

Akindes, Fay Yokomizo. 2001. "Sudden Rush: *Na Mele Paleoleo* (Hawaiian Rap) as Liberatory Discourse." *Discourse* 23, no. 1 (Winter): 82–98.

Alapaʻi, David. 1995. "Nani Wale nōʻo Pele i ka Lua." In *Nā Mele Welo: Songs of Our Heritage*, translated by Mary Kawena Pukui. Honolulu: Bishop Museum Press.

Alexander, W. D. 1892. "The Relations between the Hawaiian Islands and Spanish America in Early Times." *Papers of the Hawaiian Historical Society,* no. 1 (January 28).

American Board of Commissioners for Foreign Missions. 1819. *Mission to the Sandwich Islands*. Boston: U. Crocker.

Anderson, James D. 1978. "The Hampton Model of Normal School Industrial Education, 1868–1900." In *New Perspectives on Black Educational History*, edited by Vincent P. Franklin and James D. Anderson, 61–96. Boston: G. K. Hall.

Andrews, Lorrin. 1875. "Remarks on Hawaiian Poetry." *Islander* 1, no. 7 (April 16): 26–27.

Archuleta, Margaret L., Brenda J. Child, and K. Tsianina Lomawaima, eds. 2000. *Away from Home: American Indian Boarding School Experiences, 1879–2000*. Phoenix, Ariz.: Heard Museum.

Arensberg, Mary, ed. 1986. *The American Sublime*. Albany: State University of New York Press.

Armstrong, Clarissa. 1885. *C.C.A.: May 15, 1885, 80 Years*. Hampton, Va.: Normal School Steam Press.

Armstrong, M. F. 1885. *Hampton Institute: Its Work for Two Races, 1868 to 1885.* Hampton, Va.: Normal School Press Print.

Armstrong, Mary F., and Helen W. Ludlow. 1874. *Hampton and Its Students.* New York: G. P. Putnam's Sons.

Armstrong, Samuel Chapman. 1880. "Address by General S. C. Armstrong." *Hawaiian Gazette,* August 30.

————. 1883. *The Indian Question.* Hampton, Va.: Normal School Steam Press.

————. 1884. "Lessons from the Hawaiian Islands." *Journal of Christian Philosophy,* January, 226–28.

————. 1887. "Reminiscences." In *Richard Armstrong: America, Hawaii.* Hampton, Va.: Normal School Steam Press.

————. 1919. *Education for Life.* Hampton, Va.: Press of the Hampton Normal and Agricultural Institute.

Baldwin, James. 1899. *Our New Possessions: Cuba, Puerto Rico, Hawaii, Philippines.* New York: American Book Company.

Barman, Jean. 1995. "New Land, New Lives: Hawaiian Settlement in British Columbia." *Hawaiian Journal of History* 29:1–32.

————. 2004. *Maria Mahoi of the Islands.* Vancouver: New Star Books.

Barman, Jean, and Bruce McIntyre Watson. 2006. *Leaving Paradise: Indigenous Hawaiians in the Pacific Northwest, 1787–1898.* Honolulu: University of Hawai'i Press.

Barrère, Dorothy B., Mary Kawena Pukui, and Marion Kelly. 1980. *Hula: Historical Perspectives.* Pacific Anthropological Records, no. 30. Honolulu: Bishop Museum Press.

Beaglehole, J. C., ed. 1967. *The Voyage of the Resolution and the Discovery, 1776–1780.* Parts 1 and 2. Cambridge: Cambridge University Press.

Beckwith, Martha Warren. 1949. "Function and Meaning of the Kumulipo Birth Chant in Ancient Hawaii." *Journal of American Folklore* 62, no. 245 (July–September): 290–93.

————. 1970. *Hawaiian Mythology.* Honolulu: University Press of Hawai'i.

————, ed. and trans. 1972. *The Kumulipo: A Hawaiian Creation Chant.* Honolulu: University of Hawai'i Press.

Bell, Susan N. 1976. "Owhyhee's Prodigal." *Hawaiian Journal of History* 10:25–32.

Bennett, Guy Vernon. 1913. "Early Relations of the Sandwich Islands to the Old Oregon Territory." *Washington Historical Quarterly* 4, no. 2 (April): 116–26.

Bergin, Billy. 2004. *Loyal to the Land: The Legendary Parker Ranch, 750–1950.* Honolulu: University of Hawai'i Press.

Berlin, Ira, Joseph P. Reidy, and Leslie S. Rowland, eds. 1998. *Freedom's Soldiers: The Black Military Experience in the Civil War*. Cambridge: Cambridge University Press.

Bevens, Darcy, ed. 1992. *On the Rim of Kilauea: Excerpts from the Volcano House Register, 1865–1955*. Hawai'i National Park: Hawai'i Natural History Association.

Beyer, Carl Kalani. 2003. "Manual and Industrial Education during Hawaiian Sovereignty: Curriculum in the Transculturation of Hawai'i." Ph.D. dissertation, University of Illinois, Chicago.

———. 2004. "Manual and Industrial Education for Hawaiians during the 19th Century." *Hawaiian Journal of History* 38:1–34.

Bingham, Hiram. 1847. *A Residence of Twenty-one Years in the Sandwich Islands*. New York: Converse.

Bird, Isabella L. [1881] 1998. *Six Months in the Sandwich Islands among Hawai'i's Palm Groves, Coral Reefs, and Volcanoes*. Honolulu: Mutual Publishing.

Blackburn, Mark. 2000. *Hula Girls & Surfer Boys*. Atglen, Pa.: Schiffer Publishing.

Blue, George Verne. 1924. "A Hudson's Bay Company Contract for Hawaiian Labor." *Oregon Historical Quarterly* 25 (March): 72–75.

Bongie, Chris. 1991. *Exotic Memories: Literature, Colonialism, and the Fin de Siècle*. Stanford, Calif.: Stanford University Press.

Breault, William J. 1998. *John A. Sutter in Hawaii and California, 1838–1839*. Rancho Cordova, Calif.: Landmark Enterprises.

Brennan, Joseph. 1974. *The Parker Ranch of Hawaii: The Saga of a Ranch and a Dynasty*. New York: John Day.

———. 1978. *Paniolo*. Honolulu: Ku Pa'a.

Brigham, William T. 1909. *The Volcanoes of Kilauea and Mauna Loa on the Island of Hawaii*. Memoirs of the Bernice Pauahi Bishop Museum 2, no. 4. Honolulu: Bishop Museum Press.

Brinton, Christian. 1916. *Impressions of the Art at the Panama-Pacific Exposition*. New York: John Lane.

Broussard, Albert S. 1990. "Carlotta Stewart Lai, a Black Teacher in the Territory of Hawai'i." *Hawaiian Journal of History* 24:129–54.

Brown, J. Ross. 1968. *Etchings of a Whaling Cruise*, edited by John Seelye. Cambridge, Mass.: Harvard University Press.

Brumberg, Joan Jacobs. 1980. *Mission for Life: The Story of the Family of Adoniram Judson. . . .* New York: Free Press.

Buck, Elizabeth. 1993. *Paradise Remade: The Politics of Culture and History in Hawai'i*. Philadelphia: Temple University Press.

Buffalohead, W. Roger, and Paulette Fairbanks Molin. 1996. "'A Nucleus of Civilization': American Indian Families at Hampton Institute in the Late Nineteenth Century." *Journal of American Indian Education* 35, no. 3 (Spring): 59–94.

Burlingame, Burl, and Robert Kamohalu Kasher. 1978. *Da Kine Sound: Conversations with the People Who Create Hawaiian Music.* Kailua, Hawai'i: Press Pacifica.

Byrd, Jerry. 1975. "Musical Diggings." *Ha'Ilono Mele* 1, no. 2 (February): 4, 6.

Chamberlain, Paul H., Jr. 1968. *The Foreign Mission School.* Cornwall, Conn.: Cornwall Historical Society.

Chambliss, Randolph L. 1982. "The Blacks." *Social Process in Hawaii* 29:113–15.

Chappell, David A. 1997. *Double Ghosts: Oceanian Voyagers on Euroamerican Ships.* Armonk, N.Y.: M. E. Sharpe.

Charlot, John. 1983. "A Pattern in Three Hawaiian Chants." *Journal of American Folklore* 96, no. 379 (January–March): 64–68.

Cheever, Henry T. 1851. *Life in the Sandwich Islands: Or, The Heart of the Pacific, as It Was and Is.* New York: A. S. Barnes.

Church, Mary Brinsmade. 1913. "Elias Boudinot: An Account of His Life Written by His Granddaughter." Unpublished paper of the Woman's Club, Washington, Conn., October 1.

Clark, Robert Carlton. 1934. "Hawaiians in Early Oregon." *Oregon Historical Quarterly* 35, no. 1 (March): 22–31.

Cleland, Robert Glass. 1927. *A History of California: The American Period.* New York: Macmillan.

Clifford, James. 1997. *Routes: Travel and Translation in the Late Twentieth Century.* Cambridge, Mass.: Harvard University Press.

Coan, Titus. 1882. *Life in Hawaii: An Autobiographical Sketch of Mission Life and Labors (1835–1882).* New York: Anson D. F. Randolph.

Cook, James. 1852. *The Voyages of Captain James Cook Round the World.* Vol. 2. London: John Tallis.

Cook, Warren L. 1973. *Flood Tide of Empire: Spain and the Pacific Northwest, 1543–1819.* New Haven, Conn.: Yale University Press.

Cordes, Frederick C., ed. and trans. 1960. "Letters of A. Rotchev, Last Commandant of Fort Ross and the Resumé of the Report of the Russian-American Company for the Year 1850–51." *California Historical Society Quarterly* 39, no. 2 (June): 97–115.

Costa, Mazeppa King. 1951. "Dance in the Society and Hawaiian Islands as Presented by the Early Writings, 1767–1842." M.A. thesis, University of Hawai'i.

Cox, Ross. 1831. *Adventures on the Columbia River. . . .* Vol. 1. London: Henry Colburn and Richard Bentley.

Cumming, C. F. Gordon. 1883. *Fire Fountains: The Kingdom of Hawaii, Its Volcanoes, and the History of Its Missions*. Edinburgh: W. Blackwood.

Cutter, Donald. 1980. "The Spanish in Hawaii: Gaytan to Marin." *Hawaiian Journal of History* 14:16–17.

Dale, Edward Everett, and Gaston Little. 1939. *Cherokee Cavaliers: Forty Years of Cherokee History as Told in the Correspondence of the Ridge-Watie-Boudinot Family*. Norman: University of Oklahoma Press.

Damon, Samuel C. 1927. *A Journey of Lower Oregon & Upper California, 1848–49*. San Francisco: John J. Newbegin.

Dana, Richard Henry, Jr. [1840] 1981. *Two Years before the Mast: A Personal Narrative of Life at Sea*. New York: Penguin Books.

Daws, Gavan. 1968. *Shoal of Time: A History of the Hawaiian Islands*. Honolulu: University Press of Hawai'i.

Day, A. Grove. 1987. *Mad about Islands: Novelists of a Vanished Pacific*. Honolulu: Mutual Publishing.

———. 1990. "Foreword." In *Roughing It in the Sandwich Islands*, by Mark Twain, ix–xxxiii. Honolulu: Mutual Publishing.

de Boer, Jelle Zeilinga, and Donald Theodore Sanders. 2002. *Volcanoes in Human History: The Far-Reaching Effects of Major Eruptions*. Princeton, N.J.: Princeton University Press.

Dening, Greg. 1980. *Islands and Beaches: Discourse on a Silent Land, Marquesas, 1774–1880*. Honolulu: University Press of Hawai'i.

Desmond, Jane C. 1999. *Staging Tourism: Bodies on Display from Waikiki to Sea World*. Chicago: University of Chicago Press.

Dillon, Richard H. 1955. "Kanaka Colonies in California." *Pacific Historical Review* 24, no. 1 (February): 17–23.

Douglass, Frederick. 1855. *My Bondage and My Freedom*. New York: Miller, Orton and Mulligan.

Dulles, Foster R. 1933. *Lowered Boats: A Chronicle of American Whaling*. New York: Harcourt, Brace.

Duncan, Janice K. 1972. "Minority without a Champion: The Kanaka Contribution to the Western United States, 1750–1900." M.A. thesis, Portland State University.

———. 1972. *Minority without a Champion: Kanakas on the Pacific Coast, 1788–1850*. Portland: Oregon Historical Society.

———. 1973. "Kanaka World Travelers and Fur Company Employees, 1785–1860." *Hawaiian Journal of History* 7:93–111.

Dwight, E. W. 1818. *Memoir of Henry Obookiah, a Native of the Sandwich Islands, Who*

Died at Cornwall, Connecticut, February 17, 1818, Aged 26. New York: American Tract Society.

Edmond, Rod. 1997. *Representing the South Pacific: Colonial Discourse from Cook to Gauguin.* Cambridge: Cambridge University Press.

Edmond, Rod, and Vanessa Smith, eds. 2003. *Islands in History and Representation.* London: Routledge.

Ellis, Leonard Bolles. 1892. *History of New Bedford and Its Vicinity, 1602–1892.* Syracuse, N.Y.: D. Mason.

Ellis, William. [1827] 1963. *Journal of William Ellis: Narrative of a Tour of Hawaii, or Owhyhee; with Remarks on the History, Traditions, Manners, Customs and Language of the Inhabitants of the Sandwich Islands.* Honolulu: Advertiser Publishing.

———. 1829. *Polynesian Researches during a Residence of Nearly Eight Years in the Society and Sandwich Islands.* Vol. 4. London: Fisher, Son and Jackson.

Emerson, Nathaniel B. [1909] 1998. *Unwritten Literature of Hawaii: The Sacred Songs of the Hula.* Honolulu: Mutual Publishing.

———. 1915. *Pele and Hiiaka: A Myth from Hawaii.* Honolulu: Honolulu Star-Bulletin.

Engs, Robert Frances. 1999. *Educating the Disfranchised and Disinherited: Samuel Chapman Armstrong and Hampton Institute, 1839–1893.* Knoxville: University of Tennessee Press.

Fernández-Armesto, Felipe. 1995. *Millennium: A History of the Last Thousand Years.* New York: Charles Scribner's Sons.

Finney, Ben R. 1976. "New, Non-Armchair Research." In *Pacific Navigation and Voyaging.* Polynesian Society Memoirs, no. 39, compiled by Ben R. Finney. Wellington, New Zealand: Polynesian Society.

———. 1979. *Hokule'a: The Way to Tahiti.* New York: Dodd, Mead.

———. 1985. "Voyagers into Ocean Space." In *Interstellar Migration and the Human Experience,* edited by Ben R. Finney and Eric M. Jones, 164–79. Berkeley: University of California Press.

———. 2003. *Sailing in the Wake of the Ancestors: Reviving Polynesian Voyaging.* Honolulu: Bishop Museum Press.

Finney, Ben, and James D. Houston. 1966. *Surfing: The Sport of Hawaiian Kings.* Rutland, Vt.: Charles E. Tuttle.

———. 1996. *Surfing: A History of the Ancient Hawaiian Sport.* Rohnert Park, Calif.: Pomegranate Artbooks.

Fisher, Richard V., Grant Heiken, and Jeffrey B. Hulen. 1997. *Volcanoes: Crucibles of Change.* Princeton, N.J.: Princeton University Press.

Forbes, David W. 1992. *Encounters with Paradise: Views of Hawaii and Its People, 1778–1941*. Honolulu: Honolulu Academy of Arts.

Forbes, David W., and Thomas K. Kunichika. 1983. *Hilo, 1825–1925: A Century of Paintings and Drawings*. Hilo, Hawai'i: Lyman House Memorial Museum.

Fowles, John. 1978. *Islands*. Boston: Little, Brown.

Franchère, Gabriel. 1854. *Narrative of a Voyage to the Northwest Coast of America, 1811–1814*, translated by J. V. Huntington. New York: Bedfield.

Francis, Peter. 1993. *Volcanoes: A Planetary Perspective*. Oxford: Clarendon Press.

Frierson, Pamela. 1991. *The Burning Island: A Journey through Myth and History in Volcano Country, Hawai'i*. San Francisco: Sierra Club Books.

Fritz, Henry E. 1963. *The Movement for Indian Assimilation, 1860–1890*. Philadelphia: University of Pennsylvania Press.

Frost, Rossie, and Locky [Frost]. 1977. "The King's Bullock Catcher." *Hawaiian Journal of History* 11:175–87.

Gabriel, Ralph Henry. 1941. *Elias Boudinot: Cherokee & His America*. Norman: University of Oklahoma Press.

Garcia, Shirley. 1999. "For the Life of the Land: Hula and Hawaii's Native Forests." In *Hawai'i: New Geographies*, edited by D. W. Woodcock. Honolulu: Department of Geography, University of Hawai'i, Mānoa.

Gibson, Arrell Morgan. 1993. *Yankees in Paradise: The Pacific Basin Frontier*. Albuquerque: University of New Mexico Press.

Gillis, John. 2004. *Islands of the Mind: How the Human Imagination Created the Atlantic World*. New York: Palgrave Macmillan.

Goldmark, Joe. 1994. *The International Steel Guitar and Dobro Discography*. San Francisco.

Golson, Jack, ed. *Polynesia Navigation: A Symposium on Andrew Sharp's Theory of Accidental Voyages*. Polynesian Society Memoirs, no. 34. Wellington, New Zealand: Polynesia Society.

Greer, Richard A. 1967. "Wandering Kamaainas: Notes on Hawaiian Emigration before 1848." *Journal of the West* 6, no. 2 (April): 221–25.

———. 1970. "California Gold—Some Reports to Hawaii." *Hawaiian Journal of History* 4:157–73.

Grimshaw, Patricia. 1989. *Paths of Duty: American Missionary Wives in Nineteenth-Century Hawaii*. Honolulu: University of Hawai'i Press.

Gudde, Erwin Gustave, ed. and trans. 1940. "Edward Vischer's First Visit to California." *California Historical Society Quarterly* 19, no. 3 (September): 193–216.

Haddon, A. C., and James Hornell. 1936. *Canoes of Oceania*. Vol. 1, *The Canoes of Polynesia, Fiji, and Micronesia*. Special Publication 27. Honolulu: Bernice P. Bishop Museum.

————. 1937. *Canoes of Oceania.* Vol. 2, *The Canoes of Melanesia, Queensland, and New Guinea.* Special Publication 28. Honolulu: Bernice P. Bishop Museum.

————. 1938. *Canoes of Oceania.* Vol. 3, *Definition of Terms, General Survey, and Conclusions.* Special Publication 29. Honolulu: Bernice P. Bishop Museum.

Haifley, Julie Link. 1981. *Titian Ramsay Peale, 1799–1885.* Washington, D.C.: George Washington University.

Halstead, Murat. 1898. *Our New Possessions: Natural Riches, Industrial Resources of Cuba, Porto Rico, Hawaii, the Ladrones, and the Philippine Islands.* Chicago: Dominion.

Halter, Marilyn. 1993. *Between Race and Ethnicity: Cape Verdean American Immigrants, 1860–1965.* Chicago: University of Illinois Press.

Hanapi, Emperor. 1977. "Mike Keliiahonui Hanapi." *Ha'Ilono Mele* 3, no. 10 (October): 6–7.

Hand, Jim. 1991. "From the Beginning." *Pedal Steel Newsletter* 18, no. 5:8–10.

Handa, Al. 1998. "The National Steel Guitar Part Four." (July). http://www.nationalguitars.com/part4.html.

Handy, E. S. Craighill, and Elizabeth Green Handy. 1972. *Native Planters in Old Hawaii: Their Life, Lore, and Environment.* Bernice P. Bishop Museum Bulletin 233. Honolulu: Bishop Museum Press.

Handy, W. C. 1941. *Father of the Blues: An Autobiography*, edited by Arna Bontemps. New York: Macmillan.

Hargrove, Hondon B. 1988. *Black Union Soldiers in the Civil War.* Jefferson, N.C.: McFarland.

Harris, Paul William. 1999. *Nothing but Christ: Rufus Anderson and the Ideology of Protestant Foreign Missions.* New York: Oxford University Press.

Haskin, Frederic J. 1920. "The White Man in the Tropics." *Mid-Pacific Magazine* 20, no. 1 (July): 17–19.

Haskins, C. W. 1890. *The Argonauts of California.* New York: Fords, Howard and Hulbert.

Hau'ofa, Epeli. 1994. "Our Sea of Islands." *Contemporary Pacific* 6, no. 1 (January): 49–60.

Hood, Mantle. 1996. "Musical Ornamentation as History: The Hawaiian Steel Guitar." In *The Hawaiian Steel Guitar and Its Great Hawaiian Musicians*, edited by Lorene Ruymar, 12–15. Anaheim Hills, Calif.: Centerstream Publishing.

Ho'omanawanui, Ku'ualoha. 2001. "Yo Brah, It's Hip Hop Jawaiian Style: The Influence of Reggae and Rap on Contemporary Hawaiian Music." *Hawai'i Review* 56 (Summer): 136–75.

Horan, James D., ed. 1960. *C.S.S. Shenandoah: The Memoirs of Lieutenant Commanding James I. Waddell.* New York: Crown Publishers.

Howay, F. W. 1933. "Brig Owhyhee in the Columbia, 1827." *Oregon Historical Quarterly* 34, no. 4 (December): 324–29.

Howe, K. R. 1984. *Where the Waves Fall: A New South Sea Islands History from First Settlement to Colonial Rule*. Honolulu: University of Hawai'i Press.

———. 2000. *Nature, Culture, and History: The "Knowing" of Oceania*. Honolulu: University of Hawai'i Press.

Hultgren, Mary Lou, and Paulette Fairbanks Molin. 1989. *To Lead and to Serve: American Indian Education at Hampton Institute, 1878–1923*. Virginia Beach: Virginia Foundation for the Humanities.

Ii, John Papa. 1959. *Fragments of Hawaiian History*, translated by Mary Kawena Pukui. Honolulu: Bishop Museum Press.

Illerbrun, W. J. 1972. "Kanaka Pete." *Hawaiian Journal of History* 6:156–66.

Imada, Adria L. 2004. "Hawaiians on Tour: Hula Circuits through the American Empire." *American Quarterly* 56, no. 1 (March): 111–49.

Jackson, Miles N. 2001. *And They Came: A Brief History and Annotated Bibliography of Blacks in Hawaii*. Durham, N.C.: Four-G.

Jaggar, Thomas A. 1945. *Volcanoes Declare War: Logistics and Strategy of Pacific Volcano Science*. Honolulu: Paradise of the Pacific.

———. 1956. *My Experiments with Volcanoes*. Honolulu: Hawaiian Volcano Research Association.

Jefferson, Thomas. 1954. *Notes on the State of Virginia*, edited by William Peden. Chapel Hill: University of North Carolina Press.

Johnson, Rubellite Kawena. 1981. *Kumulipo: The Hawaiian Hymn of Creation*. Vol. 1. Honolulu: Topgallant Publishing.

Jones, W. H. S., trans. 1923. *Hippocrates*. Vol. 1. Cambridge, Mass.: Harvard University Press.

Kaeppler, Adrienne L. 1973. "Music in Hawaii in the Nineteenth Century." In *Musikkulturen Asiens, Afrikas und Ozeaniens*, edited by Robert Günther, 311–38. Germany: Gustav Bosse Verlag Regensburg.

[Kahanamoku], Duke Paoa. 1911. "Riding the Surfboard." *Mid-Pacific Magazine* 1, no. 1 (January): 3.

Kahn, Daniel. 1976. "Steel Guitar Development." *Ha'Ilono Mele* 2, no. 3 (March): 6–7; 2, no. 4 (April): 4–6; and 2, no. 5 (May): 1–5.

Kalakaua, David. [1888] 1990. *The Legends and Myths of Hawaii: The Fables and Folk-Lore of a Strange People*. Honolulu: Mutual Publishing.

Kamakau, Samuel Manaiakalani. 1964. *Ka Po'e Kahiko: The People of Old*, edited by Dorothy B. Barrère and translated by Mary Kawena Pukui. Honolulu: Bishop Museum Press.

————. 1992. *Ruling Chiefs of Hawaii*. Honolulu: Kamehameha Schools Press.

Kanahele, George S. 1973. *Ki ho'alu: The Story of Slack Key*. Honolulu: Hawaiian Music Foundation.

————. 1977. "Charles E. King, Consensus Dean of Hawaiian Music." *Ha'Ilono Mele* 3, no. 8 (August): 5–6; and 3, no. 9 (September): 6–7.

————. 1977. "Ernest Kaai, a Giant in Hawaiian Music." *Ha'Ilono Mele* 3, no. 11 (November): 3–4.

————, ed. 1979. *Hawaiian Music and Musicians: An Illustrated History*. Honolulu: University Press of Hawai'i.

————. 1999. *Emma: Hawai'i's Remarkable Queen*. Honolulu: Queen Emma Foundation.

Kanahele, Pualani Kanaka'ole, and Davianna Pomaika'i McGregor. 1995. "Pele Beliefs, Customs, Practices." Unpublished manuscript, August. Hawai'i Geothermal Project.

Kanahele, Pualani Kanaka'ole, and Duke Kalani Wise. *Ka Honua Ola (The Living Earth)*. Honolulu: Center for Hawaiian Studies, University of Hawai'i, Mānoa.

Kane, Herb Kawainui. 1987. *Pele: Goddess of Hawai'i's Volcanoes*. Captain Cook, Hawai'i: Kawainui Press.

Karttunen, Frances. "Far-Away Neighbor Islands: Pacific Islanders on Nantucket during the Whaling Era." Unpublished paper.

Keller, Gary D. 1997. *A Biographical Handbook of Hispanics and United States Film*. Tempe, Ariz.: Bilingual Press.

Kelsey, Theodore. 1941. "Unknown Poetry of Hawaii." *Paradise of the Pacific* 53, no. 6 (June): 26–28, 31.

Kenn, Charles W. 1955. "Sutter's Canacas." Conference of California Historical Societies, *Newsletter* 2, no. 2:3–6.

————. 1956. "Descendants of Captain Sutter's Kanakas." In *Proceedings of the Second Annual Meeting of the Conference of California Historical Societies*, edited by Richard Coke Wood, 87–101. Stockton, Calif.: College of the Pacific.

Kent, Noel J. 1983. *Hawaii: Islands under the Influence*. New York: Monthly Review Press.

Kienzle, Rich. 1979. "Steel Guitar: The Western Swing Era." *Guitar Player* 13 (December): 48, 50–52.

Kimura, Larry. 1964. "Old-Time Parker Ranch Cowboys." *Hawaii Historical Review* 1, no. 9 (October): 161–68.

King, John, and Jim Tranquada. 2003. "A New History of the Origins and Development of the 'Ukulele, 1838–1915." *Hawaiian Journal of History* 37:1–32.

Kipling, Rudyard. 1940. *Rudyard Kipling's Verse*. New York: Doubleday, Doran.

Kittelson, David. 1963. "Hawaiians and Fur Traders." *Hawaii Historical Review* 1, no. 2 (January): 16–20.

————. 1965. "John Coxe: Hawaii's First Soldier of Fortune." *Hawaii Historical Review* 1, no. 10 (January): 194–98.

Kuykendall, Ralph S. 1938. *The Hawaiian Kingdom.* Vol. 1, *Foundation and Transformation, 1778–1854.* Honolulu: University Press of Hawai'i.

————. 1953. *The Hawaiian Kingdom.* Vol. 2, *Twenty Critical Years, 1854–1874.* Honolulu: University of Hawai'i Press.

————. 1967. *The Hawaiian Kingdom.* Vol. 3, *The Kalakaua Dynasty, 1874–1893.* Honolulu: University of Hawai'i Press.

Kyselka, Will. 1987. *An Ocean in Mind.* Honolulu: University of Hawai'i Press.

La Farge, John. 1916. *Reminiscences of the South Seas.* Garden City, N.Y.: Doubleday.

Lagler, Karl F., et al. 1977. *Ichthyology.* 2d edition. New York: John Wiley and Sons.

Lane, M. Melia. 1985. "The Migration of Hawaiians to Coastal British Columbia, 1810 to 1869." M.A. thesis, University of Hawai'i.

Larson, Edward J. 2001. *Evolution's Workshop: God and Science in the Galapagos Islands.* New York: Basic Books.

Lee, Lloyd L. 1948. "A Brief Analysis of the Role and Status of the Negro in the Hawaiian Community." *American Sociological Review* 13, no. 4 (August): 419–37.

Lewis, David. 1972. *We, the Navigators: The Ancient Art of Landfinding in the Pacific.* Honolulu: University of Hawai'i Press.

Lewis, Martin W., and Kären E. Wigen. 1997. *The Myth of Continents: A Critique of Metageography.* Berkeley: University of California Press.

Lipscomb, Andrew A., et al., eds. 1903. *The Writings of Thomas Jefferson.* 20 vols. Washington, D.C.: Thomas Jefferson Memorial Association.

Lomawaima, K. Tsianina. 1996. "Estelle Reel, Superintendent of Indian Schools, 1898–1910: Politics, Curriculum, and Land." *Journal of American Indian Education* 35, no. 3 (Spring): 5–31.

London, Jack. 1907. "A Royal Sport: Surfing at Waikiki." *A Woman's Home Companion,* October.

————. 1911. *The Cruise of the Snark.* New York: Macmillan.

Ludlow, Helen W. n.d. *Clarissa Chapman Armstrong.* Honolulu: Hawaiian Mission Children's Society.

————, ed. 1888. *Ten Years' Work for Indians at the Hampton Normal and Agricultural Institute, at Hampton, Virginia, 1878–1888.* Hampton, Va.: Hampton Institute.

Luomala, Katherine. 1951. Review of *The Kumulipo: A Hawaiian Creation Chant,* edited and translated by Martha Warren Beckwith. *Journal of American Folklore* 64, no. 254 (October–December): 429–30, 432.

————. 1961. "Survey of Research on Polynesian Prose and Poetry." *Journal of American Folklore* 74, no. 294 (October–December): 431, 435.

————. 1972. "Foreword." In *The Kumulipo: A Hawaiian Creation Chant*, edited and translated by Martha Warren Beckwith, ix–xix. Honolulu: University of Hawaiʻi Press.

Lyons, Curtis J. 1892. "Traces of Spanish Influence in the Hawaiian Islands." *Papers of the Hawaiian Historical Society*, no. 2 (April 27).

Lyons, Jeffrey K. 2004. "Memoirs of Henry Obookiah: A Rhetorical History." *Hawaiian Journal of History* 38:35–57.

MacArthur, Robert H., and Edward O. Wilson. 1967. *The Theory of Island Biogeography.* Princeton, N.J.: Princeton University Press.

Macdonald, Gordon A. 1972. *Volcanoes.* Englewood Cliffs, N.J.: Prentice-Hall.

Macdonald, Gordon A., and Agatin T. Abbott. 1970. *Volcanoes in the Sea: The Geology of Hawaii.* Honolulu: University Press of Hawaiʻi.

Malloy, Mary. 1990. *African Americans in the Maritime Trades: A Guide to Resources in New England.* Kendall Whaling Museum Monograph Series, no. 6. Sharon, Mass.: Kendall Whaling Museum.

Malo, David. [1903] 1951. *Hawaiian Antiquities*, translated by Nathaniel B. Emerson. Honolulu: Bishop Museum Press.

Malone, Bill C. 2002. *Country Music, U.S.A.* Austin: University of Texas Press.

Martin, Margaret Greer, ed. 1992. *The Lymans of Hilo.* Hilo, Hawaiʻi: Lyman House Memorial Museum.

Marty, Martin E. 1970. *Righteous Empire: The Protestant Experience in America.* New York: Dial Press.

Marzio, Peter C. 1979. *The Democratic Art: Pictures for 19th-Century America.* Boston: David R. Godine.

Maxon, Helen Hitchcock. 1987. *D. Howard Hitchcock: Islander.* Honolulu: Topgallant Publishing.

McBeth, Sally J. 1983. *Ethnic Identity and the Boarding School Experience of West-Central Oklahoma American Indians.* Lanham, Md.: University Press of America.

McClain, Charles J. 1994. *In Search of Equality: The Chinese Struggle against Discrimination in Nineteenth-Century America.* Berkeley: University of California Press.

McGregor, Davianna Pomaikaʻi. 1993. "Pele vs. Geothermal: A Clash of Cultures." In *Bearing Dreams, Shaping Visions: Asian Pacific American Perspectives*, edited by Linda A. Revilla et al., 45–60. Pullman: Washington State University Press.

Meany, Edmond S. 1909. *History of the State of Washington.* New York: Macmillan.

Meares, John. 1790. *Voyages Made in the Years 1788 and 1789, from China to the North West Coast of America*. London: Logographic Press.

Melville, Herman. [1851] 1967. *Moby-Dick*, edited by Charles Child Walcutt. Toronto: Bantam Books.

Memoirs of Henry Obookiah, a Native of Owhyhee, and a Member of the Foreign Mission School; Who Died at Cornwall, Conn., Feb. 17, 1818, Aged 26 Years. Elizabeth-Town, N.J.: Edson Hart, 1819.

"Memoirs of Thomas Hopoo." *Hawaiian Journal of History* 2 (1968): 42–54.

Menard, H. W. 1964. *Marine Geology of the Pacific*. New York: McGraw-Hill.

———. 1986. *Islands*. New York: Scientific American Books.

"Menzies' California Journal." *California Historical Society Quarterly* 2 (January 1924): 265.

Miller, David G. 1988. "Ka'iana, the Once Famous 'Prince of Kaua'i.'" *Hawaiian Journal of History* 22:1–19.

Missionary Album: Portraits and Biographical Sketches of the American Protestant Missionaries to the Hawaiian Islands. Honolulu: Hawaiian Mission Children's Society, 1969.

Missionary Spelling Book, and Reader. Prepared at the Foreign Mission School, Cornwall, Conn. and Designed Especially for Its Use. Hartford, Conn.: George Goodwin and Sons, 1822.

Mitchell, Donald D. Kilolani, and George S. Kanahele. 1979. "Steel Guitar." In *Hawaiian Music and Musicians: An Illustrated History*, edited by George Kanahele, 366–67. Honolulu: University Press of Hawai'i.

Molin, Paulette Fairbanks. 1988. "'Training the Hand, the Head, and the Heart': Indian Education at Hampton Institute." *Minnesota History* 51, no. 3 (Fall): 82–98.

Morgan, Murray. 1948. *Dixie Raider: The Saga of the C.S.S. Shenandoah*. New York: E. P. Dutton.

Morison, Samuel Eliot. 1920. "Boston Traders in the Hawaiian Islands, 1789–1823." *Proceedings of the Massachusetts Historical Society* 54 (October): 9–47.

———. 1921. *The Maritime History of Massachusetts, 1783–1860*. Boston: Houghton Mifflin.

Mortimer, George. 1791. *Observations and Remarks Made during a Voyage to the Islands of Teneriffe. . . .* London: T. Cadell.

Munford, James Kenneth, ed. 1963. *John Ledyard's Journal of Captain Cook's Last Voyage*. Corvallis: Oregon State University Press.

Nā Mele Paniolo: Songs of Hawaiian Cowboys. CD collection. Honolulu: Hawaii State Foundation on Culture and the Arts, 1990 and 2004.

A Narrative of Five Youth from the Sandwich Islands, Now Receiving an Education in This Country. New York: J. Seymour, 1816.

National Security Strategy of the United States of America, September 2002, www.whitehouse .gov/nsc/nss.html.

Naughton, E. Momilani. 1983. "Hawaiians in the Fur Trade: Cultural Influence on the Northwest Coast, 1811–1875." M.A. thesis, Western Washington University.

Navarro, José-Manuel. 2002. *Creating Tropical Yankees: Social Science Textbooks and U.S. Ideological Control in Puerto Rico, 1898–1908*. New York: Routledge.

Nimmo, H. Arlo. 1992. *The Pele Literature: An Annotated Bibliography of the English-Language Literature on Pele, Volcano Goddess of Hawai'i*. Bishop Museum Bulletin in Anthropology no. 4. Honolulu: Bishop Museum Press.

Noble, Gurre Ploner. 1948. *Hula Blues: The Story of Johnny Noble, Hawaii, Its Music and Musicians*. Honolulu: Tongg Publishing.

Nordon, Van. 1911. "Hawaii for the White Man." *Mid-Pacific Magazine* 1, no. 6 (June): 629, 634.

Nordyke, Eleanor C. 1988. "Blacks in Hawai'i: A Demographic and Historical Perspective." *Hawaiian Journal of History* 22:241–55.

O'Brien, Patty. 2006. *The Pacific Muse: Exotic Femininity and the Colonial Pacific*. Seattle: University of Washington Press.

Okihiro, Gary Y. 2001. *The Columbia Guide to Asian American History*. New York: Columbia University Press.

———. 2001. *Common Ground: Reimagining American History*. Princeton, N.J.: Princeton University Press.

———. 2006. "Afterword: Toward a Black Pacific." In *AfroAsian Encounters: Culture, History, Politics*, edited by Heike Raphael-Hernandez and Shannon Steen, 313–30. New York: New York University Press.

———. 2006. "Islands of History: Hawai'i and Okinawa." *Okinawan Journal of American Studies* 3:1–6.

———. 2006. "Toward a Pacific Civilization." In *Transcultural Localisms: Responding to Ethnicity in a Globalized World*, edited by Yiorgos Kalogeras, Eleftheria Arapoglou, and Linda Manney, 15–25. Heidelberg, Germany: Universitätsverlag Winter GmbH Heidelberg.

Olmsted, Francis Allyn. 1841. *Incidents of a Whaling Voyage*. New York: D. Appleton.

O'Neil, Marion. 1930. "The Maritime Activities of the North West Company, 1813 to 1821." *Washington Historical Quarterly* 21, no. 4 (October): 243–67.

Oreskes, Naomi, ed. 2003. *Plate Tectonics: An Insider's History of the Modern Theory of the Earth*. Boulder, Colo.: Westview Press.

Osorio, Jonathan Kay Kamakawiwoʻole. 2002. *Dismembering Lāhui: A History of the Hawaiian Nation to 1887*. Honolulu: University of Hawai'i Press.

Oyabe, Jenichiro. 1898. *A Japanese Robinson Crusoe*. Boston: Pilgrim Press.

Pearson, Charles H. 1893. *National Life and Character*. London.

Pease, Zephaniah W. 1918. *History of New Bedford*. Vol 1. New York: Lewis Historical Publishing.

Pfister, Joel. 2004. *Individuality Incorporated: Indians and the Multicultural Modern*. Durham, N.C.: Duke University Press.

Phillips, Clifton Jackson. 1968. *Protestant America and the Pagan World: The First Half Century of the American Board of Commissioners for Foreign Missions, 1810–1860*. Cambridge, Mass.: East Asian Research Center, Harvard University.

Porter, Kenneth W. 1931. *John Jacob Astor: Business Man*. 2 vols. Cambridge, Mass.: Harvard University Press.

Porterfield, Nolan. 1992. *Jimmie Rodgers: The Life and Times of America's "Blue Yodeler."* Urbana: University of Illinois Press.

Portlock, Nathaniel. 1789. *A Voyage Round the World: But More Particularly to the North-West Coast of America. . . .* London: John Stockdale.

Pratt, Richard Henry. 1964. *Battlefield and Classroom: Four Decades with the American Indian, 1867–1904*, edited by Robert M. Utley. New Haven, Conn.: Yale University Press.

———. 1973. "The Advantages of Mingling Indians with Whites" and "A Way Out." In *Americanizing the American Indians: Writings by "Friends of the Indians,"* edited by Francis Paul Prucha, 260–76. Cambridge, Mass.: Harvard University Press.

Price, A. Grenfell, ed. 1971. *The Explorations of Captain James Cook in the Pacific as Told by Selection of His Own Journals, 1768–1779*. New York: Dover Publications.

Pukui, Mary Kawena. 1949. "Songs *(Meles)* of Old Ka'u, Hawaii." *Journal of American Folklore* 62, no. 245 (July–September): 247–58.

Pukui, Mary Kawena, and Samuel H. Elbert. 1986. *Hawaiian Dictionary*. Honolulu: University of Hawai'i Press.

Pukui, Mary Kawena, Samuel H. Elbert, and Esther T. Mookini. 1974. *Place Names of Hawaii*. Honolulu: University of Hawai'i Press.

Pukui, Mary Kawena, and Alfons L. Korn, eds. and trans. 1973. *The Echo of Our Song: Chants & Poems of the Hawaiians*. Honolulu: University of Hawai'i Press.

Ralston, Caroline. 1989. "Changes in the Lives of Ordinary Women in Early Post-Contact Hawaii." In *Family and Gender in the Pacific: Domestic Contradictions and the Colonial Impact*, edited by Margaret Jolly and Martha Macintyre, 45–64. Cambridge: Cambridge University Press.

Report of the Hawaiian Volcano Observatory of the Massachusetts Institute of Technology and the Hawaiian Volcano Research Association, January–March 1912. Boston: Society of Arts of the Massachusetts Institute of Technology, 1912.

Reyes, Luis I. 1995. *Made in Paradise: Hollywood's Films of Hawai'i and the South Seas.* Honolulu: Mutual Publishing.

Rich, E. E. 1959. *The History of Hudson's Bay Company, 1763–1820.* Vol. 2. London: Hudson's Bay Record Society.

Richard Armstrong: America, Hawaii. Hampton, Va.: Normal School Steam Press, 1887.

Roberts, Helen H. 1926. *Ancient Hawaiian Music.* Bernice P. Bishop Museum Bulletin 29. Honolulu: Bishop Museum Press.

Robinson, William H. 1977. "Indian Education at Hampton Institute." In *Stony the Road: Chapters in the History of Hampton Institute,* edited by Keith L. Schall, 1–33. Charlottesville: University of Virginia Press.

Rogers, John, and Tim Knott. 1975. "The Paniolos." *Ko Kākou* 1, no. 2 (February): 13–15.

Ronda, James P. 1990. *Astoria and Empire.* Lincoln: University of Nebraska Press.

Ross, Alexander. 1956. *The Fur Hunters of the Far West,* edited by Kenneth A. Spaulding. Norman: Oklahoma University Press.

Ruschenberger, William Samuel W. 1838. *Narrative of a Voyage Round the World.* Vol. 2. London: Richard Bentley.

Said, Edward W. 1993. *Culture and Imperialism.* New York: Vintage Books.

Sampaio, Philip, Joy Kalawaia, and Debra Arii. 1975. "Sol Bright: 'Hawaiian Cowboy.'" *Ko Kākou* 1, no. 2 (February): 11–12.

Sánchez-Eppler, Karen. 2007. "Copying and Conversion: An 1824 Friendship Album 'from a Chinese Youth.'" *American Quarterly* 59, no. 2 (June): 301–39.

Sanneh, Lamin. 1999. *Abolitionists Abroad: American Blacks and the Making of Modern West Africa.* Cambridge, Mass.: Harvard University Press.

Scarth, Alwyn. 1994. *Volcanoes: An Introduction.* College Station: Texas A&M University Press.

Schiffer, Nancy N. 1998. *Surfing.* Atglen, Pa.: Schiffer Publishing.

Schmitt, Robert C. 1963. "Migration Statistics of Hawaii, 1823–1962." *Hawaii Historical Review* 1, no. 4 (July): 59–68.

———. 1965. "Population Characteristics of Hawaii, 1778–1850." *Hawaii Historical Review* 1, no. 11 (April): 199–211.

———. 1968. *Demographic Statistics of Hawaii: 1778–1965.* Honolulu: University of Hawai'i Press.

———. 1968. "South Seas Movies, 1913–1943." *Hawaii Historical Review* 2, no. 11 (April): 433–52.

———. 1988. *Hawai'i in the Movies, 1898–1959.* Honolulu: Hawaiian Historical Society.

Schurz, William Lytle. 1985. *The Manila Galleon.* Manila, Philippines: Historical Conservation Society.

Scruggs, Marc. 1992. "Anthony D. Allen: A Prosperous American of African Descent in Early 19th Century Hawai'i." *Hawaiian Journal of History* 26:55–93.

Sereno, Aeko. 1990. "Images of the Hula Dancer and 'Hula Girl': 1778–1960." Ph.D. dissertation, University of Hawai'i.

Sharp, Andrew. 1963. *Ancient Voyagers in Polynesia.* Sydney, Australia: Angus and Robertson.

Shinseki, Kyle Ko Francisco. 1997. "El pueblo mexicano de Hawai'i: Comunidades en formación." M.A. thesis, University of California, Los Angeles.

Sibley, Hi. 1935. "Better Ways to Build Surf Boards." *Popular Science Monthly,* August, 56.

Silva, Noenoe K. 2004. *Aloha Betrayed: Native Hawaiian Resistance to American Colonialism.* Durham, N.C.: Duke University Press.

Simpson, George. 1847. *Narrative of a Journey Round the World, during the Years 1841 and 1842.* Vol. 2. London: Henry Colburn.

Simpson, MacKinnon. 1993. *The Lymans of Hawai'i Island: A Pioneering Family.* Hilo, Hawai'i: Orlando H. Lyman Trust.

Simpson, MacKinnon, and Robert B. Goodman. 1986. *Whale Song: A Pictorial History of Whaling and Hawai'i.* Honolulu: Beyond Words Publishing.

Smith, Bernard. 1960. *European Vision and the South Pacific.* New Haven, Conn.: Yale University Press.

Smith, John David. 2002. "Let Us All Be Grateful That We Have Colored Troops That Will Fight." In *Black Soldiers in Blue: African American Troops in the Civil War Era,* edited by John David Smith, 1–77. Chapel Hill: University of North Carolina Press.

Smith, Philip Chadwick Foster. 1984. *The Empress of China.* Philadelphia: Philadelphia Maritime Museum.

Spaeth, Sigmund. 1938. "Hawaii Likes Music." *Harper's Monthly Magazine,* March, 423–27.

Sparks, Jared. 1829. *The Life of John Ledyard, the American Traveller.* Cambridge, Mass.: Hilliard and Brown.

Spate, O. H. K. 1979. *The Spanish Lake.* Minneapolis: University of Minnesota Press.

Spivey, Donald. 1978. *Schooling for the New Slavery: Black Industrial Education, 1868–1915.* Westport, Conn.: Greenwood Press.

Spoehr, Alexander. 1986. "Fur Traders in Hawai'i: The Hudson's Bay Company in Honolulu, 1829–1859." *Hawaiian Journal of History* 20:27–66.

———. 1988. "A 19th Century Chapter in Hawai'i's Maritime History: Hudson's Bay Company Merchant Shipping, 1829–1859." *Hawaiian Journal of History* 22:70–100.

Spring, Gardiner. 1820. *Memoirs of the Rev. Samuel J. Mills.* New York: New York Evangelical Missionary Society.

Start, Edwin A. 1892. "General Armstrong and the Hampton Institute." *New England Magazine,* n.s., 6:444.

Staudenraus, P. J. 1961. *The African Colonization Movement, 1816–1865*. New York: Columbia University Press.

Stauder, Catherine. 1972. "George, Prince of Hawaii." *Hawaiian Journal of History* 6:28–44.

Stebbins, Theodore E., Jr. 1976. *American Master Drawings and Watercolors: A History of Works on Paper from Colonial Times to the Present*. New York: Harper and Row.

Steinberg, Philip E. 2001. *The Social Construction of the Ocean*. Cambridge: Cambridge University Press.

Stewart, Charles Samuel. 1839. *A Residence in the Sandwich Islands*. Boston: Weeks, Jordan.

Stewart, Watt. 1970. *Chinese Bondage in Peru: A History of the Chinese Coolie in Peru, 1849–1874*. Westport, Conn.: Greenwood Press.

Stillman, Amy K. 1989. "History Reinterpreted in Song: The Case of the Hawaiian Counterrevolution." *Hawaiian Journal of History* 23:1–30.

———. 1998. "Hula Hits, Local Music and Local Charts: Some Dynamics of Popular Hawaiian Music." In *Sound Alliances: Indigenous Peoples, Cultural Politics and Popular Music in the Pacific*, edited by Philip Hayward, 89–103. London: Cassell.

———. 1998. *Sacred Hula: The Historical Hula ʻAlaʻapapa*. Bishop Museum Bulletin in Anthropology 8. Honolulu: Bishop Museum Press.

Stoddard, Charles Warren. 1889. "Halcyon Hawaii." *Paradise of the Pacific* 2, no. 12 (December): 2, 3.

Stoddard, Lothrop. 1920. *The Rising Tide of Color against White World-Supremacy*. New York: Charles Scribner's Sons.

Takara, Kay Brundage. 1977. "Who Is the Black Woman in Hawaii?" In *Montage: An Ethnic History of Women in Hawaii*, edited by Nancy Foon Young and Judy R. Parrish, 85–93. Honolulu: General Assistance Center for the Pacific, University of Hawaiʻi.

Talbot, Edith Armstrong. 1904. *Samuel Chapman Armstrong: A Biographical Study*. New York: Doubleday, Page.

Tatar, Elizabeth. 1979. "Chant." In *Hawaiian Music and Musicians: An Illustrated History*, edited by George Kanahele, 53–68. Honolulu: University Press of Hawaiʻi.

———. 1987. *Strains of Change: The Impact of Tourism on Hawaiian Music*. Bishop Museum Special Publication 78. Honolulu: Bishop Museum Press.

Tate, Merze. 1961. "The Sandwich Island Missionaries Lay the Foundation for a System of Public Instruction in Hawaii." *Journal of Negro Education* 30, no. 4 (Fall): 396–405.

———. 1962. "Decadence of the Hawaiian Nation and Proposals to Import a Negro Labor Force." *Journal of Negro History* 47, no. 4 (October): 248–63.

Taylor, Albert P. 1915. "Hawaii: The Best-Known Building at the Panama-Pacific Exposition, 1915." *Hawaiian Almanac and Annual for 1916.* Honolulu: Thos. G. Thrum.

Tchen, John Kuo Wei. 1999. *New York before Chinatown: Orientalism and the Shaping of American Culture, 1776–1882.* Baltimore: Johns Hopkins University Press.

Thayer, Ward Warren. 1917. *Report to Hon. Lucius E. Pinkham, Governor of Hawaii . . . Concerning Hawaii's Exhibit at the Panama-Pacific International Exposition.* Honolulu: Hawaiian Gazette.

Theroux, Joseph. 1992. "Volcano Painter: Pioneer Artist Charles Furneaux Built on Success." *Hawaii Magazine* 9, no. 5 (October): 70–75.

Thomas, Nicholas. 1997. *In Oceania: Visions, Artifacts, Histories.* Durham, N.C.: Duke University Press.

Todd, Frank Morton. 1921. *The Story of the Exposition: Being the Official History of the International Celebration Held in San Francisco in 1915 to Commemorate the Discovery of the Pacific Ocean and the Construction of the Panama Canal.* New York: G. P. Putnam's Sons.

Topolinski, John R. Kaha'i. 1976. "Musical Diggings: Na Mele Ohana (Family Songs)." *Ha'Ilono Mele* 2, no. 1 (January): 3–6.

———. 1976. "Musical Diggings: The Sumner Family: A Legacy of Family Mele and Chants." *Ha'Ilono Mele* 2, no. 2 (February): 2–6.

———. 1976. "Musical Diggings: The Sumner Family." *Ha'Ilono Mele* 2, no. 3 (March): 3–7.

Trennert, Robert A. 1982. "Educating Indian Girls at Nonreservation Boarding Schools, 1878–1920." *Western Historical Quarterly* 13, no. 3 (July): 271–90.

Trimillos, Ricardo D. 1990 and 2004. "*He Mo'olelo*: Historical and Artistic Notes." In *Nā Mele Paniolo: Songs of Hawaiian Cowboys.* CD collection. Honolulu: Hawai'i State Foundation on Culture and the Arts.

Trudeau, Noah Andre. 1998. *Like Men of War: Black Troops in the Civil War, 1862–1865.* Boston: Little, Brown.

Tuan, Yi-Fu. 1974. *Topophilia: A Study of Environmental Perception, Attitudes, and Values.* Englewood Cliffs, N.J.: Prentice-Hall.

Tucker, Sherrie. 2000. *Swing Shift: "All-Girl" Bands of the 1940s.* Durham, N.C.: Duke University Press.

Twain, Mark. [1872] 1993. *Roughing It.* Berkeley: University of California Press.

Twombly, Alex. Stevenson. 1900. *Kelea: The Surf-Rider, a Romance of Pagan Hawaii.* New York: Fords, Howard, and Hulbert.

Valeri, Valerio. 1985. *Kingship and Sacrifice: Ritual and Society in Ancient Hawaii.* Chicago: University of Chicago Press.

Waddell, Eric, Vijay Naidu, and Epeli Hauʻofa, eds. 1993. *A New Oceania: Rediscovering Our Sea of Islands.* Suva, Fiji: University of the South Pacific.

Ward, David C. 2004. *Charles Willson Peale: Art and Selfhood in the Early Republic.* Berkeley: University of California Press.

Washington, Booker T. [1901] 1995. *Up from Slavery.* Oxford: Oxford University Press.

———. 1909. *Some Results of the Armstrong Idea.* Hampton, Va.: Institute Press.

Weintraub, Andrew N. 1998. "Jawaiian Music and Local Cultural Identity in Hawaiʻi." In *Sound Alliances: Indigenous Peoples, Cultural Politics and Popular Music in the Pacific,* edited by Philip Hayward, 78–88. London: Cassell.

Weiskel, Thomas. 1976. *The Romantic Sublime.* Baltimore: Johns Hopkins University Press.

Wellmon, Bernard Brian. 1970. "The Parker Ranch: A History." Ph.D. dissertation, Texas Christian University.

Wendt, Albert. 1976. "Towards a New Oceania." *Mana* 1, no. 1 (January): 49–60.

Westervelt, W. D. 1987. *Myths and Legends of Hawaii,* edited by A. Grove Day. Honolulu: Mutual Publishing.

Wexler, Laura. 2000. *Tender Violence: Domestic Visions in an Age of U.S. Imperialism.* Chapel Hill: University of North Carolina Press.

Wilkes, Charles. 1845. *Narrative of the U.S. Exploring Expedition during the Years 1838–1842.* Vol. 4. Philadelphia: Lee and Blanchard.

Willard, Michael Nevin. 2002. "Duke Kahanamoku's Body: Biography of Hawaiʻi." In *Sports Matters: Race, Recreation, and Culture,* edited by John Bloom and Michael Nevin Willard, 13–38. New York: New York University Press.

Williamson, Judith. 1986. "Woman Is an Island: Femininity and Colonization." In *Studies in Entertainment: Critical Approaches to Mass Culture,* edited by Tania Modleski, 99–118. Bloomington: Indiana University Press.

Wilson, Keith P. 2002. *Campfires of Freedom: The Camp Life of Black Soldiers during the Civil War.* Kent, Ohio: Kent State University Press.

Wist, Benjamin O. 1940. *A Century of Public Education in Hawaii, 1840–1940.* Honolulu: Hawaii Education Review.

Withey, Lynne. 1987. *Voyages of Discovery: Captain Cook and the Exploration of the Pacific.* Berkeley: University of California Press.

Wood, Houston. 1999. *Displacing Natives: The Rhetorical Production of Hawaiʻi.* Lanham, Md.: Rowman and Littlefield.

Woodson, Carter Godwin. [1933] 1972. *The Mis-education of the Negro.* New York: AMS Press.

Wyllie, Robert. 1844. "Notes." *The Friend* 2, no. 9 (September 4): 79.

Ziegler, Alan C. 2002. *Hawaiian Natural History, Ecology, and Evolution.* Honolulu: University of Hawai'i Press.

Zitkala-Sa. 1985. *American Indian Stories.* Lincoln: University of Nebraska Press.

Zmijewski, David. 2004. "Mark Twain's Dual Visions of Hawai'i: Censoring the Creative Self." *Hawaiian Journal of History* 38:112–17.

DISCOGRAPHY

Georgia Jumpers. "Guitar Rhythm." *King Bennie Nawahi: Hawaiian String Virtuoso, Acoustic Steel Guitar Classics from the 1920s.* Yazoo Records, 2000.

Ho'opi'i, Sol. "Hula Blues" and "I Like You." *Sol Hoopii: Master of the Hawaiian Guitar,* vol. 2. Rounder Records, 1991.

———. "Twelfth Street Rag" and "Farewell Blues." *Sol Hoopii: Master of the Hawaiian Guitar,* vol. 1. Rounder Records, 1991.

Kaapana, Led, Alison Krauss, and Sam Bush. "Waltz of the Wind." *Led Kaapana and Friends.* Dancing Cat Records, 1998.

Kapena. "The Solid Rock." *Wild Heart.* KDE Records, 1993.

Dick McIntire and His Harmony Hawaiians. "Hilo March." *Ticklin' the Strings: Hawaiian Memories.* Unlimited Media, 2006.

Tau Moe Family. "E Mama Ea." *Ho'Omana'o I Na Mele o Ka Wa U'i.* Rounder Records, 1989.

Nawahi, Ben. "Black Boy Blues." *King Bennie Nawahi: Hawaiian String Virtuoso, Acoustic Steel Guitar Classics from the 1920s.* Yazoo Records, 2000.

Rodgers, Jimmie. "Everybody Does It in Hawaii." *Classic Sides,* CD 2. JSP Records, 2002.

Tarlton, Jimmie. "My Little Blue Heaven." *Slidin' on the Frets: The Hawaiian Steel Guitar Phenomenon, Classic Rural, Popular and Foreign Performances on the Acoustic Steel Guitar.* Yazoo Records, 2000.

Weaver, Sylvester. "Guitar Rag." *Slidin' on the Frets: The Hawaiian Steel Guitar Phenomenon, Classic Rural, Popular and Foreign Performances on the Acoustic Steel Guitar.* Yazoo Records, 2000.

Weldon, Casey Bill. "Can't You Remember." *Casey Bill Weldon, 1936–37,* vol. 2. Document Records, 2005.

Bob Wills and His Texas Playboys. "Steel Guitar Rag." *The Essential Bob Wills and His Texas Playboys.* Sony, 1992.

Woods, Oscar "Buddy." "Don't Sell It—Don't Give It Away." *Slidin' on the Frets: The Hawaiian Steel Guitar Phenomenon, Classic Rural, Popular and Foreign Performances on the Acoustic Steel Guitar.* Yazoo Records, 2000.

INDEX

abolitionism, 92–94, 158, 160–61, 236n48, 241n36

Aborigines' Protection Society, London, 149

Acapulco, Spanish trade port, 170

Adams, George, 159

Adams, Henry, 38

Adams, Peter, 162

Adams, William W., 117

Ae'a, Joseph Kapaeau, 201

Africa: colonization site for free blacks, 89–90; Hawaiians lumped racially with Zulus of, 189; missions, 91; seamen from, 158; in social evolution and design, 208

African Americans: African Free Schools, 89, 93, 236n48; Census racializations, 159; "civilized" by whites, 89, 123–25; "civilizing" American Indians, 120–21; Civil War Colored Troops, 104–5, 122, 161–64; colonization of free blacks, 89–90, 93–94, 237n63; education in South, 89, 100, 105–8, 114–23, 129–32, 202, 216; at Hampton, 100, 105–8, 106fig, 107fig, 114–25, 131, 132, 216; Hawaiians lumped racially with, 105–6, 114, 152–53, 154, 158, 195–200; Hawai'i migrant labor from South, 134; Jim Crow era, 130; manual labor training, 105–7, 115–20, 122–23; military service and gender gap among, 257n118; missionaries, 89–90, 91, 93, 215; music, 196–201, 203, 218; "Negro movement," 105; "Negro problem," 92–93; physical descriptions by white missionaries, 101; in racial hierarchy, 107, 120, 130–31; seamen, 158; segregated, 92–94, 130, 160, 216; slaves, 2, 74, 91–94, 120, 122–23, 161; teacher training, 105–8

African Free Schools, New York City, 89, 93, 236n48

agricultural deities, 50

agricultural labor, 103, 129, 133, 134

Ah-Kam, 99

Alapa'i, David, 41–42

Aleutian Trench, off Alaska, 17

algae, in coral reefs, 7–8

Ali Baba Trio, 200, 218

Aloha (1931), 67–68

Aloha 'Aina, 42

Aluli, Noa Emmett, 42

American Board of Commissioners for Foreign Missions, 59, 81–82, 86–88, 94, 98, 103

American Colonization Society, 89

American continent: natural wonders, 213; at periphery of Oceania/Hawai'i, 2, 5, 206, 210–11; in social evolution and design, 208. *See also* Atlantic Northeast; California; Hawai'i; Pacific Northwest; South; Spanish America; United States government

American Eagle, 85

American Foreign Mission movement, 87

Designer:	Sandy Drooker
Text:	10/14 Adobe Garamond
Display:	Bank Gothic Medium, Caslon Antiqua
Indexer:	Barbara Roos
Cartographer:	Bill Nelson
Compositor:	Integrated Composition Systems
Printer and binder:	Maple-Vail Manufacturing Group